God Beyond Borders

God Beyond Borders

Interreligious Learning Among Faith Communities

SHERYL A. KUJAWA-HOLBROOK

PICKWICK *Publications* · Eugene, Oregon

GOD BEYOND BORDERS
Interreligious Learning Among Faith Communities

Horizons in Religious Education 1

Pickwick Publications
An Imprint of Wipf and Stock Publishers
199 W. 8th Ave., Suite 3
Eugene, OR 97401

www.wipfandstock.com

ISBN 13: 978–71-62564–458-9

Cataloguing-in-Publication data:

Kujawa-Holbrook, Sheryl A.

God beyond borders : interreligious learning among faith communities / Sheryl
A. Kujawa-Holbrook.

xlii + 174 pp. ; 23 cm. Includes bibliographical references.

Horizons in Religious Education 1

ISBN 13: 978–71-62564–458-9

1. Religious Education. I. Series. II. Title.

BL65 F2 K85 2014

Manufactured in the U.S.A.

To my mentor, friend, colleague
Edward W. Rodman

God beyond borders
we bless you for strange places
and different dreams
for the demands and diversity
of a wider world
for the distance
that lets us look back and re-evaluate
for new ground
where the broken stems can take root,
grow and blossom.
We bless you
for the friendship of strangers
the richness of other cultures
and the painful gift of freedom
Blessed are you,
God beyond borders.
But if we have overlooked
the exiles in our midst
heightened their exclusion
by our indifference
given our permission
for a climate of fear
and tolerated a culture of violence
Have mercy on us,
God who takes side with justice,
confront our prejudice
stretch our narrowness
sift out our laws and our lives
with the penetrating insight
of your spirit
until generosity is our only measure.
Amen[1]

1. Kathy Galloway, *Maker's Blessing* (Glasgow: Wild Goose Publications, 2000). Used with Permission.

Contents

Series Foreword

THE EDITORIAL BOARD OF Horizons in Religious Education is delighted to select *God Beyond Borders: Interreligious Learning Among Faith Communities* by Sheryl A. Kujawa-Holbrook as the first book in the series. Indeed this book leads us towards the horizons of the field. What could be more timely in our world of rapid technology, almost instant communication, shifting political boundaries and alliances, and conflict, some of which results from religious communities? Her attention to how we can come to know and understand each other contributes hope to our world. Dr. Kujawa-Holbrook teaches in an interfaith environment and has comprehensively researched efforts across the continent to engage in interfaith learning and education.

From its founding the Religious Education Association has crossed religious boundaries in an effort to learn from each other and to contribute to the education of the wider public world. That is precisely what Dr. Kujawa-Holbrook's book does. Her survey of the scholarship on interfaith education is a foundation on which other scholars and practitioners will draw. The book offers rationale for interfaith education, describes processes of education, provides multiple examples of concrete practices, and highlights the profoundly transforming outcomes that occur. Her work builds on and extends the mission of the Religious Education Association. We are honored to publish it. We encourage you to draw deeply of this book and further extend the horizons of our work for the flourishing of the world we share.

Preface
by Eboo Patel

SHERYL KUJAWA-HOLBROOK'S IMPORTANT BOOK on congregations and interfaith cooperation reminds me of a crucial moment in American history. When, as a seminary student, Martin Luther King Jr. was introduced to the *satyagraha* ("love-force") philosophy of the Indian Hindu leader Mahatma Gandhi, King did not reject it because it came from a different religion. Instead, he sought to find resonances between Gandhi's Hinduism and his own interpretation of Christianity. Indeed, it was Gandhi's movement in India that provided King with a twentieth-century version of what Jesus would do. King patterned nearly all the strategy and tactics of the civil rights movement—from boycotts to marches to readily accepting jail time—after Gandhi's leadership in India. King called Gandhi "the first person in history to lift the love ethic of Jesus above mere interaction between individuals to a powerful and effective social force."

Following Gandhi was King's first step on a long journey of learning about the shared social justice values across the world's religions, and partnering with faith leaders of all backgrounds in the struggle for civil rights. In 1959, more than a decade after the Mahatma's death, King traveled to India to meet with people continuing the work Gandhi had started. He was surprised and inspired that this movement included Indians of all faith backgrounds working for equality and harmony, discovering in their own traditions of Islam, Buddhism, Jainism, Sikhism and Humanism the same inspiration for love and peace that Gandhi found in Hinduism and King in Christianity.

King's experience with religious diversity in India shaped the rest of his life. He readily formed a friendship with the Rabbi Abraham Joshua

Heschel, finding a common bond in their love of the Hebrew prophets. The two walked arm-in-arm in the famous civil rights march from Selma to Montgomery. In his famous sermon "A Time to Break Silence," King was unequivocal about his Christian commitment and at the same time summarized his view of the powerful commonality across all faiths: "This Hindu-Muslim-Christian-Jewish-Buddhist belief about ultimate reality" is that the force of love is "the supreme unifying principle of life."

One of the great gifts of Sheryl's book is that it shines a light on this path that King walked, showing all of us involved with religious congregations how we can be interfaith leaders. There are too many out there who would say off-handedly, "The reason religions fight is because they've always fought." But when we tell the history of America as it speaks to interfaith cooperation, we know that's just not true. Rev. King and Rabbi Heschel are two examples of interfaith leaders—people who have the knowledge and skills to stop that fiction with knowledge, build relationships between their communities, and work together to better our common world.

What is especially important to emphasize about each of these leaders is that they had what I call a *theology of interfaith cooperation*, or knowledge of one's religion's inspiration to cooperate with others. At the organization I founded, Interfaith Youth Core, we believe that religion in the 21st century can be a bubble of isolation; a barrier of division; a bomb of destruction; or a bridge of cooperation. Faith communities make these choices, in part, guided by their theology of engaging the religious other. If you ask the people who are building barriers, "What in your faith inspires you to separate yourself from people of other faiths?" they will cite you chapter and verse. They know the scripture, they know the heroes, and they know the stories. So, if somebody asked you and me, "What is your theology of interfaith cooperation? What in the Christian tradition, in the Jewish faith, in Islamic civilization inspires you to build interfaith cooperation?" what would you and I say to that? This is an increasingly critical question to answer, and it ought to be answered everywhere from kindergarten religious education classes in churches, synagogues and mosques all the way to seminary. This book is an important guide on that journey.

Here is a small snapshot for what a theology of interfaith cooperation might look like for me as a Muslim. I hope as you read this, you'll be thinking about the scripture and stories in your own faith that would make up your theology of interfaith cooperation. In the Holy Qur'an God tells the Prophet Muhammad that he was sent to be nothing but a special mercy upon all the worlds." The Prophet is described as, *a special mercy upon all the worlds*—not a kindness for Muslims alone, not an enrichment for the Arabs of the seventh century, but *a mercy upon all the worlds*. That to me is a vision of interfaith cooperation that transcends the lines of tribe.

Here is another story from Islam along these lines. There is a story of a group of Christians who came to visit the Prophet in the city of Medina, and they argued with the Prophet about the nature of Jesus, and about theology. When it came time for the Christians to pray, they asked the Prophet if he would give them leave, so they could exit and could give their prayers outside the city of the Prophet. Muhammad said, "Why would you leave? Offer your prayers in my mosque." And the Christians said, "But we've spent the last several hours arguing theology. We were afraid you wouldn't even let us leave." The Prophet said, "Just because we differ on theology doesn't mean I don't offer you hospitality. It doesn't mean I don't seek cooperation with you. It doesn't mean I don't see you with human dignity."

These are the building blocks of my Muslim theology of interfaith cooperation. The stories go on and on, and the scripture is seemingly endless. Just like in Judaism and Christianity, just like in Buddhism and Hinduism. But it is not enough to individually know these stories. We must share them with our congregations and colleges, and not only be inspired to love one another but to act on those theologies and build interfaith cooperation in our communities.

In other words, we must take upon ourselves the responsibility of bridge-building.

Acknowledgments

When I began this project ten years ago, after I completed *A House of Prayer for All Peoples*, there were many fewer sources available for studying interreligious work in congregations. Times have changed dramatically, and a major part of the work of the book has been keeping up with this growing field. This research has been funded in part through Conant Sabbatical Grants from the Episcopal Church Center, New York, New York, and a grant from the Elizabeth Ann Bogert Memorial Fund for the Study and Practice of Christian Mysticism, Friends World Committee for Consultation, The Religious Society of Friends (Quakers). Sections of this book were expanded as I participated in the Christian Leadership Initiative, sponsored by the American Jewish Committee and the Shalom Hartman Institute, Jerusalem, Israel. My own training in interreligious learning was once again expanded through ongoing participation in the Inter-Religious Studies Project for faculty through a grant made by the Jewish Community Foundation to the Academy of Jewish Religion, California. Special thanks to my hevruta partner for two years, and colleague, Marvin Sweeney.

My deepest thanks to the Religious Education Association (REA) who deemed this work worthy of inclusion in the Horizons series. Special thanks to Jack Seymour for his wisdom and encouragement.

Christine J. Hong, formerly of Claremont School of Theology, and now Associate for interfaith Relations of the Presbyterian Church, U.S.A.was an invaluable research assistant, and has helped keep me current regarding denominational materials.

John Ratti, colleague, commentator, and wise-one, provided keen editorial assistance with the manuscript. Zev Hayyim-Feyer was also a keen proof reader and asked marvelous questions. Richard Bass supported the project and always believed in the value of the book.

Acknowledgments

Countless colleagues have been generous with their time for interviews, as well as with emails, suggestions, and advice. This book is about the deep commitment to interreligious community lived out every day in our local communities, congregations and religious institutions. I am tremendously grateful and honored that I was able to learn about (and write about) the work of the many, many people who directly contributed content to this book:

David E. Abrahams, Beth Adams, Michael Allen, Susan Andrews, Shaheen Akhtar, Daniel Alder, J. Edwin Bacon, Dwight Bailey, Wendy Claire Barrie, Thomas Bridenthal, Martin Brokenleg, Tess Browne, Lamar Burton, Jerry Campbell, Peter J.B. Carman, Nick Carter, Bill Catherwood, Clare J. Chapman, Kathleen Kline Chesson, Sandra Chisolm, Heather Collins, Sherrie Connelly, Louis Crew, Sandra D'Amico, Nancy Davidge, Penny Davis, Tom Davis, Maria DeCarvalho, Kristi L. Denham, Brett Donham, Susan Donnelly, Ian Douglas, Christopher Duraisingh, Cathy Dutch, Bradley Dyche, Christopher Epting, Paul Fairley, Jerry Folk, Greg Foraker, Grant Lynn Ford, Tuomi Joshua Forrest, Mark Frazier, Murray Frick, Hank Galganowicz, Jane Stormont Galloway, Michael Gillespie, Kimberly George, Neil D. Gold, Gary Goldacker, Tom Goddhue, June Goudey, Grattan, David Gray, Gary Greenebaum, Charlie Haas, Bob Hanson, Forrest Harms, Hal T. Ley Hayek, Sherilyn Henry, Joyce Herman, Joanna Helmbacher, Bob Hudak, Deborah Hunley, Mitchell Hurvitz, Bob Husselrath, Chester Jones, Frederick Jones, Jay Kanzler, Salma Kazmi, Alexander Kern, Soumaya Khalifa, Ahmed Kobeisy, Penny Kohn, George Kroupa, Frank Larkey, Eric H. F. Law, Bruce Lawrence, Ian Lawton, Mel Lehman, Robert Levy, Ama Zenya Lewis, Asair Lummis, Iain MacDonald, Gordon McBride, Elizabeth Magill, Ernesto Medina, Bryce Miller, Douglas Mills, Lori Mills-Curran, Ricardo Moreno, Fred Moser, Lucinda Mosher, Edward Mullins, Richard Murphy, Aly Nahas, Mary Ogus, Sonia Omulepu, Elizabeth Orens, Lily Oster, David Parks-Ramage, Lester Ruiz, Cameron Partidge, Jennifer Peace, Bruce Pehrson, Janet Penn, Daniel Polish, Julia K. Powell, Shanta Premawardhana, James Purdy, Ronald Quay, Mahmood Rahman, Mawdudur Rahman, James C. Rhodenhiser, Greg Rickel, Edward W. Rodman, Joseph Rosenbloom, Bill Salyers, Stefani Schatz, Anita Schell-Lambert, Franklin Sherman, S. Samuel Shermis, David S. Shields, Phil Snider, Bowie Snodgrass, Joel Soffin, Marston Speight, Jane Spickett, Isabel Steilberg, Jep Streit, Paul Stumme-Diers, Cynthia Bronson Sweigert, Marsha Swenson, Angel Suarez-Valera, Musa Syeed, Sayyid Syeed, Najeeba Syeed-Miller, Sara

Tatum, Charles Taylor, John Tenhula, Steve Thom, Robert V. Thompson, Sara L. Vurek, Cindy Visscher, Isaac Weiner, Mark Wilhem, Ann Roberts Winsor, Ellen K. Wondra, Denise Yarbrough, Liz Zivanov.

As is the case with most authors who spend hours (and years) writing, this book would not be possible without the support and forbearance of family, most especially my husband Paul Holbrook and our daughter Rachel Holbrook.

Faithfully,

Sheryl A. Kujawa-Holbrook
Claremont, California
Martin Luther King Jr. Day, 2013

Introduction

When religion becomes the bridge that leads to God, it stretches us to live to the limits of human possibility. It requires us to be everything we can possibly be: kind, generous, honest, loving, compassionate, just. It sets out to enable us to be fully, human beings.

JOAN CHITTISTER, OSB (2013)

THE UNITED STATES IS one of the most religiously pluralistic countries in the world. We live in a time where interreligious learning is critical for human survival. Somewhere on this earth people die because of religiously-motivated conflicts every day. Increasingly we find ourselves having to learn different religious traditions in order to understand the nature of current events. Discussions about the current American religious landscape often ignore one salient fact: that the Abrahamic religions and cultures have been deeply intertwined and intricately related from their inception. After the 1965 Immigration Act, other religions, such as those with origins in Asia, grew. Within a five-mile radius of my own location in Southern California, there are places of worship for Jewish, Muslim, Christian, Hindu, and Buddhist communities. Los Angeles is considered the most diverse Buddhist city in the world. In states like California, there is no majority race, ethnicity, or religion. Demographic shifts toward similar diversity, while uneven across the United States, will occur virtually everywhere in the next 50 years and will no longer be confined to the coasts and cities more often associated with religious diversity.

MAJOR RELIGIONS

The United States and the World

	United States	**World**
1	Christianity 78.4%	Christianity 33%
2	Unaffiliated/Non-Religious 16%	Islam 21%
3	Judaism 1.7%	Unaffiliated/Non-Religious 16.1%
4	Unitarians/ Liberal Faiths 0.7%	Hinduism 14%
5	Buddhism 0.7%	Chinese Traditional 0.6%
6	Hinduism 0.4%	Buddhism 0.6%
7	Islam 0.6%	Indigenous/African 0.6%
8	Hinduism 0.4%	Sikhism .36%
9	New Age 0.4%	Juche 0.3%
10	"Other World Religions" 0.3%	Spiritism .23%
11	Native American Religions 0.3%	Judaism .22%

Other ranked World Religions: 12. Baha'i; 13. Jainism; 14. Shinto; 15. Cao Dai; 16. Zoroastrianism; 17. Tenrikyo; 18. Neo-Paganism; 19. Unitarian Universalism; 20. Rastafarisnism; 22. Scientology

U.S. Data: Pew Forum on Religion & Public Life, "Statistics on Religion in America," Accessed April 1, 2013; World Data: "Major Religions of the World Ranked by Number of Adherents," www.adherents.com; Accessed April 1, 2013. The "unaffiliated in the United States and across the world includes atheists, agnostics, humanists, "spiritual but not religious," and people answering "none" or no religious preference. Worldwide, half this group includes persons who are theistic but not nonreligious.

For much of its history the United States was considered a majority white Protestant country with significant religious diversity. However, by the early 21st Century the United States moved from being a religiously diverse white Protestant country to being a genuinely pluralistic nation where no single religious group has a majority (Public Religion Research Institute 2012; Butler Bass 2013).

"The issue of living in a pluralist society and thinking theologically about the questions it poses today is important for every community of faith," writes Diana Eck, professor of comparative religion and Indian studies at Harvard University, and director of the Pluralism Project. "How do we think about our own faith as we come into deeper relationship with people of other faiths and as we gain a clearer understanding of their religious lives?" (Eck 2001, 4)

Eck's definition of religious pluralism moves past statistical diversity, which is a given, to a more proactive "energetic engagement with diversity." This engagement moves past the "thin" foundation of religious tolerance, to "the active seeking of understanding across lines of difference." This new paradigm for pluralism is not relativism or watering down religious traditions, but "the encounter of commitments," requiring us to bring our religious identities and our commitments to our interreligious relationships, and remaining in relationship despite even our deepest differences. Such pluralism involves both speaking and listening on both sides of the learning process. "Dialogue does not mean everyone at the 'table' will agree with one another. Pluralism involves the commitment to being at the table—with one's commitments" (Eck 2006).

For Christians, the transformation of the religious landscape marks a significant shift in the way many Americans think about religion. Our Christian faith "has become a matter of decision and choice among alternatives," notes theologian Douglas John Hall. "At a very obvious, though still frequently ignored, level it means that everything we think, say, write, sing and pray as Christians must now be done in the lived recognition that ours is a particular religious tradition, a choice we have made and (if we are to continue as Christians) must continually reaffirm" (Hall 1991, 208–9). The purpose of this book is to investigate how individuals and faith communities participate in interreligious learning, and how those realities need to inform our practice in the future. The assumption here is that religious pluralism is more than a reality to be tacitly accepted. Rather, it is a sign of Divine activity in our midst, a tremendous gift, and an opportunity for the Christian church to deepen the faith of its own adherents, to participate fully in civic life, and to work for the good all humanity. But for Christians to thrive in the midst of religious pluralism we need to understand and to articulate our own faith on a deeper level, we need to make it our business to study the beliefs and practices of others, we need skills in navigating other traditions and cultures, and we need to build authentic partnerships in our local communities. Mahatma Gandhi, who lived in an era of many religious conflicts in his native India, once commented that if reconciliation and peace was the goal, he would have to show Muslims that he loved them as much as his fellow Hindus. What would a Christian church look like that loved all God's people as much as it did its own members? The task of interreligious learning is to equip us to live more fully into this vision.

Introduction

The book examines the many ways Christian faith communities and religious organizations engage interreligious learning in the present, makes suggestions to enrich current practices, and urges deeper engagement in the future. The introduction and chapter 1 provide the theological and theoretical basis for interreligious learning. Thereafter, each chapter begins with an example of the particular aspect of interreligious learning that is its focus. Each chapter also provides educational principles, illustrations drawn from interviews and site visits, and then concrete strategies for interreligious learning. The structure of the book follows the following pattern: The remainder of this introduction provides background to the subject of interreligious learning from a Christian perspective; religious pluralism and the Christian tradition; Christian privilege in the United States; connections between interreligious learning and cultural competency; and some definitions for frequently used terms. Chapter 1 is an exploration of the ways of understanding interreligious learning, its development as a field, and the range of approaches found within Christian congregations and religious organizations. Chapter 2 reflects on the transformative power of interreligious encounter. The practices of interreligious learning are the focus of chapter 3, including pilgrimages, shared meals, text studies, clergy exchanges, and work with children and youth. Chapter 4 delves into the sharing of sacred spaces and prayer as forms of interreligious learning. Compassionate action in local communities as interreligious learning is the focus of chapter 5. The importance of intentional interreligious communities and their unique contributions to interreligious learning is the focus of chapter 6. The concluding chapter of this book, chapter 7, takes a look at the future of interreligious learning, and suggests directions for further study and action.

A primary goal of this book is to push beyond seeing interreligious learning as a specialized program, or an optional activity, toward seeing it as integral to the vocation of faith communities. In order to accomplish this vision, we need to begin to see all of organized religious practice—education, worship, social action, hospitality, pastoral care—through the lens of interreligious learning. This book is aimed at religious educators, clergy, congregational leaders, seminarians, and concerned folk. It is written from a Christian perspective, though the research partners are from diverse religious traditions, and also include intentionally interreligious organizations. My hope is that while the book is written in a Christian voice, that it contains some wisdom to share with all who read it.

THE HISTORY OF CHRISTIANITY
AND RELIGIOUS PLURALISM

The history of encounter across the borders of religious difference is an ancient one, and includes humankind's efforts to seek alliances with neighbors and to live in peace. We know that Christianity was born in the midst of religious diversity and is not the only tradition to have interreligious encounters throughout its history. For instance, Akbar the Great, a Muslim leader in seventeenth-century Mughal India, encouraged religious tolerance, in this case in a nation which included Muslims, Hindus, Sikhs, and Christians. In the Balkans, though recently the site of ethnic and religious violence, Roman Catholic and Orthodox Christians, Muslims, Jews, and Sufis lived together in peace for hundreds of years.

The Hebrew people lived in a religious context that included the Hittites, Babylonians, Egyptians, and Assyrians. Despite admonitions against foreign gods, we know that the ancient Hebrews adapted Canaanite practices in their worship. Of course, Christianity began as a Jewish sect and developed within the context of a religiously pluralistic society that included adherents of the state religion, mystery religions, and Greek philosophy, to name a few. After the death and resurrection of Jesus, early Christian communities adopted practices, such as baptism from Judaism, and appropriated portions of the Jewish liturgy for worship. They also adopted cleansing rituals from Near Eastern bathing customs. The apostle Paul strongly believed that gentile converts did not need to adopt Jewish practices, such as circumcision, to belong to the community.

For Christians, the life and ministry of Jesus of Nazareth remains the greatest single source of insight on issues of religious pluralism. His example was one of respect and compassion to the most outcast of his society. He was an observant Jew, and yet he spoke and ate with all kinds of "sinners," including people of other religions, such as Roman soldiers, the Syro-Phoenician woman, and Samaritans, even when such actions clearly drew criticism among members of his own religious community. Often during his public ministry, Jesus exhorted his followers to "love your neighbor as yourself," and he sought out ways to demonstrate the importance of this practice. He believed that all people were children of God, and thus worthy of love and respect. This is not to say, however, that all of those around him shared his beliefs or were appreciative of his response to religious pluralism. On at least one occasion, the temple authorities accused Jesus of being a Samaritan, or a heretic, or possessed by demons, due to his open relationships with those normally seen as outside his own tradition (John 8:48). Episcopal priest and diplomat Frederick Quinn sees Jesus' encounters with people of other religious traditions as an integral part of his mission: ". . . it is possible to envision an unfolding process represented broadly in the Reign of God and more specifically in the loving Jesus who gave his followers the example of the Good Samaritan, the Roman officer, a tax collector, the Syro-Phoenician woman and other outcast and marginal people welcomed into his divine presence" (Quinn 2012, 171). Openness to religious pluralism is a basic Christian value if we are to consider the example of Jesus. Openness to learning about other traditions and extending hospitality and friendship are a mandate if we are to follow his example in the world. From a Christian perspective, interreligious learning is not about watering down Christian identity or making relative other religious traditions, but a positive sign of faithfulness to the gospel.

The longest text in the gospels that focuses on Jesus' interaction with a person of another religious tradition is his conversation with the Samaritan woman found in the Gospel of John (4:3–42). The passage actually documents the longest conversation in the New Testament that Jesus had with anyone. Throughout the gospels Jesus used the example of Samaritans on three occasions that illustrate interactions with the religious "other." In addition to the story of Jesus and the Samaritan woman, there is the parable of the Good Samaritan (Luke 10:25–37). As that story goes, the Samaritan is the only traveler willing to stop and care for a person in need, despite their religious and cultural differences. In the story of the ten lepers, it is the Samaritan who returns to thank Jesus for healing, and thus, was healed (Luke 17:11–19).

The story of the Samaritan woman at the well is one that many Christians, no doubt, have heard preached many times. In the story, Jesus stops at Jacob's well at noon and asks a Samaritan woman for a drink. She is astonished that a Jew would even speak to her, much less ask her for a drink of water, and she is annoyed that this mysterious stranger did not have the sense to bring his own bucket. A conversation between the two ensues, about the shared religious history of Jews and Samaritans, their religious differences, and the meaning of "living water." Struck by her encounter with this man, and his uncanny ability to understand her, the Samaritan woman is moved to consider Jesus a prophet, and questions if he could be the Messiah. She then runs to tell everyone in town about the conversation she had with Jesus. Her testimony is so convincing that the community invites him to stay and teach there for a time. The text suggests that, through their encounters with Jesus, others in the Samaritan community were also moved by his teaching.

Often sermons on the text of Jesus and the Samaritan woman focus on the way Jesus spoke openly to a woman, or on his relationships to women in general, in ways uncharacteristic of his culture and era. Those interpretations of the passage remain important. He does, after all, linger at a well, despite the fact that wells were considered women's territory. Reading the passage through an interreligious lens, however, adds another important dimension to the story, one seldom heard from the pulpit. From an interreligious perspective, the story of Jesus and the Samaritan woman is a dialogue with a person representing a different religious tradition, and, from the perspective of a Jew of the era, a despised tradition at that. The story is astonishing for its sheer length; unlike other stories, it is not cryptic or rushed but is a detailed meeting between two unlikely people at a well in the center of town. It is almost as if the gospel writer wants those listening to or reading the story to pause and to linger at the well with Jesus and the Samaritan woman, to eavesdrop on their conversation.

Scholar Sandra M. Schneiders has written extensively on the gospel of John, and has noted that while much is made of the Samaritan woman's numerous husbands, fairly little has been written about her apostolic role in witnessing to her whole community about Jesus. Although the text says that the disciples were shocked to find Jesus talking openly with the woman, it also seems clear, according to Schneiders, that they knew better than to question their master's intentions to include women among his followers. From the beginning, the dialogue between the woman at the well and Jesus is deeply theological. The woman questions Jesus directly on key issues of Samaritan belief in tension with Jewish tradition. She questions his breaking Jewish tradition by speaking to her in public and sharing drinking utensils with a Samaritan. She also questions his offer of living water, which suggests that he is on par with Jacob, who gave the well to Israel. Similarly, she is concerned about the issue of "true" worship, and questions Jesus about where it is to take place, on Mt. Gerizim, as the Samaritans believed, or in Jerusalem, as the Jews believed (Schneiders 2003, 138–41).

To a Jew of Jesus' day, the ritual purity of a Samaritan was suspect, and the custom was to avoid contact. Jesus would have grown up with the notion that, despite their shared heritage, Samaritans were only marginally better than gentiles, and certainly were not full members of the house of

Israel. They were considered foreigners. Still, Jesus went out of his way to enter the town of Sychar, and to invite dialogue on topics that were traditionally considered controversial and painful. Jesus reached out to the Samaritans as individuals and as a community in ways that transcended the barriers of separation between them. As one commentator suggests, Jesus used his knowledge of Samaritan religion and culture to communicate with them in terms that were important to them, knowing they were looking for a messiah who would restore belief and reveal truth. Had he used the words and phrases of a Jewish context, he might not have been able to overcome their mistrust and suspicion. Yet, as soon as the Samaritan woman realized that Jesus' message was to reveal truth, she immediately began to talk about faith. She took risks not only by speaking with him, but by inviting him into her own community. Although Western Christianity does not record her name, the Samaritan woman is known as St. Photina, Equal to the Apostles, in the Orthodox tradition (Schneiders 2003, 138–41).

As Christianity spread throughout the Roman Empire, it absorbed and adapted religious customs and practices of local people. Yet, as the church grew as an institution and solidified its political power, Christians in the West initiated waves of persecution against those of other religious traditions, including Jews and Muslims, as well as others whose beliefs were held in suspicion, such as heretics and witches. As European powers participated in colonial expansion, Christians were brought into contact with indigenous religions, often condemning native traditions and practices. From the late Enlightenment period onward, Christian mission was cast as a civilizing mission bringing the culture and values of the West to colonized peoples increasingly defined by racial differences, and denigrated as inferior. "In terms suggested by the evolutionary theory of the nineteenth century," writes postcolonial theologian Kwok Pui Lan, "Christianity was hailed as the highest stage of human religious development" (Kwok 2011, 534–35).

As independence movements of the former colonies of Europe grew in the modern era, the Christian church was challenged to rethink its mission. At the same time, mass migrations of people into the West changed the religious landscape. "As people of many faiths come to settle in the metropolis, the question for Western Christians is no longer how to missionize non-believers in far-away lands, but how to live among religious neighbors whose children go to the same schools as theirs," writes Kwok Pui Lan. "Such a situation is by no means new; many Christians in

Africa and Asia have been faced with similar questions for a long time. This simply means that people in the Western world are experiencing the pluralistic condition that has defined the religiosity of the majority of the world's population. As religious pluralism has become a global phenomenon, how to live harmoniously together as people of faith is a critical key to world peace" (Kwok 2011, 535–36).

In addition to growing religious pluralism, the Christian population of the world has also shifted. In 1900, Europe comprised two-thirds of the Christian world. It is estimated that by 2050 the Christian world will have "turned upside down." By that year, a third of the world's Christians, approximately a billion people, will live in Africa, and they will outnumber European Christians by two to one. The largest percentage of non-Arab Muslims are also those who live in Africa (Jenkins 2010, 45).

In response to the need to bring religious leaders from around the world together to promote peace and mutual understandings, Christian leaders came together with others to form interreligious organizations. For example, the first Parliament of the World's Religions was held in Chicago in 1893 to bring together the world's religious and spiritual communities to cultivate peace and mutual understanding. Continuing in this tradition, the latest Parliament of the World's Religions in 2009 brought together 10,000 participants in Melbourne, Australia, to foster interreligious dialogue on important local, national, and world issues. Throughout the 20th century, dialogues between the Abrahamic faiths, Christianity, Judaism, Islam, and Baha'i, became prominent, particularly after the Second Vatican Council, and in the United States during the 1960s through the Civil Rights movement and other social movements. The Second Vatican Council took the unprecedented step of including interreligious relations as a topic of serious study, exhorting all Roman Catholics to dialogue with other believers (Knitter 2002, 75–76). The World Council of Churches (WCC) at its general assemblies in Uppsala (1968) and Nairobi (1975), also addressed the need for greater understanding of different religious traditions, somewhat controversially, as some member churches believed that interreligious learning meant an abdication of Jesus' commission to preach the gospel to the ends of the earth. Subsequently, the WCC organized interreligious dialogue within the subunit, "Dialogue with People of Living Faiths" (Kwok 2011, 536).

During the first decade of the twenty-first century, several world-wide initiatives for greater interreligious cooperation emerged, some directly in response to the tragedies of September 11, 2001, such as the educational programs offered by The Interfaith Center of New York for high school and college students, healthcare workers, social workers, city officials, and judges, focused on the social concerns of different faith communities. On an international scale, in 2008 King Abdullah of Saudi Arabia initiated an interreligious conference representing Buddhism, Taoism, Hinduism, Christianity, Judaism, and Islam, hosted by King Juan Carlos of Spain. The following year, the Dalai Lama started the "World-Religions and Symphony" conference as a means to deal with strife among religious groups. In 2010, the Claremont School of Theology, the Academy for Jewish Religion, and the Islamic Center of Southern California, announced a joint agreement which will provide theological education of Christians, Jews, and Muslims, as well as students from other faith groups, through the new Claremont Lincoln University. The hope of the partnership is to educate religious leaders and scholars across religious boundaries better prepared to work in the context of religious pluralism to improve local communities and to heal and repair the world (Kujawa-Holbrook, 2010).

CHRISTIAN PRIVILEGE IN THE UNITED STATES

Those concerned with interreligious learning in faith communities in the United States, must take into account the manner in which "Christian privilege" operates throughout the religious landscape. In many ways, Christian privilege operates in ways similar to white privilege within American culture. The automatic privilege received by European Americans within the United States is the topic of a landmark paper by Peggy McIntosh, associate director of the Wellesley Centers for Women, entitled, "White Privilege: Unpacking the Invisible Knapsack." Now considered a classic among anti-racism educators and trainers, McIntosh's paper uses the image of white privilege as an invisible, weightless knapsack of special provisions, maps, code books, tools, visas, and blank checks to symbolize the subtle but powerful advantages given to those of the dominant racial group. White privilege is given to those born white; it is not chosen. Similarly, white privilege is oppressive to people of color, whether those of us who are beneficiaries choose to be oppressive or not. White people are socialized, according to McIntosh, "to think of themselves as mentally neutral, normative, and average, and also ideal, so that when we work to benefit others, this is seen as work that will allow "them" to be more like "us" (MacIntosh 1990, 31–36).

Psychologist Lewis Schlosser has adapted Peggy McIntosh's work to extend to "Christian privilege," or the advantages inherited by adherents of the dominant religion in the United States, although he is careful to point out that all Christians are not treated equally, either. Roman Catholics have experienced religious discrimination throughout the history of the United States, as have members of other groups like the Church of Jesus Christ of Latter-day Saints, also known as the Mormons, and Seventh Day Adventists, each of which is not always regarded as Christian by other Christians. Yet, despite these inequities, Schlosser argues that overall, these groups on the whole are more privileged than other religious groups in American society (Schlosser 2003, 44–51).

What are examples of Christian privilege? Christians can expect to hear music from their religious group on the radio, or programs on television shows, often corresponding with major holidays such as Christmas or Easter. Christians can reliably expect that our religion will be covered within the context of classes on civilization and in history books read in our schools. Many of us who are Christians do not need to raise our children to expect religious persecution or bias. Within the United States, a church building is considered to be the normative place of worship, where people sit in pews and are presided over by a member of the clergy. The prayer postures of Muslims or Native Americans or Buddhists, are not seen as normative. In the United States, a steeple is considered normative for religious architecture while a minaret or a dome is less so. Federal and state religious holidays and worship are structured around the Christian calendar. It is still considered unique to have candidates for national offices to come from religious backgrounds other than those in the Christian tradition. When Senator Joseph Lieberman was selected as the vice presidential running mate in 2002, much of the media surrounding his candidacy revolved around the fact that he was, in his own words, "an observant Jew" with leanings toward Orthodoxy, and setting off a flurry of anti-Semitic commentary.

Like other forms of unearned privilege, Christian privilege also has a negative impact on Christians. Christians in interreligious contexts often feel that their level of religious literacy is not as high, in terms of knowledge of other religious as well as Christianity itself, as those with a minority religious status. The lack of acknowledgement of Christian privilege can make it difficult for some Christians to understand how some religious groups came to view them with mistrust or dread. There are theological terms, such as "saved" or "scripture" that are taken for granted in Christian vocabulary and that affect interreligious relationships but that cannot be explained with precision by many Christians. The sheer variety of Christianities in the United States, while a tribute to the richness of American religions, are a source of some confusion to other religious groups, and not well explained among Christians. There is no one way to be a follower of Jesus, and our denominational traditions each convey valuable pieces of the total picture, along with some fairly selective history. Intra-religious dialogue, or building relationships between various forms of Christianity is as challenging for Christians as inter-religious dialogue, if not more so due to "family" divisions with deep and complicated histories. Similarly, political terms such as "conservative" or "liberal" when used to describe forms of Christianity are not particularly useful in interreligious contexts; no one form of the Christian tradition is by definition more tolerant of religious differences than another. Rather, different Christianities tend to shape their encounters with other religious traditions around different questions or emphases, such as sacred texts, or compassionate action, or spiritual practices. Still other Christian discourse tends to frame evangelism and religious pluralism in opposition, rather than seeing each as a different Christian response to context. For Christians concerned about evangelism, there is much that can be done among cultural Christians who know little about the tradition, lapsed Christians, Christians who have suffered religious abuse, the unaffiliated, and among Christian church-goers yearning for renewal, rather than focusing efforts on the committed adherents of other religious traditions. On the other hand, Christian responses to religious pluralism that are focused on understanding and caring for those who have found meaning in other religious traditions, and who wish to live in peace and work for the good of all humanity, are sorely needed in the world today.

Letting go of Christian privilege means acknowledging that Christian churches are not as welcoming as we would like to believe, and that how we interact with people of other religious groups in our communities needs to be examined and reshaped if authentic interreligious learning is to be a reality. Rather than holding onto outdated models of a mono-religious American culture, we have an opportunity to re-envision our religious mosaic, and enrich our faith communities and neighborhoods at the same time. In the beyond-Christian-privilege vision of religious America, religious differences are considered a valuable asset and a means to work for the common good.

Adherents of many religious communities in the United States, including American Indians, Africans and African Americans, Jews, Muslims, and Roman Catholics, experience discrimination and violence based on their religious identities. American history has shown that religious freedom is linked to struggle in much the same way as other aspects of civil rights. We also know from studies on psychological conditioning that it contributes to both positive and negative bias in terms of cultural and religious groups (Ratcliff 1997, 103–4). Recent studies indicate that the relationship between some religious groups and the media in the United States does contribute to a form of negative conditioning (Boudreau 2009, 297). Meaning that if the media consistently portray certain religious groups as negative, the impact of those messages will affect the way that group is perceived by many in the society. At the same time, looking at the demographics, it is unrealistic to talk about Christianity in the United States—or any other religious group—in isolation from the other religious communities which surround it, either in this country or abroad. For example,

- The number of persons who report that they are Protestant Christians is barely 51% and this statistic encompasses hundreds of denominations including evangelical churches (26.3%); mainline churches (18.1%), and historically black churches (6.9%) (Pew Forum 2010).

- Although the United States remains 80% Christian, religious minority faiths are growing the fastest. Seventy-two percent of all Muslim congregations and 68% of Jewish congregations reported more than 5% growth since 1995. By contrast, 19% of mainline and evangelical Protestants reported that they lost 5 % or more of their membership since 1995 (Hartford Institute, 2010).

- Including all religions congregations in the United States, the highest percentage of interreligious participation is from Jewish Reform and Conservative temples. Reform and Conservative Jewish congregations also have the highest percentage of full-time clergy—88% (Hartford Institute 2010).

- The fastest growing congregations in the United States are (in order) mega-churches, Muslim, Latter-day Saints, and Assemblies of God. Of the Muslims interviewed, 71% had visited a school or church to talk about Islam. Most mosques (93%) are intercultural, serving more than one ethnic group. The Hartford Institution for Religion Research found that Muslims, Orthodox Christians, and Roman Catholics place a high emphasis on family devotions, fasting and holy day observances, and that Muslims and Evangelical Protestants share similar views on premarital sex, alcohol and drugs (Hartford Institute 2010).

- Among the congregations surveyed by the Hartford Institute in 2005, the highest rates of participation in interreligious worship (40%) and interreligious community service (64%) were among traditions other than Christians. Professor David Roozen suggests that these statistics make sense, in particular "because as minority faith traditions in the U.S. context, they arguably have the most to gain from increased understanding and tolerance; also because of demographics, they tend to be concentrated in cosmopolitan areas where there are larger numbers of Christian congregations seeking to partner with relatively small numbers of other religious communities" (Hartford Institute 2010).

- Among people who are married, approximately 37% are married to a spouse with a different religious affiliation. Hindus and Mormons are the most likely to be married to someone of the same religious background (Pew Forum 2010).

- In contrast to Islam and Hinduism, Buddhism in the United States is made up of native-born adherents, whites, and converts. One-third of American Buddhists are Asian; three-quarters of all American Buddhists are converts (Pew Forum 2010).

Interreligious learning is an antidote to negative conditioning about other religious traditions, and lingering fear about religious differences. A truism about interreligious learning is that it more often deepens the existing religious identity of an individual or group, than it converts them to another religion. Research shows that individuals who learn in religiously diverse environments usually do not convert to another tradition; only a small percentage of adherents change their religious affiliation as a direct result of interreligious encounter. Among those who do change religions, those conversions are more characteristic of a spiritual search which began before any specific interreligious encounter took place. It is also true that some religious traditions actively proselytize, while some discourage it, and some are traditionally indifferent. For example, many contemporary Buddhists welcome participation in their spiritual practice without encouraging persons to call themselves Buddhists. "We don't need more Buddhists," said His Holiness the Dalai Lama, "what we need are more people practicing compassion" (Tenzin Gyatso 2001, 12). Generally speaking, in contexts of interreligious learning, the purpose of the encounter between persons of different religious traditions is for understanding, and parties involved are requested to mutually refrain from proselytizing.

From my own experience as a Christian, I can attest from first-hand experience that interreligious learning expanded both my spirit and my vision. Interreligious learning has helped me to articulate on a deeper level what it means to be a follower of Jesus of Nazareth than if I had restricted my religious relationships to people who shared my religious worldview. Interreligious learning encourages me to learn more about my own religious tradition, its strengths, and its challenges for those who adhere to other truths. As a Christian I also realize that interreligious learning does not remove the theological, philosophical, and cultural differences within my own faith tradition and with other religious groups. For instance, for some Christians, interreligious learning means discerning what salvation means for them and their relationship with persons of other religious traditions. For others, the concern of who is saved is not as central as is the need to form mutually beneficial relationships. For some Christians, the central questions are about belonging to a community with a shared history and practice. As a Christian, I am interested in supporting the kind of interreligious learning within faith communities that encourages religious literacy in our own tradition as well as those of others, to promote mutual respect and understanding, and to bring reconciliation and healing. As Rabbi Gary Greenbaum, the former U.S. Director for Interreligious Affairs of the American Jewish Committee, said, "By knowing more about what I believe and how I express that belief, your own faith can be strengthened. Meanwhile, my understanding of my own belief system grows stronger as I better comprehend your beliefs. Less smoke. More heat. Real fire. No mirrors" (Kujawa-Holbrook, 2010).

INTERRELIGIOUS LEARNING
AND CULTURAL COMPETENCY

Human beings are multi-faceted. Assuming that individuals and groups inhabit many different cultures simultaneously, individuals and faith communities are better prepared for interreligious learning when challenged to become both culturally competent and religiously literate. Without a functional understanding of the interlocking relationships between social identities of race, ethnicity, and culture, there is no foundation upon which to build greater interreligious understanding. In terms of cultural competence, the ability to recognize and respond to varying aspects of cultural differences, including religious differences, and to have the capacity to maintain relationships across differences is needed for authentic religious pluralism. Cultural competence with religious literacy is the outcome of engaging a multi-level process of education and change built in cultural awareness, which enables individuals and groups to do the following (Kujawa-Holbrook 2003, 29–42; 2002, 16–19):

1. *Get in touch with one's own religious culture and beliefs, as well as issues of prejudice and stereotypes towards persons of other religions.* Cultural competence with religious literacy requires each person and each faith community to develop an understanding about how these traits impact persons and faith communities from different religious traditions. When dealing with cultural and religious differences, feelings of anxiety, fear, awkwardness, and discomfort are natural. Often the fear is as much about feeling discomfort in expressing one's own religious beliefs as about a lack of religious literacy. Sometimes there is a feeling that discussing religious differences is wholly negative, or that if one lacks a specialized vocabulary it will insult the other group. Biases about other religions are often apparent on a "feeling level" rather than a cognitive level. At this stage it is important to help people develop their confidence in discussing their own religious histories, cultures, and beliefs through sharing stories.

2. *Know the difference between race, religion, ethnicity, and culture, and be able to apply this knowledge within community contexts.* Religion is but one of the many different dimensions of culture which constitute the social identities of the people who comprise our local communities. Other forms of identity, including race, ethnicity, nationality, immigration status, age, etc., work together and constitute the profiles of members of our religious communities. It is important for members of congregations to recognize that cultural differences are real and that, after all, we will surely see matters differently. On a personal level, it means that individual Christians must understand how culture shapes religious identities and how the hegemonic Christian culture may have an impact on persons of different religious groups.

3. *Challenge the myth that all religions are the same, and uphold their particularities in relationship.* Religious literacy requires knowledge of one's own religious culture, including history, traditions, values, family

systems, languages, interpersonal styles, and artistic expressions, as well as of other religions. While there are *some* similarities among different religious groups, authentic religious cooperation is not built on denying the reality or importance of differences, but rather on the acknowledgement of difference and the commitment to build relationships with that recognition as a given. Often, well-intentioned people promote the idea that "all religions really are the same" in an effort to encourage cooperation, without realizing that the denial of differences actually becomes an impediment to interreligious learning.

4. *Recognize that there are multiple centers of truth, whose legitimacy is often determined by the amount of power any given perspective may have in a particular context.* Although there is a human tendency to universalize our own experience, it is important to understand that what we may value as objective truth may be seen differently from the perspective of a person from a different religious and cultural background. For those of us who are Christians, it means we can never *really* know what it means to be a Muslim or a Jew. In the United States people from other religions generally know more about Christianity than Christians know about others religions because it is critical to their survival.

5. *Understand that the building of interreligious cooperation is a long-term commitment.* As is any change process, building authentic interreligious cooperation is a long-term process, fraught with mistakes and frustration as well as joy and celebration. Even in the face of failure, relationships deepen and interreligious learning expands. When faithful people truly embrace their religious neighbors in an environment where spiritual, emotional, and intellectual questions are acknowledged, the quality of the relationships both within and outside the faith community are enhanced.

We are all shaped by many factors—religion, racial/ethnic background, family of origin, education, nationality, regional affiliations, gender, social class, to name a few. Misunderstandings will occur even when there is good will and careful planning. Listed here are some primary categories of cultural differences which influence interreligious learning:

1. *Forms of verbal and non-verbal communication.*
Across cultures, the way we use particular words or expressions, as well as gestures, eye contact, facial expressions, all impact dialogue, as do non-verbal factors, such as personal distance and the amount of appropriate

physical contact. Similarly, different groups place different values on the loudness or the quietness of conversations, as well as on how much assertiveness is considered respectful.

2. *Attitudes toward conflict.*

Although some cultures view conflict as a positive means to raise differences and seek resolutions, other cultures find open conflict to be embarrassing or troubling. Similarly, while some groups tend to address issues directly and in the open, others find such exchanges disrespectful or troubling and prefer to come to a resolution behind the scenes.

3. *Attitudes toward showing emotions.*

How much emotion it is appropriate to express and with whom it is appropriate to express it constitute a cultural communications factor that differs widely across groups. With some groups, the expression of anger or tears is advised or even applauded; in other groups the expression of strong emotions is a private matter, reserved for the home. In the same vein, cultures vary about the amount of personal information that should be disclosed to others outside the group or family.

4. *Balancing relationships and task management.*

In interreligious collaborations, it is not uncommon to find that some groups tend to focus on tasks to be completed and that other groups tend to be more interested, at least initially, in forming relationships before they begin work together. Both are forms of collaboration, but they differ in the way relationships and tasks are balanced in the process.

5. *Styles and levels of decision-making.*

The styles of decision-making and who is to be included in the process vary across religious and cultural groups. Some religious groups favor more hierarchical or more democratic decision- making styles. In any given interreligious group there are likely to be people who feel comfortable participating in decision-making as well as those who look to others of their group for guidance or consult.

6. *Differences in learning styles*

Just as learning styles vary in any group, interreligious groups are comprised of people who favor different ways of learning and process information differently. Some groups favor an analytical approach to issues, while others favor experiential, relational or spiritual approaches.

Navigating cultural differences takes practice and the ability to be fully present to another person or group. Well-developed listening skills and a commitment to develop relationships are key, as is the need for sensitive interreligious hospitality. Faith communities that develop cultural competency have the opportunity to get to know their neighbors better and to experience more rewarding interreligious learning. Cultural competence is a *learned* skill, not an automatic gain from most religious education. Studies have shown that culturally-competent faith communities are not organic; that is, without intentional skill-building, most instinctively attract persons like the dominant group. An inadequate understanding of the actual religious diversity within a local community and how it works across cultural contexts hampers interpersonal relationships and coalition building.

DEFINITIONS

Setting forth some basic definitions for use throughout this book is itself a form of interreligious learning; the practice creates the opportunity to frame the use of language in ways which facilitate interreligious encounter. Some of the terms listed below will vary according to different authors, though will be used throughout this book in the following manner:

Abrahamic—Monotheistic religions which look to Abraham as a spiritual ancestor and share sacred narratives and common history. (Though the appropriateness of this term has been contested as the traditions refer to Abraham in different ways.) Traditionally, Judaism, Christianity, and Islam are considered Abrahamic faiths. More recently, the Baha'i faith, Druse, and Mormonism are also recognized by some as part of the Abrahamic tradition.

Acculturation—The process of assimilation whereby one group becomes absorbed into the cultural identity of a dominant culture. Religious acculturation refers to the process whereby one religious group becomes absorbed into that of another. Most religious groups in North America struggle to maintain distinctive religious cultures within the overall dominant Christian culture.

Adherent—A follower or a believer of a particular religion.

Anti-Semitism—Anti-Jewish oppression or the systemic oppression of those of Jewish heritage and/or culture. Anti-Semitism is also referred to as the "longest hatred." It is considered by some authors to be a form of racism (Wistrich 1994, xv-xxvi).

Assimilation—The process whereby individuals from one cultural or religious group merge, or "blend," into the dominant group. The concept originated in anthropology and generally refers to a group process, although assimilation can also be experienced on an individual level. For some, assimilation means giving up languages other than English or traditions or customs not practiced in the dominant culture. At one time, assimilation—or the "melting pot" ideal—was assumed to be integral to becoming part of American culture. Generally, religious groups now reject the notion of assimilation, in favor of "integration," or the ideal that it is possible to be both Muslim, or Jewish, or Hindu, and to be an "American," without sacrificing distinctive religious identity.

Bigotry—An intensive and negative form of prejudice usually marked by fear, intolerance, hatred, or suspicion. Intolerance and hatred based in forms of religious identity is religious bigotry.

Christian Privilege—Relates to the idea of Christian hegemony and assumes that the Christian religion and its values are normative for American public life.

Cross-Cultural—The interaction, communication, or connection between people from two or more different cultures.

Culture—The body of learned beliefs, traditions, behavior patterns, communication styles, concepts, values, institutions, and standards that are commonly shared among members of a particular group. These elements are socially transmitted to individuals and individuals are expected to conform to them. Persons belong to a variety of cultural groups simultaneously, as, for example, racial cultures, ethnic cultures, regional cultures, and religious cultures.

Cultural Identity—The part of us that relates to the cultural groups to which we belong, also referred to as *social location*. Individual persons, in fact, encompass multiple identities that relate to a variety of cultural groups, including race, ethnicity, gender, nationality, sexual identity, and so on. Religious identity is a form of cultural identity and thus is interconnected with the other cultural groups to which we belong that form our social location.

Dialogue—In the interreligious sense, refers to the two-way (or more) method of cross-cultural communication in an effort to promote greater understanding, respect, and cooperation among members of different religious groups. Authentic interreligious dialogue is always a multi-directional conversation; it involves listening and speaking, giving and receiving, owning one's own truth and remaining open to the truth of the other. Its chief goal is not to convert, but to promote deeper relationships among adherents of different religious groups.

Diversity—Differences among people or peoples reflected in a variety of cultural forms, included but not limited to race, ethnicity, age, religion, and so on. *Religious Diversity* refers to the varieties of religious experience reflected in a community. Technically, to say that a community or a congregation is religiously diverse does not assume that there are relationships with people across differences. However, the amount of religious diversity in a community and the variety of religious groups represented do point to opportunities for interreligious encounter.

Ecumenical or *Ecumenism*—Refers to the relationships between different denominations of a religious group on the local, regional, national or international levels in a effort to seek greater cooperation and a deeper unity. Within Christian circles, the term describes the relationship between different churches, such as the Concordat between the Episcopal Church and the Evangelical Lutheran Church in America.

Genocide—The systematic destruction of or conspiracy to destroy a group identity because of common racial, national, tribal, cultural, linguistic, or religious characteristics. For example, the Holocaust is one example of religious genocide.

Inter-faith—Refers to understanding, dialogue, and engagement among persons of different religious groups. The term is most commonly associated with relationships among adherents of the Abrahamic faiths, although in various contexts it is inclusive of other religious groups as well.

Inter-religious—Refers to understanding, dialogue, and engagement among persons of different religious groups. Technically, it is a broader and more inclusive group than "interfaith," in that it seeks to include those who are adherents of groups that do not consider themselves "faith" groups, such as some Buddhists, as well as well as those philosophically committed to the common good but not necessarily theistic in belief, such as Humanists.

Often used within the context of academic and monastic dialogues, the term is used in this book because it encompasses dialogue within the widest spectrum of religious belief systems, including the "spiritual but not religious."

Intra-religious—Refers to understanding, dialogue and engagement among persons of a single religious group. Often, the skills needed to facilitate interreligious dialogue are also helpful in dialogue across differences among persons who are technically adherents of the same religious group. For instance, the Orthodox-Anglican dialogues are an example of dialogue between two related but distinct branches of the Christian Church. There are also examples of intra-religious dialogue among other religious communities, for instance dialogue between different branches of Judaism or of Islam.

Integration (also known as Accommodation/Inculturation)—A response of minority religious communities that embraces some aspects of the dominant culture yet strives to retain its own religious culture, including language, traditions, customs, and values.

Isolation—A response of minority religious communities that rejects everything identified with the dominant religious groups. It can mean rejecting the dominant religious language and staying outside the social and political frameworks of the dominant religious culture.

Linguicism—Discrimination and oppression based on language. Linguicism can be conscious or unconscious, active or passive. Within the context of the United States, it is often associated with national origin and English proficiency. Within the context of religion, it also surfaces in conversations on "sacred" languages and on those languages used in prayer and worship.

Multi-cultural—The co-existence of a variety of distinct cultures within a given context. Religion is one aspect of culture, as are race, ethnicity, national origin, language, etc.

Multi-faith—The co-existence of a variety of distinct faith groups within a given context or project. The term is used often to describe joint efforts of the Abrahamic traditions or other religious groups who self-describe as "faith" groups and who are in relationship to work for the common good. "Multifaith" also supports the ideal that all religious are equal, and that no one religion is superior to another. Although the term is often used interchangeably with "interfaith," it does not presume dialogue about religion as part of the relationship between the distinct religious groups.

Multi-religious—The co-existence of a variety of religious groups within a context. Technically, it is a more inclusive term than "multifaith" because it includes those who are adherents of religions who do not self-describe as a "faith" group. Although the term is often used interchangeably with "inter-religious," it does not imply dialogue on religion between group members.

Racism—The systemic oppression of one race by another. In the United States, racism operates on the personal, interpersonal, institutional, and cultural levels and, as a system, differentiates between whites and people of color. Because the social systems and institutions within the United States are controlled by white people, they have the social power to make and enforce decisions and have greater access to resources. Racist attitudes and behaviors can be intentional or unintentional. A shorthand definition for racism is prejudice plus social power. Some argue that anti-Semitism is a form of racism, as well as the anti-Arab or Anti-Middle Eastern oppression that is currently on the rise.

Religious Oppression—Refers to the subordination of minority religions by a dominant religious majority. This subordination is the result of unequal power relationships of religious minority groups with the Christian majority culture in the United States. In the United States, religious oppression is supported through cultural norms and values associated with Christian hegemony, as well as individuals through religious prejudice, to marginalize and exclude religious minority groups from the privileges and access afforded citizens of the dominant religious culture.

Religious Pluralism—Based in interreligious dialogue, religious pluralism describes an active engagement with religious diversity that seeks understanding across religious differences. Although often confused with religious relativism, the ideal of religious pluralism has grown to include what Diana Eck refers to as "the encounter of commitments." This vision of religious pluralism calls people to bring all of their religious identities and commitments to the table and suggests that even our deepest disagreements should be upheld in relationship to each other (Eck 2010).

Religious Tolerance—Based on the belief that persons of different religious backgrounds should be allowed to practice their religion without fear of discrimination or persecution.

Supersessionism—The traditional Christian belief that biblical Judaism was fulfilled or replaced by Christianity, and that the Mosaic Covenant between God and Israel as the chosen people has been abrogated.

I envision the Christian church as a deep well, not unlike the well where Jesus and the Samaritan woman had their encounter. It's a place of living water, a place to meet the stranger, a place to have deep conversations, a place to take risks, a place to practice compassion and to receive mercy. A gathering place for people who come from our own cultures and traditions, but also unlikely people, people from different religious backgrounds, different countries, different traditions, even those we have historically considered our enemies. A faith community with porous boundaries, that includes people who are affluent and privileged sharing a table with those who suffer from prejudice and marginalization. Here is a vision of a church where we can linger in the sun and engage in dialogue about our truths. Interreligious learning often begins with one conversation between two people, then expands to include wider communities, and then gradually dismantles the borders between us, the walls of theology and ideology, the barriers of practices and social roles.

Jesus modeled a way to meet our neighbors by going to their sacred places, by visiting their wells. For us, it will mean going out of our way, and perhaps feeling discomfort, at entering our neighbor's temple, or synagogue, or mosque. It will mean offering hospitality and inviting others into our midst. Getting to know each other and building trust will take more than one conversation. It will mean times of rejection and criticism. At times we will be tempted to pull back and focus inward. To cross the border between the stranger and the neighbor, between enmity and understanding, is both rewarding and costly. Where might you find the opportunities for such conversations in your wider community?

This book is based in hope. Its primary focus is to encourage interreligious learning in faith communities on a long-term basis. Interreligious learning is integral to the mission of faith communities serious about making positive contributions and to local neighborhoods and the wider world. Almost all of those interviewed, including members of faith communities with long-standing interreligious learning of some sort, attested to fears and failures in the process. Yet they all bear witness to the positive impact that interreligious learning made on them spirituality, as well as to the ongoing importance of those relationships to their transformation. They experienced a glimpse of the type of community that Kathy Galloway of the Iona Community in Scotland envisioned in her poem "God Beyond Borders," found at the beginning of this book, where she states "generosity is our only measure" (Galloway 2000, 3). In reading this book, I hope you will learn something and be encouraged in your own efforts in interreligious learning.

REFLECTION QUESTIONS

1. Reflect on your own faith journey with religious pluralism. How old were you when you first encountered another religion, and what was the quality of that experience? How do you experience religious pluralism now? What are your hopes and fears for interreligious community?

2. Follow your local newspaper or television or radio station for a week. How are various religious traditions portrayed in your local media? What are the messages about religious difference? How might your congregation encourage healthy attitudes toward religious pluralism in your community?

3. Who are your neighbors? Research the religious diversity of your community or your neighborhood. What other faith communities are located less than ten miles from your congregation? Does your congregation have ongoing relationships with other religious traditions? If so, how might these relationships deepen? If your congregation does not have such relationships, what are the possibilities in your community?

1

Ways of Understanding Interreligious Learning

I sense in some of the most strident Christian communities little awareness of this new religious America, the one Christians now share with Muslims, Buddhists, and Zoroastrians. They display a confident, unselfconscious assumption that religion basically means Christianity, with traditional space made for Jews. But make no mistake: in the past thirty years, as Christianity has become more publicly vocal, something else of enormous importance has happened. The United States has become the most religiously diverse nation on earth.

DIANA ECK, *A NEW RELIGIOUS AMERICA* (ECK 2001, 4)

INTERRELIGIOUS LEARNING IS NOW a growing interdisciplinary field of scholarly inquiry and pedagogical practice. The purpose of this chapter is to examine the ways of understanding interreligious learning, its development as a field of inquiry, and the range of approaches found within Christian faith communities and religious organizations. Integral to interreligious learning is the importance of personal narratives, both the learning and the *unlearning* of stories of religious pluralism, and the histories of faith communities from an interreligious perspective. The importance of religious literacy as a critical component of interreligious learning is discussed, as are the methodological tools which shape effective interreligious learning. Finally, this chapter will look at the Interreligious Transformation Continuum across Christian congregations and religious organizations, the implications of these varying approaches for interreligious learning, as well as suggestions for supporting future growth.

WHAT IS INTERRELIGIOUS LEARNING?

Interreligious learning is an emerging discipline with the aim to help all participants to acquire the knowledge, attitudes and skills needed to interact, understand, and communicate with persons from diverse religious traditions; to function effectively in the midst of religious pluralism; and to create pluralistic democratic communities that work for the common good. Interreligious learning is an interdisciplinary field that draws content, conceptual frameworks, processes and theories from religious education, religious studies, multicultural education, racial and ethnic studies, women's studies, youth studies, sociology, peace and reconciliation studies, congregational studies, and public policy studies. It also applies, challenges, and interprets insights from these fields to pedagogy and curriculum development in diverse educational settings, including faith communities, schools, and organizations.

Interreligious learning begins with stories and identifying shared values. As a process it should be grounded in the spiritual journeys of individuals and groups, and connected to a vision for humankind to love one another as neighbors. Interreligious learning, like other transformational experiences, will best occur within groups. While this does not exclude the need for individual interreligious learning and reflection, these experiences alone do not replace the importance of forming relationships across religious traditions within the process. Learners and their life histories and experiences should be at the center of interreligious teaching and learning. Learning which occurs in contexts that are familiar to people, that addresses multiple learning styles, and encourages critical thinking, shapes transformative interreligious encounters.

Interreligious learning values cultural differences and religious pluralism in learners, their communities, and in religious leaders and teachers. It requires cultural competency that understands the complexities of religious, cultural, racial, linguistic, regional, and national differences, as well as differences due to gender, sexual identities, economic status, immigration status, and age. Interreligious learning challenges discrimination and addresses intolerance and oppression. Throughout the learning process, sensitivity to feelings, conflicts, prejudices, generalizations, and other impediments to community building across differences need to be acknowledged and addressed openly. Power analysis and openness to structural equality and the redistribution of power among diverse groups are key values and skills in working for the common good. Shared leadership and facilitation is ideal in interreligious encounters, as is the need for democratic space and the expectation that learners are actively engaged in their own learning.

Religious literacy is integral to interreligious learning, including knowledge and understanding of one's own religious tradition, as well as other religious traditions. Interreligious learning builds on and expands the formation of positive and critical religious identities for all ages. It assumes that adherents are the experts of their own religious experience, and have perspectives and information which is of value to others. Interreligious learning strives to first recognize the good in one's own religious tradition and that of others, at the same time acknowledging that all religious traditions also have limitations as human interpretations of the Divine. In interreligious learning, dialogue is as much about listening as it is about speaking. Learners must be religiously literate and capable of forming relationships with individuals, families and communities in order to create environments that are supportive of multiple religious traditions, a variety of life experiences, and democratic action.

THE INTERRELIGIOUS DIALOGUE TRADITION

The fiftieth anniversary of the beginning of Vatican II is a reminder of the importance of the council in opening the door of the Roman Catholic Church, as well as other Christian churches, to the possibilities of interreligious learning through deeper relationships with other religious traditions. Shortly after the council there was a burst of educational activity and publications from Christian organizations and denominations interested in pursuing interreligious dialogue. Given that Christians had maintained for centuries that there was no salvation outside of the church, and that other religions were seen as obstacles to mission, it is not surprising that potential dialogue partners from other traditions were skeptical at first about Christian motivations for interreligious encounter. Indeed, given that the slogan for the Edinburgh Missionary Conference in 1910 was "Christianization of the World in this Century," it is somewhat amazing that so many interreligious dialogues did occur in the years immediately after Vatican II. In these early years, a spirit of enthusiasm often carried the day, and at times the need to develop intentional processes and language for encounter with other religions were neglected. Some of those most engaged in interreligious dialogue in the early years were criticized for losing touch with their own faith communities; others maintained a more conservative reaction to the quick pace of changing attitudes toward other religious traditions. The rise in fundamentalism across religious traditions also contributed to an attitude that positive religious pluralism and lasting peace were unrealistic dreams (Evers 2012, 228–29).

Despite these challenges, the field of interreligious dialogue has expanded over the past 60 years. It should be noted here that the term "dialogue" originated and is most often used in Christian circles, though it sometimes is adopted by members of other religious traditions. (The term "theology" is another Christian term that is used irregularly across religious traditions with a variety of meanings.) In some cases "interreligious dialogue" is used synonymously with "interreligious learning." In other cases, interreligious dialogue refers to specific processes designed for interreligious encounters; including dialogues between experts, interpersonal dialogues between persons of different religious traditions; and community dialogues that are linked to social engagement and peace-building initiatives. Interest in dialogue as a methodology for interreligious encounters also spread beyond its Roman Catholic roots. The importance of grounding Christian theology in a religiously pluralistic world is the premise behind one of the first works on interreligious dialogue to be published through the World Council of Churches, *My Neighbor's Faith—And Mine* (1986). Based in small group learning, the purpose is "to promote an awareness of our neighbors as people of living faiths, whose beliefs and practices should become integral elements in our theological thinking about the world and the human community" (WCC 1986, viii).

The many ways of understanding interreligious learning continues to expand today, including the tradition of dialogue, but also including a variety of approaches and methodologies to support and enrich encounters between different religious traditions. Leonard Swidler, professor of Catholic Thought and Interreligious Dialogue at Temple University, publishes widely and is credited by many with developing the philosophy and pedagogy of interreligious thought and practice. In particular, sources concerned with interreligious dialogue often begin with Swidler's work as a starting point. Recently Quaker teacher and editor Rebecca Kratz Mays published a collection of essays which update and expand Swidler's work from the perspective of local communities, in *Interfaith Dialogue at the Grass Roots* (2008).

Interest in dialogue as a primary methodology for interreligious encounters continues to be a primary theme in the literature of interreligious learning. One who expands the more traditional frameworks of interreligious dialogue is Bud Heckman. In his *Interactive Faith,* Heckman builds on the work of the Pluralism Project at Harvard University and explores ways to balance dialogue and action in terms of learning styles, ethos, organizational structures, and mission (2008, 223). In *What Do We Want The Other To Teach About Us?* (2006), David L. Coppola of the Center for Christian-Jewish Understanding of Sacred Heart University in Fairfield, Connecticut, encourages dialogue as a process which first views the other in relationship with God, before tackling the more abstract elements of religious belief. His book is a collection of essays on Jewish-Christian-Muslim dialogue written by experienced scholars and activists and geared for religious educators in local synagogues, churches, and mosques. "Dialogue and education are tools for each to approach the other as people in relationship with God first, and not as objects spouting abstract beliefs" (Coppola 2006, xv). Presently, Christian interreligious scholar Douglas Pratt, from the University of Waikato, New Zealand, and the University of Bern, Switzerland, is now exploring the various models of interreligious dialogue gathered from international organizations and prevalent over the last 30–50 years with intent to expand "the praxis of dialogue" in the future (2012).

Dialogical Jewish-Christian "conversations" as a means for greater interreligious understanding is the focus of the work of Joseph D. Small and Gilbert S. Rosenthal's edited volume of essays on covenantal partnership, sponsored by the Presbyterian Church (U.S.A.) and the National Council of Synagogues. The book is offered as a model to local communities to encourage the same conversations, including controversial topics such as the State of Israel, conversion and proselytizing, and intermarriage (2010). The use of dialogue as a methodology is also found in literature on Christian-Muslim and Christian-Buddhist relationships. For example, Jane Idelman Smith, professor of Islamic Studies at Harvard University and Hartford Seminary writes on the history, practice and challenges of current Muslim-Christian dialogues (Smith 2007). The release in 2007, "A Common Word

Between Us and You," a letter between 138 Muslim leaders worldwide sent to the leaders of major Christian denominations, and the Christian response, "Loving God and Neighbor Together," affirmed both the differences between the two traditions, as well as the shared commitment to love God and to love our neighbors. The published letters and responses, *A Common Word,* are one example of the emergent dialogue between the two traditions (Volf, Muhammad, Yarrington 2010). Paul Ingram of Pacific Lutheran University studies the processes of Buddhist-Christian dialogue, mapping out the conceptual, socially-engaged, and interior dimensions of each tradition.

INTERRELIGIOUS LEARNING
AND RELIGIOUS EDUCATION

Interreligious learning today includes the interreligious dialogue tradition, as well as additional approaches. The importance of interreligious learning was argued by religious educators in the early twentieth century, particularly as people of faith struggled to make sense of catastrophic world wars. As early as the 1930s and 1940s, progressive religious educator Adelaide Teague Case worked with the Fellowship of Reconciliation (FOR) and other peace organizations to draft studies and curricula focused on the need to bridge cultural and religious differences around the world. From the 1940s onward, religious educator Norma H. Thompson encouraged ecumenism, and later religious pluralism, and played a key role in Jewish-Christian dialogues. Case and Thompson are only two of the many religious educators who practiced, taught, and wrote about the importance of religious pluralism, often before the interest of mainstream churches and denominations.

No critical exploration of interreligious learning would be completed without mention of the ground breaking work of religious educator Mary C. Boys, now professor of practical theology at Union Theological Seminary in New York. Through her scholarship, Boys skillfully interweaves religious education with biblical studies, liturgy, and systematic theology. Boys' work not only emphasizes the need for Jewish-Christian dialogue, but goes a step further by challenging inherent and inherited Christian supersessionism. That is, the belief that the validity of the Christian faith means supplanting the Jewish tradition. While it is important for Christians to encounter many of the religious traditions of the world, Boys asserts that for those Christians interested in fully engaging interreligious learning, understanding the shared history with Judaism is inescapable. This is not to say that Christians should never engage traditions beyond Judaism. Rather, it is to highlight the understanding that, "There is no way to talk about Christianity without reference to Judaism" (Boys 2000, 7). Because of the historic ties between the two traditions, Boys argues that it is integral for Christian interreligious learning to take seriously our relationship with Judaism. Boys argues for the importance of educating Christians for fuller participation in a pluralistic world through teaching, preaching and worship that deconstructs inherited supersessionism, helps people understand what is wrong with it, and then helps them reconstruct a new "story line" that does not define Christianity over against Judaism. For Mary Boys, interreligious learning in inextricably linked to justice in "discovering the right way in which we might understand the people from whom we came and with whom we are linked to the God of Abraham and Sarah so that we ourselves might walk our journey of faith in a more trustworthy fashion" (Boys 2000, 8).

In *Christians & Jews in Dialogue. Learning in the Presence of the Other* (2006), Mary C. Boys and Jewish educator Sara S. Lee, director emerita of the Rhea Hirsch School of Education and adjunct professor emerita of Jewish Education at Hebrew Union College—Jewish Institute of Religion in Los Angeles, weave together interreligious teaching and learning from the perspectives of both Judaism and Christianity. Through personal stories, case studies and observations tested through years of personal teaching experience, Boys and Lee make the connection between interreligious learning and the need to heal religious divisions by bringing people together to talk through difficult subjects such as religious identity, the Holocaust, and the State of Israel. Boys and Lee's theory of interreligious learning provides a platform for the emergent field today, including an emphasis on 1) "study in the presence of the other"; 2) intentionally connected content and process; 3) a hospitable environment which enables learners to cross religious boundaries, and 4) the need to "get inside" the religious tradition of another (Boys and Lee 2006, 95).

PERSONAL NARRATIVES AND INTERRELIGIOUS LEARNING

Austrian-born Jewish philosopher Martin Buber believed that personal narratives, or the telling of stories, brings healing and is sacred action. Buber tells a story about a man who was the student of a holy rabbi, the Baal

Shem Tov. The rabbi used to jump and dance as he prayed. The story of the rabbi at prayer was so powerful that the act of telling it brought healing to the man as, ". . . he stood up while he was telling the story and the story carried him away so much that he had to jump and dance to show how he [holy Baal Shem Tov] had done it." From that moment, the story-teller was healed. "This is how stories ought to be told" (Buber 1973, 71).

The poet Maya Angelou writes, "History, despite its wrenching pain, cannot be unlived, but, if faced with courage, need not be lived again (Angelou 1993). Stories have the ability to transform both the storyteller and the listener. Each person is the authority of their own personal story of religious pluralism. It doesn't matter if a person does not have a formal theological education, or skipped Sunday school, or has not studied the Talmud or Torah or Qur'an. Efforts at interreligious cooperation are empowered by storytelling because stories convey lived religious experiences. Rather than beginning conversations with doctrinal debates or theological abstractions, beginning with personal stories enables people to appreciate each other's human experience. Our personal experience is at the root of how we experience religious differences as well as how we experience God. "Telling my story is not in itself theology but a *basis* for theology," writes theologian Jung Young Lee, "indeed, the primary context for doing my theology. This is why one cannot do theology for another. If theology is contextual, it must certainly be autobiographical" (Lee 1995, 7).

My own family of origin is Polish-American, people who encountered prejudice on a variety of levels, including language, immigration status, nationality, social class, and religion. As Roman Catholics, they were aware of the prejudices against them from other Christians. As immigrants, they knew the isolationist practices of the Midwestern city in which they lived and strived to keep their culture alive despite discrimination. The church was the center of every major event of their lives, and probably the most important institution to which they related. Yet, in subtle ways, they also embraced the pluralism of their context. They chose to make sense of their own experience of marginalization by consciously not doing the same to other people. So, unlike my peers' families, my family had friends from other Christian denominations and Jewish friends as well. The priests in our parish church shared pulpits with the rabbi of the nearest temple and took people from the congregation to visit the local mosque when it opened. Years later, when my vocation led me to ordination in the Episcopal Church, that same family greeted the surprise of an ordained daughter with tears of joy. Although none of these actions was accompanied by splashy media coverage or elaborate programs, I have learned from my story the transformative power of local people of faith taking seriously the need to be in relationship with their neighbors and I believe that has a profound impact on faith communities.

The work of Frank D. Rogers Jr. on narrative pedagogies and young people points to the central role of personal narratives for interreligious learning. Stories transmit faith traditions, and therefore are important tools for religious literacy. They shape one's sense of personal and communal identity, and they mediate experiences of the sacred. Stories nurture critical consciousness and inspire social transformation. They also nurture and affirm creativity and public expressions (Rogers 2011). In another new book, the importance of personal narratives as a key methodology in interreligious learning for religious educators, community leaders, and activists, is the focus of *My Neighbor's Faith: Stories of Interreligious Encounter, Growth and Transformation* (2012), by Jennifer Howe Peace, Or N. Rose, and Gregory Mobley of Hebrew College and Andover Newton Theological School. Similarly, Miranda Sharp uses stories of intercultural *mis*understanding to teach the limits of our own perspectives in order to shape encounters that are mutually empowering (Sharp 2013).

The Faith Club by Ranya Idliby, Suzanne Oliver, Priscilla Warner (2006), and *Getting to the Heart of Interfaith* by Don Mackenzie, Ted Falcom, and Jamal Rahman (2009), are essentially collections of personal narratives by the authors, representative of Judaism, Christianity and Islam. Both are used extensively for the purposes of study and to spark discussions in local faith communities. The emphasis here is on interreligious formation by moving people past feelings of separation and fear to a place where they are able to discuss critical differences and remain in relationship with each other.

In the same vein, Michelle LeBaron's voluminous work on mediation and conflict transformation informs interreligious learning. LeBaron's approach views stories as pathways to healing and transformation, and much of her work is about providing narrative tools to communities in conflict. "As we acknowledge the legitimacy of stories as ways of communicating and negotiating identity and meaning, we see that they are essential to our processes. They are the fabric through which conflicts are constructed and the threads through which relationships can be rewoven (2002, 249). LeBaron's work is inclusive of many forms of difference, and is not limited to or focused on religious differences, though it speaks widely to the power of stories to build and sustain human communities. Stories connect us in relationship to others through content, feeling and meaning. They convey our deepest hopes and deepest fears. "They are openings into whole worlds," writes Michelle LeBaron. In LeBaron's work in conflict transformation, she argues that the power of stories can reframe and transform even the most deeply felt conflicts. She believes that stories are always present, in harmony or in conflict. They can be resources for relationship, or they can be resource for division. What matters is how we create, shape, interpret, and reinterpret our experiences. Stories are important resources in interreligious learning because they bring us into connection with those of other religious traditions; they stimulate empathy by engaging human relationship; they provide contextual information about another person or group; they convey their message indirectly, saving face, thus supporting a greater sense of harmony; and, they are opportunities to practice compassionate listening (LeBaron 2002, 222–23).

Interfaith families remain an important, though often neglected, source of interreligious relationships found in faith communities. Jane Kaplan analyzed stories of Jewish-Christian interfaith families in order to discern patterns that occur in almost every aspect of family life that are influenced by religious traditions (2004). These stories reveal the power of religious holidays and rites of passage, even for those who do not consider themselves observant Jews or Christians. The stories also speak to the importance of religious literacy; many of the couples interviewed wanted to ensure that their children adequately understood their religious heritage, even if the parents felt their own understanding was limited. As the numbers of intermarried families continue to rise, the need for interreligious learning that takes into account the realities of these families remains an important, if controversial, field of inquiry.

Marc Gopin, the director of the Center for World Religions, Diplomacy, and Conflict Resolution at George Mason University's School for Conflict Analysis and Resolution, writes about the inner lives of Arab and Jewish peacemakers, almost all of whom suffered violence or witnessed it against their loved ones. Gopin believes that one of the inherent skills of effective story-tellers, self-reflection, is also found in the narratives of extraordinary peacemakers. These peacemakers are conscious of their own internal life and struggles, they are prepared to face themselves ethically and spiritually, and they are more ready that the average person to share these stories with others as part of their personal growth, as well as part of their peacemaking. Gopin writes that self-reflection is a key skill if individuals and groups are going to overcome violence and despair. He argues that a central source of misery and conflict in families and communities, "is the emotional, cognitive and ethical failure to be self-reflective" (Gopin 2013, 6–7).

INTERRELIGIOUS LEARNING AND RELIGIOUS LITERACY

For Christians engaged in interreligious learning, it often seems as if other religious groups know a great deal more about their religion than we do. This fear can manifest itself in a reluctance to talk about religious beliefs, not only with other Christians, but with adherents of other faith traditions, or to avoid interreligious encounters all together. Thus, stress on religious literacy for all ages serves as a foundation for intentional interreligious learning. In his book *Religious Literacy: What Every American Needs to Know and Doesn't*, Steven Prothero raises the issue of religious *illiteracy* in the United States. In his work as a religious studies professor at Boston University, Prothero noticed that his students did not seem to understand what he believed were basic references to religious topics in his lectures. So he devised a basic quiz to determine the students' level of basic religious knowledge. Some of the basic questions in the quiz, included:

- Name the Ten Commandments
- Name the four Gospels
- Name the sacred text of Hinduism
- What is the name of the holy book of Islam?
- What is the Golden Rule?
- What are the first five books of the Hebrew Bible or the Christian Old Testament?
- What is Ramadan? In what religion is it celebrated?
- Name the Four Noble Truths of Buddhism.

In addition to his students, Prothero questioned his own children and came to the conclusion that both groups knew little about their own religion and even less about other religious traditions. This lack of religious literacy, suggests Prothero, is not only alarming inside religious communities, but is detrimental to participation in civic and political life. Prothero suggests that many key issues of our society today, such as immigration, marriage, abortion, the environment, euthanasia, poverty, capital punishment, and war are argued by invoking religion or the Bible, and thus, for people to engage these issues, they need to be religiously literate (Prothero 2007).

Diana Eck concurs with Prothero's assertion that the new religious America requires a greater degree of literacy than is now the reality. "I think it is dangerous to live at such close quarters in a society such as ours, with a series of half baked truths and stereotypes functioning as our guides to the understanding of our religious nature," she writes. "If you ask what my fear is, it's that if our diversity becomes isolated enclaves in which we do not allow ourselves to encounter one another and don't take on the difficult task of creating a positive pluralism in which we have engaged with one another, we may end up with communities that are more isolated" (Caldwell 2008).

INTERRELIGIOUS LEARNING
THROUGH COMMUNITY AND HOSPITALITY

Although much of religious curricula published through denominations or Christian publishers are predominately Christian-focused, there are some notable exceptions. Many of the denominational approaches to interreligious learning are focused on building relationships with neighbors from other religious traditions. Such relationships, it is reasoned, will enrich faith communities and local neighborhoods. For example, The General Board of Global Ministries of the United Methodist Church publishes an interfaith study guide by R. Marston Speight, *Creating Interfaith Community*, which focuses on the realities of religious pluralism in North America and on resources from the Christian faith in building community across traditions. The need for greater cultural competence in encounters with our neighbors of different faiths is the premise of Cherian Puthiyottil's *Our Neighbors: An Introduction to Cultural Diversity and World Religions* (2001). This work by Augsburg Fortress is organized through five of the major religions of the world (Buddhism, Judaism, Hinduism, Islam and Christianity), along with the religious composition of 60 nations throughout the world. Though more a resource book than praxis-oriented, *Grounds for Understanding* (1998), by S. Mark Heim, focuses on theological responses to religious pluralism from the perspective of a wide range of Christian denominations, including many major documents on interreligious relationships (Heim 1998).

Lucinda Mosher's artful and articulate "Faith in the Neighborhood" series grounds interreligious learning in everyday encounters in local communities, as well as in the spiritual needs and connections we share; belonging, praying, grieving. Mosher, an Episcopalian writing for an ecumenical audience, argues that the Ninth Commandment warns us against bearing "false witness" against our neighbors. But how can we be assured that we are not doing that to our neighbors of other religions unless we know about their traditions and practices? If we are commanded to love God and our neighbors we must "be with" our neighbors, and thus, be equipped with deeper understanding across religious differences. " Christians know that *all* humanity has been created in God's image . . . We can therefore be of better service—more loving, more respectful of dignity, more likely to establish justice and peace—if we understood how our neighbor 'establishes, maintains, and celebrates a meaningful world,' which is what religion does" (2005, xi). The "Faith in the Neighborhood" series is intended for study in Christian congregations and religious schools.

Building interreligious community through learning about Christian responses to religious pluralism is the premise of an interfaith curriculum published by LeaderResources in Massachusetts. Designed for use by youth and adults in congregations by Denise Yarbrough, an Episcopal priest, *The Many Faces of God: An Interfaith Encounter for Youth and Adults,* introduces the various Christian theological approaches to religious pluralism, along with an examination of the Nicene Creed, and specific teaching in the practice of dialogue.

The idea that interreligious learning is based in hospitality and welcome is the approach of several scholars. English Jesuit Michael Barnes in *Interreligious Learning: Dialogue, Spirituality and the Christian Imagination* (2012) argues the importance of interreligious hospitality, along with an emphasis on difference *and* particularity in the search for meaning. Barnes describes three shifts or "movements" that occur in relationship with the other. The first, "meetings," attempts to situate interreligious encounter within the context of theology and history. Here he offers the image of religious traditions as "schools of faith" where teachers and learners can meet and ask questions about beliefs, actions, prayers and rituals with integrity. The second movement, "crossings" emphasizes the need for people to be translated across cultural boundaries if they are to learn the skills necessary for dialogue. "Imaginings," the third movement concerns the return back across the threshold of engagement to reflect on the ways that faith is enhanced through interreligious learning and the need to imagine an alternative future. Barnes' movements are not intended as fixed stages, but rather as a way of reflecting on the spirituality of interreligious dialogue. "More important than any such logic is the conviction which guides me throughout that, while Christian faith and the beliefs and practices of Jews, Muslims, Hindus, and Buddhists may be saying different things, the very attempt to grapple with difference in a spirit of generous respect can be mutually supportive and illuminating" (Barnes 2012, xiii–xiv).

The importance of hospitality as seen through the biblical text, is a framework for interreligious learning used by evangelical Christian contributors to the field. For example, Pentecostal theologian Amos Yong explores scripture, the practices of Jesus, and the early church to conclude that adherents of other religions are not objects for conversion, but rather a religious neighbor to whom hospitality must be extended and received. Through a pneumatological framework, Yong argues that if hospitality plays a central role in the Christian theology of religions today, than the result is not only a set of ideas but a correlative set of practices. "Christian mission in a post-modern, pluralistic, and post-9/11 world is constituted by evangelism, social witness, and interreligious dialogue and that evangelism and proclamation always involve social engagements and interreligious dialogues of various kinds," he writes (Young 2008, 129).

INTERRELIGIOUS LEARNING AND YOUNG PEOPLE

Interreligious learning for children and youth and young adults is a growing field, although faith communities in the United States have fewer resources in this area to draw on than do those regions, such as the United Kingdom and some European countries, where religion is taught as an academic subject in schools. For example, Carl Sterken's book on *Interreligious Learning* discusses mono-religious, multi-religious, and interreligious models of religious education as they relate to primary schools (Sterkens 2001, 47). The debate on the place of teaching religion(s) in the public schools in the United States is a long and complicated one, based in the need for more widespread religious literacy and skills to participate in democracy and navigate religious pluralism on the one hand, and the affirmation of the separation of church and state and fear of proselytism on the other. "One of the greatest ironies of our intellectual life in the United States is that though we are the world's most religiously diverse nation we are also its most religiously illiterate," writes Diane L. Moore, senior lecturer in religious studies and education at Harvard Divinity School and chair of the three-year task force the American Academic of Religion on the teaching of religion in the schools. Moore's approach to overcoming religious illiteracy is rooted in cultural studies in an effort to mitigate the dangers of essentialism while retaining the critical and emancipatory dimensions of multicultural and reconstructionist theories (Moore 2007, 27, 78). Harvard Divinity School is also the home of the Religious Literacy Project, headed by Diane L. Moore, and designed to provide resources on the religious dimensions of multiculturalism in civil life for the use of public school teachers and their students.

The study of interreligious learning among children, youth and young adults based in faith communities is comprised of several approaches. First, grouped together under the unifying theme of the need to pass on religious traditions to the next generations or rites of passage, there are those studies which look at spiritual development and formation from the perspective of individual traditions. For example, James L. Heft's work looks at the challenges of religious socialization among Jews, Christians, and Muslims in the contemporary United States. Heft's work is written in response to three national studies on youth religious development; Christian Smith's study on the religious practices and understanding of teenagers in the United States; Sandy Astin's research on college students and their sense of spirituality; and, Heft's own research supported by the Lilly endowment on how synagogues, congregations and mosques connect spirituality and religious practices (Heft 2007, 8). From the perspective of Islam, Robert Hefner and Muhammqad Quasim Zaman's book on *Schooling Islam* examines the complexities of models of religious education in Muslim contexts. "We in the West would be truer to our own moral history were we to recognize that our schools and politics, too, bear the imprint of struggles over how children and citizens should ethicalize and behave . . . They are a civilizationally specific response to the challenges of pluralism, knowledge, and ethics faced by all citizens in the late modern world" (Hefner and Zaman 2007, 35).

Another volume funded through the Search Institute and the John Templeton Foundation and edited by Karen Marie Yust and others, focuses on spiritual development in childhood and adolescence in Buddhism, Christianity, Hinduism, Islam and Judaism. Here the studies focus on the role of children and adolescents within the five religious traditions; question how the traditions understand the process of spirituality in childhood and adolescence; examine which rituals and spiritual practices nurture young people, and guide them to meaning, purpose and ethical action; investigate to whom the religious assign responsibility for nurturing spirituality in children and youth; and lastly, examine how religious traditions address the social, policy and cultural forces which impact childhood and adolescent spirituality (Yust, A.N. Johnson, S.E. Sasso, E.C. Roehlkepartain 2006, 10).

Related to the field of childhood and adolescent spirituality is the growing multi- and interdisciplinary field of childhood studies. The United Nations General Assembly adopted the Convention on the Right of the Child (CRC) in 1989, thereby affirming the rights of children to practice their preferred religion, and thereby challenging scholars, policy makers, religious leaders, and educators to cooperation and joint action for the sake of the world's children. At the same time, during the 1990s the theoretical boundaries of children and childhood were expanded, affirming their voices and agency (Ridgely 2011, ix–x). The work of Don S. Browning and Bonnie J. Miller-McLemore, challenge the adult-centric approach to the study of religions, and respond to the question, "How do different religious traditions in the United States today understand children, and how do people in these religions study and guide children in the light of the prominent threats and opportunities of American life?"(Browning and Miller-McLemore 2009, 1) Browning and Marcia J. Bunge studied the attitudes towards children,. central religious practices, and the role children play internationally in Judaism, Christianity, Islam, Hinduism, Buddhism and Confucianism. "Religious images and understanding of children are not confined to the inner life of a specific tradition the spill over into the wide society, no matter how allegedly secular that society is thought to be," write the authors. They believe that study of the relationships between religion and childhood are crucial "because they are often a source of deep tension and heated debate here and abroad."(Browning and Bunge 2009, 3).

Intentional interreligious education with children is a focus in practical theologian Elizabeth F. Caldwell's *God's Big Table. Nurturing Children in a Diverse World,* where she uses the imagery of coming to the table as a metaphor for the ways churches can engage pluralism through the biblical theme of welcoming all of God's children."The wrestling that is most needed by people of faith today and by congregations is how we understand who God is in relation to difference—people who think differently than I do, people who look differently from me, people of different faiths who believe in God in ways that are unique to their traditions," writes Caldwell (Caldwell 2011, 3). Caldwell also addresses hospitality to multifaith families and ways to introduce different religious traditions to children. Interreligious hospitality is a theme in Dori Grinenko Baker's *Greenhouses of Hope: Congregations Growing Young Leaders Who Will Change the World.* Along with Katherine Turpin, the author argues that young people today live in a "new convivencia—a living mix of a multitude of religious beliefs and practices" and advocates for Christian congregations to practice radical welcome as a space for young people to reflect on their lived experience in an interreligious world (Baker 2010, 85).

Eboo Patel, director of the Interfaith Youth Core (IFYC) and research director Patrice Brodeur studied a wide range of international initiatives and projects of the "first interfaith generation" in their book, *Building the Interfaith Youth Movement: Beyond Dialogue to Action.* In addition to building a knowledge base in interreligious youth work, the work is intended to contribute to the global interfaith youth movement. "One of the goals of this movement is to empower each other to pioneer new and cooperative learning paths at the same time as we make room critical self-reflection through which scholarship can be produced as another tool for empowerment," they write (Patel and Brodeur 2006, 1, 6–7).

Literature for children and youth tends to focus on building religious literacy in one's own tradition as well as the religions of the world, an awareness of the stereotypes and common misconceptions about religious traditions, and the need for positive relationships with neighbors of other traditions to contribute to the common good and to live in peace. More so than in curricula for adults, literature for young people is organized around the idea of "world religions," despite the limitations of that term, namely, it was constructed to lump together all religions which were not Christianity; that religious pluralism is located where we live, not elsewhere in the world; and, that the term begs the question of what is considered to be a "religion." This problem with terminology aside, the importance of introducing young people to other religions in a positive way is an important consideration, and controversial in some Christian contexts. J. D. Rhodes' *World Religions,* for instance, is focused on Christian youth interested in better understanding the religions in their communities; among friends, classmates, and neighbors. A more social studies approach is taken by Margaret O. Hyde and Emily G. Hyde in *World Religions 101,* which explores spirituality and religion from the perspective of a world phenomenon rather than from belief. Included here for young people is a basic introduction to the neurobiology of the brain and its relationship to religion. Laura Buller's *A Faith Like Mine*, is a celebration of the religious traditions of the world for children from the perspective of adherents who are also children.

In the United Kingdom, where religion is taught as an academic subject in schools, there is a variety of materials available for children and youth which can also be adapted for use in faith communities. For example, Religious and Moral Education Press (RMEP) has several series which introduce religions traditions tor young people. The "Faith and Commitment" series looks at religions and denominations through the personal reflections of adherents. To create the books the authors visited local communities in Britain and interviewed people of different ages about their personal religious experiences (Sutcliffe 1984). The "Places for Worship" series introduces children into the sacred spaces of churches, synagogues, mosques, gurdwara, viharas, mondirs, and other sites (Broadbent and Logan 2009). Another series, 'Times to Remember," shares with children the major stories of religious traditions, such as the stories about Jesus found in Christianity, or the birthday of Guru Nanak, the founder of Sikhism (Broadbent and Logan 1988). Lastly, for youth, the "Faith in Action" series shares short biographies of men and women who have courageously acted according to their faith, such as Mahatma Gandhi, Aung San Suu Kyi, Desmond Tutu, Martin Luther King, Jr., etc. The stories are focused on encouraging young people to empathize with the religious leaders by describing their situations, reflecting on related local and global issues (Constant 1998).

CONCEPTUAL FRAMEWORKS AND METHODOLOGIES FOR INTERRELIGIOUS LEARNING

Integral to interreligious learning are the conceptual frameworks, processes, and methodologies which help learners develop skills to better understand other religious traditions, and to better navigate, individually and collectively, the relationships found through interreligious encounters. Judith A. Berling's book, *Understanding Other Religious Worlds: A Guide for Interreligious Education* (2004), is one of the most comprehensive of these works. As professor of Chinese and Comparative Religions in the Graduate Theological Union, Berkeley, Berling makes the clear distinction between the learning of *facts* about other religions, and *understanding* other traditions and adherents. She suggests methodologies for interreligious teaching and learning in the classroom, in faith communities, and in theological education settings.

Case Study methodologies are central to the literature of interreligious teaching and learning. For example, Paul D. Numrich, who is both a theological educator and a scholar of religion, edited an illuminating collection of case studies of Christian congregations and their actual encounters with other religious traditions, in a effort to illustrate the joys and challenges of interreligious engagement (2009). In Britain, Malcolm Torry and Sarah Thorley documented case studies of Christians engaging other religious traditions in a variety of contexts; churches, hospitals, prisons, schools, women's groups, funerals, on pilgrimage, etc. Each case study has a response authored by adherents of the partner traditions. Together they illustrate the many ways interreligious learning and engagement support spiritual growth and build more peaceful communities (2008). Kate McCarthy's work on interfaith organizations, including families and faith communities is an expansive look at the wide variety of contexts where interreligious engagement takes place today. Importantly, her research delves into the subject of the online interreligious encounters where people of different religious traditions meet every day. McCarthy's work suggests the need to explore more intentionally the way online learning shapes interreligious encounters (2007).

Fredrick Quinn's interreligious scholarship focuses on Anglican and Episcopal contexts and analyzes case studies from the United States and the United Kingdom to document how Christian responses to other religions have changed in recent decades. Quinn's goal is not to present conclusive findings, but rather, to make a case to the church that global interreligious contact is a reality, and that given this reality, Christians need to intentionally change how we teach and practice our faith. Quinn argues that in the years ahead, "Its [the church's] teaching authority will be more that of advice and guidance in sound scholarship, than a defensive reassertion of ancient dogmatic formulae. Its sacramental life will be more the offer of the unconditional and personal love of God to encourage human flourishing in an equitable and just world, than a hierarchical control of the exclusive means to eternal life. An institutional form will be more one of humble service to the community than of patriarchal dignity and control" (156).

The need to integrate interreligious learning into theological education in order to prepare leaders for a religiously pluralistic world is the focus of a number of initiatives, including *Changing the Way Seminaries Teach: Pedagogies for Interfaith Dialogue* by David A. Roozen and Heidi Hadsell. This study moves the religious literacy of seminary graduates beyond Christianity, although that need is affirmed, to addressing ways theological schools address and structure interreligious engagement within the context of their curricula. Through case studies and sample syllabi Roozen and Hadsell create "a practical literature and related conversation among theological educators on the role of the practice of interfaith dialogue in the seminary curriculum" (Roozen and Hadsell 2009, 5).

Similarly, interreligious learning from the Christian tradition as a resource for religious leadership is the premise behind the book by David R. Brockman from Southern Methodist University and Ruben L.F. Habito from the Perkins School of Theology. *The Gospel Among Religions: Christian Ministry, Theology, and Spirituality in a Multifaith World* (2010) weaves together a rich selection of historical and contemporary sources in support of interreligious dialogue and relates it to the task ministerial formation.

INTERRELIGIOUS LEARNING AND PEACE-BUILDING

The connections between peace-building and interreligious dialogue and learning made by Amos Yong are echoed in the work of educators and activists from a across religious traditions. *Peace-Building By, Between and Beyond Muslims and Evangelical Christians* (2009) edited by Mohammed Abu-Nimer and David Augsburger is a compilation of articles by Christians and Muslims on topics related to interreligious peace-building such as religious identity, religious conversion and apostasy, interreligious dialogue, conflict transformation, and human rights. David R. Smock's *Interfaith Dialogue and Peace-Building* (2000) takes up the question of the relationship of religion to peace-building, and then offers principles in support of dialogue processes (Smock 2000,129–31). Susan Brooks Thistlethwaite's *Interfaith Just Peacemaking: Jewish, Christian and Muslim Perspectives on the New Paradigm of Peace and War* (2012) is a result of the Interfaith Just Peacemaking conference in 2009. Here "Just Peacemaking" theory is upheld as the fourth paradigm in the historic continuum of ways peace and war are addressed, including Pacifism, Just War theory, and Crusade. The focus of the collection of articles is on peacemaking practices that individuals and governments employ to save lives, and on the role of religion in informing those practices (Thistlethwaite 2012, 5–7).

Another approach to interreligious peace-building is provided by Peter Dula and Alain Epp Weaver through the Mennonite Central Committee in *Borders and Bridges* (2007). Here the authors refute the "clash of civilizations" thesis portrayed by the media and commentators which suggests that the tragedies of September 11, 2001 are the result of the divides between the (Christian) West and the Muslim world. Instead they urge a more nuanced, culturally competent, and religiously literate reading of world events. The book shares reflections of religious conflicts throughout the world, and the people and organizations who build bridges across the divide through interreligious and ecumenical cooperation, relief and development, and peace-building. Another contribution of the authors' approach is their clear articulation of biblically-based Christian identity amidst a deep commitment to religious pluralism.

As the field of interreligious learning continues to grow, more research needs to be done in the areas named here and beyond, including making the connections between these diverse fields of inquiry. In addition, curricula and resources for local faith communities which build religious literacy among all age groups, and at the same time affirm the values of religious pluralism, are needed across traditions.

INTERRELIGIOUS TRANSFORMATION CONTINUUM

What ultimately distinguishes authentic interreligious learning from episodic programs is the commitment to long-term change that transforms the lives of the individuals and groups involved. Each faith community needs to reflect deeply on its own story to discern what kind of interreligious learning might benefit the community. Though organizational theories differ, most suggest a five- or six-stage process. Though fairly few Christian faith communities will change to the extent that they are fully interreligious, the final stages in the change process apply to neighborhood organizations, to groups within congregations, to church-related schools and chaplaincies, and to other forms of interreligious cooperation, such as interreligious families, interreligious clergy groups, etc. The integration and application of several schemes suggests the following stages leading to interreligious cooperation (Kujawa-Holbrook 2002, 16–19; Knitter 2003).

Encouraging interreligious learning in faith communities requires a commitment on all levels of institutional life. While individual programs on other religions or isolated interreligious encounters may help individuals gain a greater knowledge of religions other than their own, interreligious learning entails a commitment to a long-term educational process. Authentic interreligious learning occurs only when individuals and faith communities take responsibility to learn about other religious traditions, remain open to forming deeper relationships, and undergo a change process whereby all levels of organizational life are affected by the reality of religious pluralism. The Interreligious Transformation Continuum [see appendix] is a visual representation of the different approaches Christian congregations and religious organizations respond to interreligious learning, and the types of educational support needed throughout the process. Note that while the image of the Continuum here looks fixed and progressive, that the reality is that interreligious learning is often cyclical. The relationship between interreligious learning and faith communities and interreligious organizations ebbs and flows, and it is not uncommon for a group to see itself in several categories at the same time.

The Interreligious Transformation Continuum also reflects the theological tensions within Christianity as a whole across denominations and independent churches at this time within the United States, and in other regions of the world. The work of W. Paul Jones on navigating theological diversity within faith communities describes this as a tension of depth and breadth "from the near bankruptcy of two contrasting perspectives." Liberalism, on the one hand, which stresses openness and acceptance of pluralism, but which can also fall into a relativism that robs Christianity of its uniqueness and therefore is less likely to inspire a deep commitment from its adherents. On the other hand, conservative Christianity, which demands a deep commitment and is numerically growing, but which also interprets the faith with a narrow dogmatism that contradicts the gospel it espouses. Jones' advice to avoid both religious relativism and narrow dogmatism goes beyond liberal and conservative Christian stereotypes to argue for strengthening the capacities of individuals and faith communities to cultivate clear Christian identities, which also view religious pluralism in a positive manner (Jones 2000, 23–26).

In the first column of the Interreligious Transformation Continuum, the *exclusivist organization* does not seek interreligious relationships, either intentionally or unintentionally, and excludes other religious groups. Theologically, the organization may ascribe to a "replacement model" of Christianity. That is, the belief that Christianity is the one and only true religion, that there is no value in other religions, or that adherents of other religions are primarily seen as opportunities for evangelism. Sometimes rigid exclusivism is found where there is limited awareness of what scripture or the church actually teaches, or where there is an agenda to limit social boundaries. Interestingly, the Pew Forum's U.S. Religious Landscape Survey suggests that overall most American Christians *do not* subscribe to a total replacement theology. Rather, 80% of American Christians believe that many religions can lead to eternal life, and at least eight in ten cite at least one non-Christian religion that can do so (Pew Forum 2010).

While many American Christians find the total replacement model harsh, a compromise is found in what theologian Paul F. Knitter calls "the partial replacement model," or an approach that believes that God does speak through other faiths, yet finds salvation ultimately through Jesus Christ. The partial replacement model sees other religions as a way to prepare the way for the gospel, and thus encourages dialogue across traditions. Overall, the partial replacement model shows more compassion and mercy than does the total replacement model (Knitter 2003, chapters 1 and 2).

In organizations where both the total replacement and partial replacement models are operative, questions about who are saved and who are not saved are key and should not be avoided. Rather, what is meant by "salvation" should be explored, as the concept of what is meant by salvation varies significantly across religious groups. The late Krister Stendahl, a New Testament scholar, Lutheran bishop of Stockholm, Sweden, and proponent of interreligious dialogue, believed that ultimately the question of salvation remains a mystery. Stendahl framed his perspective from the apostle Paul as he encountered feelings of superiority among gentile Christians toward the Jews. "[Paul] is trying to come to grips with the fact that there is this feeling of superiority and he doesn't like it. And he ultimately says: 'I'll tell you a mystery, lest you be conceited. And that is that the whole of Israel will in due time be saved and it's none of your business because God won't go back on his promises." (Stendhal 1993, 3).

Another perspective articulated by theologian Mark Heim suggests that a way to avoid the pitfalls of all the models is to assert that all religions are valid paths, yet with different goals (Heim 1995, 6). Thus, within the context of conversations on salvation, there is opportunity for a wider concept, as well as discussion about the many ways Jesus himself welcomed those of other religions. Questions about Jesus' own responses to religious pluralism, as well as his command to love our neighbors, are important foci for potential interreligious learning.

While some exclusivist organizations have theological reasons for not pursuing interreligious learning, there are other exclusivist congregations where belief is not the challenge. Some organizations are simply in denial about the extent of religious diversity in their midst, or are so inwardly-focused that they participate in few initiatives beyond the maintenance of their own organization. Here, as well as in other exclusivist congregations, is the challenge to examine the question, "Who are our neighbors?" Such organizations would also benefit from conversations about the religious diversity in their home communities, as well their perspectives on the mission of the local church.

The *inclusivist organization* typically has limited contact with adherents of other religions, but also believes that God can be found outside the Christian church. This model recognizes the love of God for all humankind and believes that other religions have value. At the same time this perspective, also known as the "fulfillment model," emphasizes that God's love was made real uniquely through Jesus Christ, and therefore Christianity is the fulfillment of other religions. This means that any Hindu, or Muslim, or Jew who experiences the love of God through their religion is already connected to Jesus, and is therefore to an extent a Christian, or an "anonymous" Christian who does not claim the name itself. Characteristic of this theology toward other religions were the Roman Catholic Church and some mainline denominations after the Vatican II, when the fulfillment model represented a new openness within institutional Christianity to other religious traditions. Fear may be expressed in such organizations about whether or not the gospel is being diluted by interreligious learning. Another concern within this model is that other religions are valued chiefly from a Christian perspective, and not from the perspective of their own adherents (Knitter 2003, chapters 5 and 6). Inclusivist organizations most commonly participate passively through episodic interreligious events, such as community-based Thanksgiving Day services, or breakfasts in honor of the Rev. Dr. Martin Luther King, Jr., without building any genuine relationships with members of other religious groups. While such events are significant on a symbolic level, the level of interreligious learning is limited when members of organizations simply show up without engaging their neighbors from other religions and building relationships.

For inclusivist congregations to support interreligious learning, it requires tools such as dialogue skills, the study of Christianity, and the study of other religions. Opportunities for members of these organizations to meet informally with persons of other religions, perhaps in the context of a shared meal, or in home study groups, can begin the learning process. Follow-up gatherings after interreligious events that move faith communities together toward discerning common local needs are a good way to begin cooperation.

The *tolerant organization* is one which supports religious pluralism and interreligious learning on a "symbolic" level. Such organizations may pride themselves on their religious diversity, yet on deeper examination may essentially reflect an assimilation model, in that there is little genuine interreligious cooperation in terms of the structure, policies, and culture of the organization. Tolerant organizations are respectful, if not always enthusiastic about other religious traditions, and at the same time have not made a commitment actually to change in order to accommodate deeper interreligious learning. Religious tolerance works much the same way within the United States on the whole. Mutual respect among adherents of different religions is crucial in a democracy and should not be discounted. "I function in this world as a believer, as a follower of Jesus, as an evangelical Christian—whatever label I want to attach to it," said Randall Balmer, professor of religion at Barnard College. "But I am also a citizen of a gloriously pluralistic and diverse society, which means that my behavior in that larger society has to conform to the basic etiquette of democracy." Balmer feels that as a follower of Jesus he has to navigate living in two worlds, church and state. "That's not easy to do," he says (Balmer 2006). At the same time tolerance alone does not automatically contribute to building positive relationships. Such organizations typically welcome persons from other religious backgrounds and may have programs that support religious diversity, particularly "religious unity." One fairly common characteristic of this model is to have religious leaders from other traditions preach at a Sunday service, or to include religious practices from another religious tradition in community worship, or to house interreligious organizations in the church building. Here the misappropriation of the spiritual practices of other traditions is a danger. Such activities are laudable, yet they are not vehicles for interreligious learning unless people from different traditions engage each other. In this way the tolerant organization must move past its conflict avoidant stance to look at religious differences as well as commonalities, and then apply interreligious learning to all of community life.

Many mainline Christian organizations have difficulty moving beyond the tolerant stage, either because of the lack of denominational support for interreligious learning or because their own membership begins to get fearful when the religious culture actually begins to change. Interreligious leaders in tolerant organizations often express the desire "to do more" but find resistance within the organization as a whole. Such organizations fare well by actively seeking one or two partners from other religious traditions also desiring long-term and sustained interreligious relationships, rather than attempting to engage many other religious traditions at the same time.

A *pluralist organization* intentionally develops an interreligious organization, consciously striving for deeper levels of understanding and accountability. Theologically-based in a "mutuality" model centered in the belief that there are many true religions, the pluralist organization takes seriously its call to interreligious learning. For Christians in a pluralist context, central to the theological task is the search for understandings of Christ and the church that move beyond traditional definitions that impede interreligious learning. The challenge for Christian pluralists is to avoid religious relativism which claims all religions are focused on the same path, and instead work on defining how Jesus is wholly God without being "the whole" of God. Theologian Paul Knitter suggests that while the pluralist model was a minority perspective among Christians just a few decades ago, theological positions that argue for the mutuality of religions now seem to be replacing inclusivism (Knitter 2003, chapter 7). "I see the world's great religions as siblings separated at birth," says Richard G. Watts, a retired Presbyterian pastor. 'We've grown up in different neighborhoods, different homes, with different family rituals, songs and stories. But now we are being brought together, and when we look into each other's faces we can see the family resemblance. That is a cause for great rejoicing" (Watts 2010, 12).

Although the pluralist perspective maintains a Christian worldview and perspective on other religions, its gift to interreligious learning lies in the readiness to ask new questions, as well as to reexamine scripture and tradition from the perspective of religious diversity, including our vision of Jesus Christ. Krister Stendahl believed that, within the context of religious pluralism, Christians see themselves "as particular, even a peculiar people, somehow needed by God as a witness, faithful, somehow doing what God has told them to do, but somehow not claiming to be the whole" (Stendhal 1993, 3). Although some congregations committed to interreligious learning sustain the religious pluralist model, it is more common in intentional interreligious communities, such as college and university chaplaincies, prayer and study groups, retreat centers, and neighborhood organizations. The emphasis in a pluralist context is on learning about our neighbor's religion from the perspective of religious experience. Intentional about the need to monitor the quality of community life, pluralist communities intentionally and continually monitor and evaluate their group process and practices from the perspective of interreligious learning. The pluralist model attracts seekers and pilgrims, and thus may be challenging for institutions needing to maintain an organizational life inclusive of more traditional or denominationally-centered Christian perspectives.

The *redefining organization* is prepared to rebuild every aspect of its community life to become authentically interreligious. Not a characteristic approach of many confessional churches, redefining organizations are more characteristic of chaplaincies, religious organizations, and other intentionally interreligious groups. Theologically, redefining organizations are committed to, as Knitter suggests, "making peace with radical difference" (Knitter 2003, 173). Theologically, the redefining congregation or organization embraces "the acceptance model," the belief that the religious traditions of the world are different and that we need to accept those differences, rather than seeing one religion as superior or seeking commonalities. Such religious organizations intentionally make room for co-existing truths, and exhibit comfort with multiple religious belonging. Postmodern in approach, this model maintains the distinctions among religions as an integral aspect of interreligious learning. The goal in interreligious learning is not to remove the barriers between religions, but for each religious tradition to be authentically itself while in relationship with the other. "In other words, by trying to adapt the Christian message to what we think is a message common to all our religious neighbors, we can easily lose the distinctiveness of what Christ has to say," writes Knitter. "But it may also be shortchanging the other religions and the broader culture, for what our confused suffering world may need from Christians (and from each religion) is not a voice that *fits in* but a voice that *disturbs* and offers an alternative vision" (Knitter 2003, 183). In addition, the redefining organization learns collaborative approaches for working with other religious groups, as well as how to stand as allies with those suffering from religious oppression. More common among organizations or groups affiliated with churches than whole congregations, this model offers a way of "living interreligiously" that goes beyond the set structures of institutional religious life.

The *transformed interreligious* organization is one that fully reflects the belief that religious and cultural differences are assets. A transformed organization is a fully multicultural organization that reflects religious and other forms of diversity in its structures and purpose. Such organizations uphold a *future* vision where religious differences are assets and no longer set limits on human potential. Here, the boundary between the organization and the wider religious community is porous; the organization exists to continue the dialogue, to educate about the importance of interreligious community, and to form alliances and networks to serve others. Although intentional interreligious congregations do exist, there are also other communities, sometimes at the margins, which reflect the gifts of transformed interreligious relationships. Interreligious families, clergy groups, women's groups, schools, retreat centers, local organizations, all offer religious organizations opportunities to participate in the transformative process which occurs through transformational interreligious learning.

MOVING PAST RESISTANCE

Christian theologian Fumitaka Matsuoka offers advice to those who hope to support interreligious learning. "The starting point is not to find ways of uniting people divided by fear and violence, but to recognize, celebrate, and learn from God's gift of one creation embodied in various cultures, languages, religions, and races. It is to restore moral integrity in the midst of the culture of decay by restoring freedom and dignity to the captives we held" (Matsuoka 1998, 104). The Christian tradition was created in dialogue with other traditions and belief systems, and so it is our call once again to retell the story and live our Christian identities in a globalized context. Over the last 60 years, all major Christian denominations have in their official statements adopted more open postures toward other religious traditions (Hedges 2010, 11). Indeed, it was not that long ago when Christians outside of one's own church were considered outside of salvation. Among exclusivist Christian groups, the trend is a toward a more inclusivist perspective, allowing a wider salvation through the mercy of God. Progress in Christian ecumenism has illustrated that just as there are differing versions of Christian truth, there is also value in understanding other religious truths.

Ultimately, faith communities and religious organizations must confront the challenge of envisioning a new way of relating to each other, where we not only show hospitality to our religious neighbors, but also seek to share power and burdens. In many organizations, the first steps of interreligious encounter cause resistance—altering the calendar, changing the food, changing the music, changing how we pray, meeting different people—that they never progress to the stage of rich and mutually fulfilling interreligious learning. Presbyterian pastor Richard G. Watt, the co-founder of an interreligious dialogue group that included Jews, Hindus, Buddhists, Baha'is, Muslims, and a diverse group of Christians, remembers a particularly poignant Sunday after the group had visited a Sikh Gurdwara for worship and fellowship. "I could hardly wait for Sunday morning to come, when I would lead worship in our own church in Normal, Illinois. Not because we now would 'get it right,' but because I knew myself to be part of a community far broader, far more inclusive than I had ever before imagined" (Watts 2010, 12). Those that make the commitment to interreligious learning ultimately discover that the journey is not only about anxiety and struggle; it also brings abundant hope and joy.

REFLECTION QUESTIONS

1. Reflecting on the diversity within your faith community, what interreligious relationships do you currently have? Are there interreligious families or organizations already present in your common life? How might these relationships be enhanced?

2. Reflecting on the Interreligious Transformation Continuum in the Appendix, where do you see your congregation? In what ways might your congregation best grow interreligiously?

3. Name three ways you can build the religious literacy and multicultural competency of your congregation.

2

The Transformative Power
of Interreligious Encounter

Please call me by my true name,
so I can wake up,
and so the door of my heart can be left open,
the door of compassion.

"CALL ME BY MY TRUE NAMES," THICH NHAT HANH (1999, 72)

"LITTLE MOSQUE ON THE Prairie" was a comedy series on Canadian television (CBC) that centers on the Muslim community in the fictional town of Mercy, Saskatchewan. In the first episode the Muslim community is trying to establish a mosque in the town. Yasir Hamoudi, a local builder and a Muslim, rents space from the mosque in the parish hall of the Anglican Church. Fearful because no one else in town would rent space to a mosque, Hamoudi signs the lease saying that he is renting office space for his business. The Muslim community's advertisement for an imam is answered by Amaar Rashid, a Toronto lawyer, who leaves his practice to come to Mercy, much to the dismay of his wealthy and non-religious parents. The new imam's travel to Mercy is complicated, however, by his detention by airport security, which sets off the local media interested in the background of the town's new Muslim religious leader. In the meantime, Duncan Magee, the local Anglican priest, and an overall supporter of the Muslim community, discovers that his renters are actually praying in the parish house. He offers a new lease to the Muslim community without consulting his bishop, this time for a mosque, but only on condition that he be told the truth in the future.

The series ran for six seasons in Canada but was never on network television in the United States. Since 2007, Little Mosque on the Prairie has been seen in France, Switzerland, French-speaking Africa, Israel, the West Bank, Gaza, United Arab Emirates, Finland, and Turkey. The show's creator, Zarqa Nawaz, a Muslim, views humor as one of the most effective ways to break down barriers and to encourage interreligious learning and understanding between cultures. The characters on Little Mosque on the Prairie are an example of how interreligious encounters are everywhere and infuse many aspects of daily life. The show artfully interweaves both intra-Muslim dialogue with Muslim-Christian dialogue through its characters, plots, and subplots. After the initial seasons, the show's creators also introduced a Jewish character. The show illustrates how interreligious encounters form and mature; and provides a fictional but believable case study on how people from different religious traditions in a community grew from feelings of fear and distance, to embrace each other as neighbors. Through this process of interreligious encounter the individuals, their religious communities, and the whole town was transformed. By the end of the six seasons of the series, even the most intractable Christians and Muslims were changed through their encounters with those of another religious tradition. In an interesting role reversal, during the last episode of the show, the Muslim community, once renters of a space to pray in the Anglican church, build their own mosque. Eventually this same Muslim community invites in their Christian neighbors after a fire burns their sanctuary to the ground.

THE PENTECOST PARADIGM

In the Christian tradition, the account of the first Pentecost (Acts 2:1–12) is an example of the power of a genuine encounter with the Spirit, and of how people who do not at first understand each other, are transformed in the way they see themselves, each other, and the world. Christian theologian Christopher Duraisingh uses the Pentecost story as an illustration of both the power and the potential of interreligious encounter. He argues that the Pentecost narrative carefully holds in creative tension the terms "all" and "each." *All* cultures and languages are affirmed by the Spirit, and yet *each* hears in their own language—Jews, Arabs, Libyans, Romans, and

Iranians—a microcosm of the plurality in the known world at that time. "This story suggests that it is in the midst of the promise and the pain that immigration entails in our postcolonial times that we discern the Spirit," writes Duraisingh. "The interwovenness, the intermingling of the plurality of peoples is not something of which to be afraid. For the Spirit breaks forth in the midst of this diversity and is made known as the transforming power of God." Duraisingh is quick to point out that the relationships across differences formed through the Pentecost paradigm are deeper than just celebrating diversity. Rather, the story suggests that the disciples are drawn to the Spirit and into communion for mutual enrichment *through* their differences. "It is as they mutually share their differences that they come to know and witness to what the author of Ephesians calls 'the multi-colored wisdom of God'" (Durasingh 2001, 13–14).

Duraisingh believes that the story of Pentecost illustrates an authentic way of encountering pluralism, one that "de-centers" individual and collective identities believed to be autonomous and self-sufficient. None of us is ever really self-sufficient. Whether we recognize it or not, we are bound together through a common humanity, despite our differences. "Pentecost points to a de-centering of centers and identities that exclude, a courageous crossing of borders and a promotion of multi-vocal, polyphonic community." For instance, in the Acts of the Apostle we are first introduced to Peter and his reluctance to cross the borders of race and religion, notably in terms of his attitudes toward the gentile Cornelius, and his fears about allowing those like him into the community. Yet the Spirit had an effect on Peter and changed what he originally held as impermeable cultural and religious boundaries. He was confronted with the possibility that God does not have favorites, and given the strength and the wisdom to negotiate the borders of his religious culture and welcome those from another religious background into the community. Many cultural and religious conflicts are based in the inability of people to move beyond the boundaries of their own groups, hence the need for faith communities and religious organizations to work conscientiously at broadening the sense of interdependence of the human community. Courageous border-crossing not only requires "passing over" to the viewpoint of another; it also requires a "coming back" process. That is, coming back to one's own religion or one's own way of life and integrating new insights, new appreciations, new experiences. "Here there is no fusion of borders so that our individual or group [religious] identities are lost. Nor is it a border diffusion or dissolution," writes Duraisingh, "but it is a crossing over and a returning so that the coordinates of one's identities may now be redrawn in a much richer way due to the gift from the other" (Duraisingh 2001, 14–15).

Living within the Pentecost paradigm has its challenges. It means giving up exclusivist claims. It means risking criticism from members of one's own religious tradition. In some cases, faith communities that have crossed borders and built interreligious community with their neighbors have lost members by doing so. Yet the Pentecost paradigm teaches that it is only through encounters across differences, crossing borders and coming back, that the creativity of the Spirit is unleashed, faith deepened, relationships formed, and new insights gained. Duraisingh writes, "The mission of the church today, I submit, is building such a highway over which people of diverse cultures, religions, and races can cross borders for both integration as well as enrichment of their particular identities" (Duraisingh 2001, 15). Within religious education it is the role of interreligious learning to build a highway where people of diverse social identities grow more deeply into their own identities, authentically encounter others across equally deep differences, and form communities with more intense connections to the wider world. For Christians, the Pentecost story reveals the power of interreligious encounter, whereby the power of the Spirit is unleashed, and faith and relationships are transformed.

On reflection on her own spiritual journey, from her beginnings in a Methodist church in Montana to Hindu communities in India, Diana Eck observes that religious traditions are more like rivers than stones; they flow and change, sometimes dramatically. "All of us contribute to the river of our traditions," she writes. "We do not know how we will change the river or be changed as we experience its currents" (Eck 1993, 2). In looking at the lives of religiously committed people in Christian faith communities and organizations, interreligious learning is both an opportunity and a challenge. The gifts of religious pluralism in local communities suggest the need for transformative interreligious encounters which lead people more deeply into their own tradition and at the same open them to the power the Spirit as she is experienced in relation to those of other traditions. The time is now to move interreligious learning beyond the scholarly world, as important as that work is, and reach more directly into faith communities, neighborhood organizations, families, schools, and workplaces. Interreligious learning transforms faith communities. Interreligious learning enlarges hearts, opens relationships, and builds more compassionate communities. The challenge is to support people at the grassroots to become better equipped for interreligious encounters. To do this faith communities and religious organizations must provide interreligious learning that builds mutual respect, and heals the divisions between members of different religious traditions.

HEALING DIVISIONS
THROUGH COMPASSIONATE LISTENING

Tenzin Gyatso, the 14th Dalai Lama, tells a story of his encounter with the late Thomas Merton, a Christian, Trappist monk, and spiritual writer. "When I was a boy in Tibet, I felt that my own Buddhist religion must be the best—and that other faiths were somehow inferior. . . . A main point in my discussion with Merton was how central compassion was to the message of both Christianity and Buddhism. In my reading of the New Testament, I find myself inspired by Jesus' acts of compassion. . . . The focus on compassion that Merton and I observed in our two religions strikes me as a strong unifying thread among all the major faiths. And these days we need to highlight what unifies us" (Dalai Lama, 2010).

A key skill for facilitating healing between members of different religious traditions is "compassionate listening," also known as "deep listening." Developed by Quaker peace activist Gene Knudsen Hoffman, and based in the teachings of Vietnamese Buddhist monk Thich Nhat Hanh, compassionate listening was developed as a spiritual practice of reconciliation, and is utilized by many religious traditions as well as in secular fields. The practice is based in Thich Nhat Hanh's "Three Steps to Peace," that emphasize listening to the suffering on all sides of a conflict, relating the suffering of all to one another, and bringing all sides together so that each may hear the other. In compassionate listening, the focus is on validating another's experience as part of the encounter, whether or not that experience resonates with one's own. It assumes that all human beings have some need for healing, and that the experience of being deeply heard by another opens a door to transformation of the self and of relationships. In compassionate listening practice we step aside from our own anxieties and convictions in order to be present to the anxieties and convictions of another. The encounter is not about judging whether or not we agree with another, but it is about being present with another in their humanity.

A Zen Buddhist way to explain the practice is listening with the heart. According to the tradition, when thousands of bodhisattvas (enlightened beings) gathered to discuss the best ways to ease the suffering of the people of the world, the Buddha selected compassionate listening. Within compassionate listening, listeners see themselves as "healers" rather than as judges or mediators. For the listener and for the speaker, the experience is transformational, because assumptions about others' experience are challenged and an appreciation of the complexity of issues that divide emerges from the encounter. Through the process of compassionate listening, both the listener and the speaker discover a new understanding of themselves and an appreciation of the humanity of another. In this way, the skill of compassionate listening contributes to healing within the human community (Hoffman, Monroe, and Green, 2008). It is also an integral part of interreligious encounters whereby one's own assumptions about another religious group are suspended, and a space is created where another is not judged as a member of a group, but is heard as a human being with both similar and divergent experiences. The practice of compassionate listening suggests that within interreligious encounter, both speaking *and* listening are of equal importance. In faith communities where the bias is on speaking, rather than on speaking and listening, it might be helpful to remember the following principles of compassionate listening:

COMPASSIONATE LISTENING: SOME ASSUMPTIONS

Compassionate Listening assumes that, before authentic encounters can occur, conflicting parties must first listen to each other. We cannot assume that we really know how it is to be another.

Compassionate Listening does not seek to change the other, but to love them. The more a person is loved, the more the person is free to respond to inner truth.

Compassionate Listening assumes that, in order to build peace, we need to acknowledge the humanity and the suffering of the other, that misunderstanding, conflicts, and violence are the result of unhealed wounds.

Compassionate Listening trusts that when people truly feel heard they will be more open to hearing the stories of those with whom they disagree.

Compassionate Listening is a practice of reconciliation and thus is rooted in the belief that mutually understanding and respect are the foundations for building communities across the borders of difference.[1]

Paul Metzger, a self-described conservative, fundamentalist, evangelical Christian, speaks to his experience of the role of compassionate listening in his interreligious encounters with Zen Abbot Kyogen Carlson: "I am an Evangelical, and that means I share Jesus with others in the hope that they might come to know him personally. But I appeal to people—I don't compel them. There are no notches in my belt to symbolize all those I have dragged into the kingdom. Because I value my personal relationship with Jesus, and my belief in a very personal God, I value my personal relationships. My friendship with Kyogen is not a ploy to 'get him saved' but springs from my desire for a personal relationship with him—no matter where our dialogue leads. And for all our differences, we share a common conviction that Buddha and Jesus invited—can I say, evangelized?—others to embrace a compassionate existence." Metzger believes that interreligious learning occurs only when there is compassionate give and take, and embrace of "the other." "This happens not by going around our differences, but by talking through them. It's been life-changing for me. I guess you could call it conversion," he says. For his part, Kyogen Carlson admitted that some in his sangha are wary of his friendship with Metzger. What he calls the "degree of polarization we have created in our culture wars," has at times made him nervous about sharing some of his views about the value of interreligious encounter with his ordained peers. "I have held my tongue for being castigated by more extreme voices on 'my' side of the divide, not only in my student days, but very recently." However, Carlson has also learned the importance for those with experience of compassionate interreligious encounters to claim some space in the dialogue. "We turn to face each other, a small step, but it's a beginning" (Tisdale 2006, 57).

Practicing compassionate listening goes against many Western conventions. It makes the distinction between genuine interreligious encounters and the need of some to debate religion. Practicing compassionate listening demands that we love our enemies; that we separate negative actions from the value of a person or group; and, that we counter feelings of hatred with love. For Christian organizations, examples of practicing compassion can be found in the life and ministry of Jesus. Often, when

1. Adapted by Sheryl Kujawa-Holbrook from Hoffman, Monroe, Green, and Rivers, *Compassionate Listening*. See chapter 6 in particular.

interreligious encounters are stalled or intractable, it is because of difficulties with practicing compassionate listening. Are we able to honor our own experiences as valid and at the same time listen to another with different experiences? Are we willing to open ourselves to the pain and suffering of others? Are we open to seeing God in others?

MODELS OF INTERRELIGIOUS ENCOUNTER

As the field of interreligious learning has grown since the 1960s, scholars have articulated slightly different ways of understanding interreligious encounters. For interreligious learning in faith communities, the four models of interreligious dialogue first identified by Pope Paul VI at the time of Vatican II and later expanded through the work of Roman Catholic scholar and interreligious leader Leonard Swidler and others, are a helpful starting point because they follow the patterns of human relationships in general. Here the idea of "dialogue" is not limited to conversation, although that element is certainly present. Rather, the dialogue is about interreligious encounter between members of different religious traditions which include conversations, but also venture into the many patterns of human relationships. Not limited to the relationships present within faith communities or other religious organizations, the following patterns of interreligious encounter reveal how Christians, or persons of other religious groups, can be about the business of interreligious learning throughout their daily lives, no matter where they live, and no matter what their occupation (Hornung 2007, 27–28).

1. *The Dialogue of Life.* This pattern of interreligious encounter is found through interactions with neighbors, families, schools, and workplaces. Much like the encounters that are a part of the television program Little Mosque on the Prairie, the dialogue of life depends upon cultivating an awareness of persons from other religious groups and a commitment to welcome the presence of others into our daily lives. The most basic level of interreligious encounter, the dialogue of life, is often overlooked in favor of more structured programs. Yet the capacity to form friendships across religious differences is integral to building interreligious community. For example, Claremont United Methodist Church in Claremont, California, sponsors supper groups with the Islamic Center of the Inland Empire. The "M & M" (Muslims

and Methodists) program has no other agenda than for people to have dinner together, visit each other's homes, and build relationships between the two communities. The capacity to form interreligious friendships enhances the interreligious learning in both communities.

2. *The Dialogue of Action.* This pattern of encounter is common among faith communities and focuses on collaborations between persons of different religious traditions addressing shared local issues. In the dialogue of action, relationships are built on several levels. Relationships are formed between those who dialogue about a particular problem, as they decide ways to address the problem. Relationships are also formed between individuals and organizations as they actually do the work of addressing the issue. By extension, interreligious learning can be extended to those in faith communities who are not directly involved in the project but support it in other ways. Lastly, those on the receiving end of the project through gaining some kind of assistance or advocacy, or those who work for the government or agency approached for service, also become part of the encounter as they learn more about the issues involved and as they form relationships across religious differences. This form of encounter is attractive to many faith communities because it yields practical results and because it directly benefits the local community. For instance, local hunger or housing task forces are common ways that faith communities share in interreligious encounters. This pattern of interreligious encounter can be enhanced, however, if those engaged in common action take the time intentionally to form relationships. For instance, are volunteers at a local pantry consciously recruited from all religious groups and scheduled to work together or are they segregated into faith community groups? Do you know the names, faces, and stories of the people served or of the other volunteers? Did they have the opportunity to learn about you?

3. *The Dialogue of Spiritual Experience.* This form of interreligious encounter is best illustrated through shared rituals, worship, prayer, silence, and retreat experiences. Experiences of corporate prayer and ritual tap into the depth of religious experience beyond the level of the spoken word. Interreligious spiritual experiences have the potential to yield a deep connection between people of different religious traditions. Authentic interreligious prayer and worship takes careful preparation and is best achieved through the direct and on-going

relationships between individuals or faith communities. It is not about Christians enacting a spiritual practice of another religious group, or spiritual practices of another religion, through a Christian lens. Rather, the dialogue of spiritual experience is about experiencing the rituals of another religious group *with* them and learning about how they understand them. For example, in many Christian faith communities it has become a common practice to organize a Passover Seder as part of Holy Week. While the goal of understanding the Jewish roots of Christian worship is a good one, this particular practice on the part of Christian congregations is not welcomed by many Jews. If the reverse were the practice, and another religious group chose to reenact an Easter Sunday service outside the Christian community, some Christians would be offended. This is not to say that Christians should never host Seders. But it does suggest that perhaps the best way to do so, a way that encourages interreligious learning, is to participate in relationship *with* Jewish people and be welcomed inside the spiritual experience by them. Here the reciprocity in the spiritual experience is an opportunity for interreligious learning.

4. *The Dialogue of Understanding.* The final pattern of interreligious encounter relates to exchanging beliefs, doctrine, and theology. Common in academic, monastic, and interreligious organizations, this pattern of interreligious encounter contributes to shared knowledge of other religious traditions and builds mutual respect across religious differences. The dialogue of understanding presents several challenges for faith communities, so challenging for some that they avoid this modality entirely. The first common challenge for Christians is the fear that we don't know enough about our own religion really to dialogue on the level of belief, doctrine, or theology. A related fear is the tension between honestly wanting to hear and affirm dialogue partners but at the same time wanting to uphold our own version of religious truth.

Generally speaking, most people do not change their religious affiliation based solely on interreligious encounters. We can support members of faith communities in the dialogue of understanding by raising religious literacy and by assisting people in building a theological vocabulary that best expresses their religious experience. Effective adult education can provide people with skills which enable the dialogue of understanding. The dialogue of understanding is not necessarily limited to erudite or abstract topics. Questions which pervade the human lifecycle include, What happens after death? How would you describe the presence of sin or evil in the world? What sustains you in the face of suffering or tragedy? All these deeply theological questions are critical to the dialogue of understanding. Interreligious families engage in the dialogue of religious understanding all the time, in regard to discussions about rites of passage for their children, arrangements for sickness or death, even in terms of what holidays or religious rituals are celebrated. One common method for the dialogue of understanding is the shared study of sacred texts between members of different religious groups. Bilateral Christian-Jewish or trilateral Christian-Jewish-Muslim dialogues based in the study of sacred texts are a powerful method of sharing in the dialogue of understanding.

These four models of interreligious encounter do not work in isolation, nor do they need to be programmed sequentially into the life of a community. Gaining an understanding of other religious traditions and learning to appreciate them is an evolutionary on-going process, not a one-time event or something to be raced through. Each of the four models provides for deep interreligious encounters.

CULTIVATING OPENNESS TO THE SPIRIT

The quality of interreligious encounter is directly linked to the spiritual maturity of an individual or group, as well as the capacity to be open to the experience of another. As the Pentecost story reminds us, openness to the Spirit is a critical ingredient to transformational change. People who have had little spiritual formation within their own faith community, or who associate religion with fear and intolerance, are ill prepared to participate positively in interreligious encounters. Spiritual formation which empowers people to lead lives of love and compassion is foundational to nurture interreligious encounters. Similarly, spiritual formation which encourages intellectual growth in a spirit of open inquiry, and that helps people integrate beliefs and practices supports the creation of deep relationships across religious differences. At the same time, spiritual formation which supports religious identities rooted in trust and community goes a long way in overcoming fear and intolerance across religious differences.

The ways people experience God, as well as the ways they relate to the wider world, informs their readiness for interreligious encounters. Educators and religious leaders need to be aware of the degree of readiness within a faith community to participate positively in interreligious encounters. The overall quality of life of a faith community, how it views itself and its role in the world, and its capacity for maintaining healthy relationships and navigating change are indications of readiness for interreligious encounter. "By definition a dialogue is somewhat open ended," writes Heidi Hadsell, president of the Hartford Seminary. "It is a journey that has not been precisely mapped. It is a process of mutually discovery which promises the possibility of something new emerging, perhaps something no one has dreamed or expected, a realigning of the self perhaps, a reshaping of one's own hopes and dreams" (Hadsell 2000). Through interreligious encounters, individuals and groups must bring their whole selves to the process—bodies, minds, hearts, and spirits. How a faith community nurtures and challenges its members in spiritually relates directly to its capacity to form healthy relationships with other religious groups and to appreciate the beauty and truth of other traditions.

Leonard Swidler writes about seven stages of ever-deepening relationship that occurs through interreligious encounter, each in itself a form of spiritual practice:

STAGES OF INTERRELIGIOUS ENCOUNTER[2]

Adapted from Leonard Swidler

Stage One—*Radical Encountering of Difference*
Encounters with other religious traditions challenge me to face my own worldview. I am tempted to withdraw.

Stage Two—*Crossing Over—Letting Go and Entering the World of the Other*
I decide to engage the world of the other, and I find I need to reassess my own assumptions. I find I need to reassess my stereotypes and prejudices and approach the other with openness.

Stage Three—*Inhabiting and Experiencing the World of the Other*
Practicing compassion opens me to learning many new things. I feel excitement and a deeper relationship with humanity.

---

2. Adapted from Leonard Swidler, "Stages in the Process of Interreligious Engagement," in *Interfaith Dialogue at the Grass Roots*, edited by Rebecca Kratz Mays (Philadelphia: Ecumenical, 2008) 105–6. Used with Permission.

Stage Four—*Crossing Back with Expanded Vision*
My sense of identity has deepened and changed. I am able to hold multiple truths, and I now hold the other in relationship.

Stage Five—*The Dialogic Awakening—A Radical Paradigm Shift.*
I experience a radical shift in my consciousness and am no longer able to go back to my former worldview. I sense an interconnectedness between myself, the other, and all creatures.

Stage Six—*The Global Awakening—The Paradigm Shift Matures.*
This stage of deep dialogue opens me to a common ground that underlies unique worlds and unique differences among religious groups. I embrace an expanded sense of community and a greater potential for ongoing dialogue.

Stage Seven—*Personal and Global Transforming of Life and Behavior.*
I experience communion with all—myself, others, and all creatures. My moral consciousness has been expanded, as has my concern for all life. I experience a deeper meaning in all relationships.

Swidler's work is critical to understanding interreligious encounters because it emphasizes the need to view learning as part of a *process* which contributes to spiritual growth. This process moves individuals from separation through awakening to mutual transformation. Many of the people who get passionately involved in interreligious learning do so because it becomes an integral part of their spiritual journey. They learn from people from another religious tradition who experience God differently than they do, or they discover the beauty of another tradition through spiritual experience. As the relationship deepens, so does the level of the conversation, moving past superficial and safe topics into more difficult territory. As times, interreligious encounter is supported through experiences of shared prayer or study and reflection. As is the case with developmental cycles, individuals and groups may find themselves at different points in the process, depending upon their own growth through interreligious encounters, as well as in their ability to integrate the challenges of religious pluralism with their own spiritual experience. As growth in interreligious encounter develops, both relationships and actions are transformed.

Swidler argues that overcoming "clash of civilizations" rhetoric which encourages harmful divisions between religious traditions involves "Deep-Dialogue with Critical Thinking" to change both the inner self and shared lives. Here the purpose of interreligious encounter is to be open to the other in order to better understand, and to experience the goodness in another tradition. Further, Swidler believes it is important that interreligious encounter challenges our un-conscious assumptions about other traditions, makes these negative assumptions conscious, and provides an opportunity to reflect analytically and synthetically on the experience. Such critical thinking then become integrated into the practice of interreligious encounter. "Deep Dialogue/Critical Thinking eventually must become a habit of the mind and spirit, traditionally known as a virtue—a new basic mentality, and consequent practice" (Race and Hedges 2009, 107–9).

THE CONTRIBUTIONS OF MAHATMA GANDHI TO INTERRELIGIOUS ENCOUNTER

The narratives of the holy men and women of in the past offer inspiration and practical advice on how to shape interreligious encounters and how best to live in the midst of religious pluralism. One such figure was Mohandas Gandhi (1869–1948), often referred to as "Mahatma," or "Great Soul," an honorific given him by Bengali poet and writer Rabindranath Tagore. Mahatma Gandhi's teachings are particularly helpful to students of interreligious learning because his whole life evolved as a path of deep encounter across religious differences. His ideas were not wholly unique; many were shared by other interreligious voices of his time. At the same time, he gave his life to find ways that Hindus, Christians, Muslims, Jews, Sikhs, and Jains in his country could both claim their distinctive religious identities, and at the same time create a peaceful society enriched by religious plurality. Gandhi lived in a time and place, not unlike our own, where interreligious learning was critical to survival amidst a climate of religious oppression, conflict, and violence. He believed that, for interreligious learning to become a way of life, it must engage the minds *and* hearts of all humanity. Interestingly, Gandhi was not as much interested in abstract or academic religion as he was in *lived* religion. Gandhi's detractors then and now accuse him of rampant idealism, and yet, he insisted that human beings are capable of a higher level of relationship than the tension, racism, and violence indicative of our societies suggests (Eck 1991, 77–79). He believed that religious traditions, while a source of divisiveness and tension, also equally had that potential to be a source of peace and reconciliation among all people. Gandhi's life work was to advocate for the peaceful use of religious traditions, and to encourage positive encounters between members of different traditions in his homeland and abroad.

As a Christian dedicated to religious pluralism, Diana Eck distilled from Gandhi's vast work nine "homespun" guidelines for interreligious encounters (Eck 1991, 79). These guidelines are not rigid rules, but rather principles which support interreligious learning, and encourage mutually enriching encounters between people of different religious traditions. These are principles were tested Gandhi himself as he experienced his own radically pluralistic religious context:

1. *The Many-Sidedness of Truth.* In her reading of Gandhi's writings, Diana Eck argues that he is preoccupied with "Truth," to the extent that he always capitalizes the word. For Gandhi, God is greater than our human understanding of God, and thus revelation does not belong solely to any one specific religion. Just as truth is many-sided, there are many faces of God. As is the case in our own society today, Gandhi's religious world included groups that made exclusivist claims, and yet he argued that each religion must recognize the limitations of the language, images, and names they have for comprehending God (Eck 1991, 79–89).

2. *All Religions are True.* Gandhi's religious upbringing was based in religious pluralism. He grew up in a region where Hindus and Jains shared many religious traditions, and his mother belonged to a branch of the Hindu tradition that used both the Bhagavad Gita and the Qu'ran in prayer. One of the images he used for the religions of the world was the many branches of a tree. At the same time he recognized the distinctiveness of religions, and argued against the negation of religious differences, or the pursuit of artificially imposed sense of religious unity. Within the context of interreligious learning, he reasoned, it is impossible to encounter "the other" if we eliminate religious differences. Gandhi's appreciation of other religions was based in the recognition of religious difference, along with an abiding belief that pluralism does not need to lead to division or conflict. For example, Gandhi affirmed the notion that the scriptures of other religions were divinely inspired; at the same time, he was against literalistic interpretations of sacred texts. The first question we should ask is: What does this text mean to its adherents? Then we need to ask what the text means to us. In this manner, Gandhi read the New Testament

and learned what the texts meant to Christians. He also believed that the message of the New Testament has something to say to him as a Hindu (Eck 1991, 80–81).

3. *All Religions are Imperfect.* Gandhi's writings remind us that religions are at best human creations and interpretations of God's revelation. Because religions are human creations, they also include the realities of human imperfections, such as troubling histories of war and persecution. So, Gandhi reasoned, it is fruitless to try to argue the superiority of one religion over another. Religions are pathways to God and communities of memory, and as important as they are, they are not God. Enhanced understanding of other religions through interreligious learning opens up the possibility of appreciation for the beauty of other religious cultures. The religions of the world have inspired and sustained their followers for thousands of years and have led them to create magnificent works of art, music, and the sciences. Gandhi's advice for interreligious learning is to acknowledge both the beauty and the tragedy of religious traditions while resisting comparisons between the greatest of one's own tradition and the limitations of another (Eck 1991, 81–82).

4. *Religions are "Experiments with Truth."* For Gandhi, religious truth is not based in rigid principles but lived and found experientially in the context of life's joys and struggles. He believed that religious truth is based in action and that belief should align with the way we live our lives in the world. For instance, Gandhi did not just speak out against the caste system; he adopted an untouchable child. He did not simply appreciate Christianity at a distance, he read the New Testament, formed relationships with Christians, and visited churches. He reminds us with this guideline that we bring our whole selves to encounters with people of other religions, not just our beliefs (Eck 1991, 82–83).

5. *Non-Violence as the Way to Truth.* For Gandhi, religious truth was incompatible with violence. This belief was at the center of his nonviolent resistance and action. He was not proposing passive resistance, but an active standing up for truth. Although Gandhi believed that all religions are paths to truth, he was not a relativist, and did not believe that being open to other religions required a suspension of moral judgment. For Gandhi, nonviolence included not only war and

persecution, but other more subtle forms of violence such as coercion, humiliation, abuse, and the denigration of other religions. Gandhi's principal of nonviolence rejects the denigration of other religions as a way of silencing our neighbors and is central to the authenticity of our own religious truth (Eck 1991, 80–81).

6. *Friendly Study of Other Religions.* "I hold that it is the duty of every cultured man or woman to read sympathetically the scriptures of the world," wrote Gandhi. "If we are to respect others' religions as we would have them respect our own, a friendly study of the world's religions is a sacred duty." Gandhi knew from personal experience how easy it is for different religious groups to stereotype each other. He grew up hearing the unflattering portrayals of the Hindu religion from Christian missionaries, and he heard Hindus condemn Christians for the practices of eating meat and drinking alcohol. Rather than perpetuating stereotypes, he believed that it was important to study other religions from the standpoint of those who loved the tradition, who are its adherents. For Gandhi, the friendly study of a tradition did not mean that it should be studied uncritically, but rather with an open mind and heart. He also stressed the need to experience a religion from the perspective of many voices. As Diana Eck reminds us, ". . . no tradition speaks with a single voice. The very process of dialogue is multivocal." Thus, Mahatma Gandhi, in his friendly study of Christianity, visited churches all over the world, remaining open to the tradition. He measured his experience of lived Christianity with what he read in the gospels about Jesus, and the Sermon on the Mount, in particular. When he attended a racially exclusive church in South Africa, he did not judge all Christians on the basis of that one negative experience. Friendly study reveals that the world's religions are not the same, but it supports interreligious encounter through understanding the rich distinctions among traditions (Eck 1991, 84–85).

7. *Deeper Understanding of Our Own Faith.* "I shall say to Hindus that your lives will be incomplete unless you reverently study the teachings of Jesus," wrote Gandhi. "I have come to the conclusion, in my own experience, that those who, no matter to what faith they belong, reverently study the teachings of other faiths, broaden their own instead of narrowing their hearts." Gandhi's experience taught him that the more he got to know other traditions, the more he learned about his own religion. In genuine interreligious learning, understanding flows

in two directions—not only do we need to understand each other; we need to grow in our understanding of ourselves as well. Gandhi spoke of his love for his own faith tradition in love language, and he knew that his relationship with Hinduism would not be weakened by his knowledge and appreciation of other religions. In fact, Gandhi found his own religious devotion strengthened as he experienced an extended network of human relationships. "I do not want my house to be walled in on all sides and my windows and doors to be stuffed," he wrote. "I want the cultures of all lands to be blown about my house as freely as possible. Mine is not a prison house" (Eck 1991, 84–85, 51).

8. *Conversion Belongs to God.* Gandhi used the image of the rose to explain the subtle and powerful attraction of Christianity (or any faith tradition) to its adherents. The inherent authority of the rose comes from its irresistible beauty and subtle fragrance; it does not need to prove itself or convert anyone. A rose knows it is a rose and it knows its beauty. Others will be attracted to it because of its authority and beauty. Gandhi believed that it was the height of intolerance (and therefore a form of violence) to believe that one's religion was superior to another. He saw the capacity for good that was in all religions, and understood that conversion was less about accepting doctrines than it was about a quality of the heart and the transformation of relationships. Conversion, according to Gandhi, was about Hindus being better Hindus and Muslims being better Muslims, and ultimately it is the work of God alone to turn human hearts. His openness allowed those who opposed him also to remain open, a critical factor in interreligious dialogue (Rohr 2007; Eck 1991, 86–88).

9. *True Religion Binds People Together.* Diana Eck reminds us that that the term "religio" means "to bind." Gandhi believed that the purpose of religion was to bring people together, and that that purpose was not fulfilled by merely bringing together those of the same tradition or the same culture. He believed that building relationships was at the core of all social action and that intolerance could never survive a transformed relationship. "I am striving to become the best cement between the two communities," he said during the partitioning crisis. My longing is to be able to cement the two with my blood, if necessary. But, before I can do so, I must prove to the Muslims that I love them as well as I love the Hindus." Ultimately, according to Gandhi,

interreligious encounters are is between real people and not abstract religious systems, and all traditions have a role to play in it (Eck 1991, 88–90).

STORIES OF LOCAL INTERRELIGIOUS ENCOUNTERS

What might faith communities look like if we lived in houses where all our windows and doors were open to all people of good will? How might opening our lives to interreligious learning help us to embrace those of other religious traditions?

How interreligious encounters enrich the lives of individuals and faith communities is evident from the stories. For instance, St. Philip's Episcopal Church in Tucson, Arizona, sponsored a Tuesday evening dialogue group modeled after *The Faith Club,* the best-seller written shortly after September 11, 2001, that tells the story of three women—one Muslim, one Jewish, one Christian—who came together to write a children's book only to have their project develop into a years-long interreligious encounter. According to Greg Foraker, associate clergy at St. Philip's, the appeal of the group was its ability to embody different faith traditions and stress "learning from the heart." The program expanded to include eight small groups, as well as to partner with Interfaith Community Services in Tucson to offer a similar group including Episcopalians, Presbyterians, Congregationalists, Reform Jews, and Muslims as participants (Foraker 2010).

Invariably, though each woman in the original Faith Club group had her own fears about entering into deep a interreligious encounter, each found the experience transformative. Out of their conversations about suffering, salvation, and sacrifice, Suzanne Oliver, the Christian member of the group, learned more about her own faith. Oliver said she learned to think of Jesus' death on the cross "not as what God has done for me, It's what God has done for everybody, God's empathy for our suffering. It's that death is not the end." Through the Faith Club, Tanya Idliby found ways to address "plurality, diversity, and flexibility," among other Muslim believers. Priscilla Warner, a Jew, was motivated to join the group by her own deep questions. "I had a deep need in me to resolve questions that could not be resolved by anyone else: not by my rabbi, not by my husband, not by my friends," she said. The Faith Club model is readily adaptable to small groups in faith communities and focuses on specific areas of exploration and dialogue based in participants' faith experience: What faith are you and why?

What are your biases and stereotypes about your faith and others? What means do scripture and prayer hold for you? Lastly, how can religious be used to foster peace as well as conflict? (Grossman 2008)

In a similar way to the Faith Club, Lutherans of the Swedish Theological Institute in Jerusalem host small groups sponsored by the Women's Interfaith Encounter. There, Christian, Jewish, and Muslim women, ages 25 to 82, meet, cook, share their stories, observe holidays, and dialogue on topics related to purity, forgiveness, and marriage. The equality among participants is emphasized, rather than speeches by experts. Yehuda Stolov, the director of the Interfaith Encounter Association in Jerusalem, attests to the power of small groups as interreligious encounters designed to bring people closer together in a context where peace-building is regarded as secular activity. "Religion invites people to come from a deeper self," he says (Sudilosky 2005, 45).

STRATEGIES FOR INTERRELIGIOUS ENCOUNTERS IN FAITH COMMUNITIES

It is challenging to structure interreligious encounters in faith communities which require people to claim their own religious identities and beliefs and which also challenge them to remain in relationship when differences surface. In many faith communities, there is likely to be a mix of people who experience religious homogeneity as normative, along with others who lived in situations of religious diversity. In some faith communities, people may feel unsure about their religious beliefs and thus be uncomfortable discussing religion with others. Learning the complexities of other religious traditions may seem daunting. It is not unlikely to have adults within churches who lack basic information about Christianity, or who have misinformation about other religions. Some may have deeply felt beliefs but do not want to offend others or appear to be proselytizing. It may be challenging for some people to separate their own beliefs from the way religion operates in institutions and in the wider culture. For others, religion is considered a private matter, and thus some have never publicly discussed their spiritual experiences at all. To accommodate these different realities, the following guidelines are designed to facilitate a generative environment for interreligious encounters:

- Begin with your own experience, using "I" statements, and do not speak for others. Be honest about your feelings.

- Agree to a norm of mutual respect in speech and in action. Honor your own experience and that of others.

- Develop compassionate listening skills. Prepare to listen to another with an open heart and mind.

- Study your own religious tradition as a basis for dialogue with others.

- Reflect on the question, "Who is my Neighbor," from a spiritual and faith perspective. In what ways do your beliefs support building community with people of other religious groups?

- Identify the religious demographics of your home community. Where are there already opportunities for relationship, dialogue, and engagement closest to home?

- Look for relationship and understanding on several levels: emotional, intellectual, and spiritual.

- Practice intercultural communications skills.

- Learn about other religious cultures.

- Identify resources and networks in your home community interested in interreligious education and action. Who are the persons and places in your community already looking to be in relationship with people and congregations from other religious traditions? How can I—and/or my congregation—participate in projects designed to support the common good?

- Face conflict and disagreements openly and with compassion.

- Prepare yourself for the mistakes you will make and learn from them. When another makes a mistake that is offensive to you, first assume good will on their part as well.

- Seek support and assistance from within and outside your congregation.

- Pray and celebrate!

The World Council of Churches affirms that one of the prevailing purposes of interreligious encounter is to affirm hope. "In the midst of many divisions, conflicts, and violence, there is a hope that it is possible to create a human community that lives in justice and peace" (WCCC

2009). Interreligious encounter is not an end in itself but a means toward building communities of mutual respect and understanding. As spiritual practice, interreligious encounter affirms the lives of all God's people. People of faith are called to interreligious encounters in the spirit of compassion and mutuality, to transform and reconcile. This call is not particular to Christians but is part of a larger interconnected humanity open to all people of good will. In this way, interreligious encounters help us transcend our limitations and offer us the opportunity to participate in a vision of the whole people of God.

REFLECTION QUESTIONS

1. Reflect on a significant encounter that you have had with a person or group from another religious tradition. Try to recall the entire experience, including the gifts, challenges, and confusions of the experience. What was the impact of that experience on your experience of interreligious dialogue? What did you learn from it that you carry into future interreligious dialogue?

2. Recall the four models of interreligious encounter in chapter 2. Which models have you already experienced? How might you or your faith community best participate in future interreligious learning?

3. Reflect on interreligious hospitality. What images, metaphors, passages, or other associations come to mind when you reflect on interreligious hospitality? How might you offer more interreligious hospitality in your own life? In the life of your faith community?

3

Practices of Interreligious Learning

Every great faith has within it harsh texts which, read literally, can be taken to endorse narrow particularism, suspicion of strangers, and intolerance toward those who believe differently than we do. Every great faith also has within it sources that emphasize kinship with the stranger, empathy with the outsider, and courage that leads people to extend a hand across boundaries of estrangement and hostility. The choice is ours. Will the generous texts of our tradition serve as interpretive keys to the rest, or will the abrasive passages determine our ideas of what we are called on to do? . . . I believe we are being called by God to see in the human other a trace of the divine Other.

JONATHAN SACKS, *THE DIGNITY OF DIFFERENCE* (2002, 207–8)
(USED WITH PERMISSION)

ONE FRIDAY DURING LENT, Greg Foraker, associate clergy at St. Philip's in the Hills Episcopal Church in Tucson, Arizona, entered the Islamic Center, the city's largest mosque, to participate in worship with its 500 members. To the left of the entrance was a group of women in traditional dress and to the right was a room where the male members of the mosque wash their hands and feet in preparation for prayer. Feeling uncertain in this unfamiliar place, he turned to the room where he was to wash when he unexpectedly heard someone from the group of women call his name. To his surprise the women turned out to be members of St. Philip's Episcopal

Church, covered in traditional Muslim attire from head to toe, in keeping with the practice of their hosts. After a few nervous laughs of recognition, the group once again parted as the women and men gathered in separate areas for prayer and worship.

For Christians living in a predominantly Christian culture, it is relatively easy to go through life without learning about other religious traditions or seriously examining our own. Greg Foraker and the women from St. Philip's who attended the Islamic Center's worship service were part of their congregation's "Varieties of Religious Experience" program, which grew out of the congregation's desire to offer a less traditional yet transformational Lenten program. The program was an experiential series of interreligious encounters focused on participation in worship with several of the many religious traditions found throughout the greater Tucson area, followed by a shared meal and conversation with local religious leaders.

The group of eighteen who shared in prayers with Tucson's Muslim community later gathered with the imam, or prayer leader, and a dozen members of the mosque for Middle Eastern food, lively conversation, and an opportunity to build relationships across religious traditions. Members of St. Philip's were impressed with the authenticity of the hospitality they received from the Muslim community, the shared dialogue experienced over the meal, and the enthusiasm displayed for forging deeper relationships between Christians and Muslims in Tucson. "What at first seemed unfamiliar revealed connections not at first evident," says Foraker (Foraker 2009).

Dr. S. Asif Razvi of the Islamic Center of Boston affirms the value of such encounters between Muslims and non-Muslims, from his own perspective. "Islam is a continuation of the other two Abrahamic faiths and it is every practicing Muslim's obligation to inform others about our faith," he says. "We find education and dialogue to be the best approach to inform non-Muslims and to correct the widespread misconceptions about Islam" (Razvi, 2008).

In addition to Friday prayers at the mosque, interreligious education at St. Philip's Episcopal Church in Tucson included an invitation to sit zazen at Zen Desert Sangha, to celebrate the festival of Ayyam-i-ha with the Tucson Baha'i, to dance and chant "Hare Krishna" at the Chaitanya Mandira, and to keep Shabbat with Temple Emanu-El. The interreligious education series for members of the congregation culminated with the Great Vigil of Easter at St. Philip's. Greg Foraker says that most participants attended every session of the program, despite varying schedules and multiple locations, and that "each person reported that the experience was in some way transformative for them personally. This program was not your typical Sunday morning at 10:00 a.m. adult education offering. The participants considered the encounters an adventure, and grew deeper in their own faith as a result of the process." Some participants in the Varieties of Religious Experience program reported that the experience of learning about different religious traditions challenged them to reflect more deeply on their faith as Christians. Others felt that the encounters opened up new spiritual practices and channels of prayer and reflection. Still others experienced a desire to continue to build interreligious relationships within the larger Tucson community. Key to the effectiveness of interreligious learning at St. Philip's, Foraker says, "is the need to create a *space* of welcome. Over time we have been able to develop a climate of trust and accountability. This work is not just about potlucks but about working through difficult things together" (Foraker, 2009).

After initial forays in interreligious learning, St. Philip's in the Hills Episcopal Church has continued to reach out and investigate other opportunities in the Tucson area. Rather than continuing to repeat the same "successful" programs, Greg Foraker says that they have learned to look for opportunities, remembering that within interreligious relationships, "not all parties have the same needs" (Foraker 2009). Recently, interreligious education efforts at St. Phillip's have focused on different aspects of study, prayer and service. St. Philip's and Temple Emanu-El, the oldest Reform Jewish synagogue in Tucson, sponsored a joint discussion series entitled, "The Times of Our Lives: Jewish and Christian Understandings and Rituals for Life Cycle Events." The popular series was designed to look at the rituals and spiritual practices which have been part of Jewish and Christian pastoral care for generations, and which give structure and beauty to life's passages. The presenters were Samuel N. Cohon, the rabbi of Temple Emanu-el and John Kitagawa, the rector of St. Philip's in the Hills. Sessions were held at both sponsoring religious communities, to encourage joint ownership and attendance. The themes of the sessions included rites of initiation (Jewish circumcision and baby-naming and Christian baptism); rites of passage in adulthood (Jewish bar and bat mitzvah and confirmation and Christian confirmation and other rites of passage); rites of marriage, blessing, and union (from both Jewish and Christian perspectives), and, rituals of death and mourning (Jewish practices and Christian last rites and burial).

The "Times of Our Lives" presentations were designed to give participants ample time to ask questions, dialogue, and reflect. "Of course, the richness came with the questions and discussions," reported John Kitagawa. "Interestingly, many of the questions to Sam were from his congregants, and many to me were from St. Philippians. There were also 'cross-cultural' questions, but I think we were both surprised about how many questions came from our own people about our own traditions," he said (Kitagawa 2010). Greg Foraker observed that the series responded to an "unspoken reality," that is, the people who were part of interreligious families and for the first time had an opportunity to talk about that experience" (Foraker 2010).

Interreligious learning has gradually become infused into the life of St. Philip's in the Hills in a variety of ways. Another Lenten program, "Take, Eat, Exploring the Eucharist," was designed from an interreligious perspective. Each section of the series included a teaching section and a ritual section; the series culminated in a celebration of the Holy Eucharist. The popular series drew up to 300 participants, including people from the community beyond St. Philip's, and met in the church sanctuary. Presenters included Gordon McBride, an assisting priest at St. Philip's, who spoke on the Christian history of the Eucharist, including traditional as well as feminist perspectives; Helen Cohn, a spiritual director and rabbi of Congregation M'kor Hayim in Tucson (a Reform Jewish congregation that shares space with the First Congregational/UCC Church), spoke on Passover and the Jewish inheritance; and, from an eastern perspective, Michael Roach, a Tibetan Buddhist monk and one of the co-founders of Star in the East Foundation, an organization dedicated to furthering the Wisdom tradition in Christianity through retreat and prayer, spoke on a Buddhist Approach to the Eucharist.

St. Philip's in the Hills's community life also reflects other religious groups traditions in more subtle ways. For instance, when an adult education class on the Hebrew Scriptures was offered, Rabbi Helen Cohn taught a session to ensure that students would hear a Jewish voice. St. Philip's also houses the Tacheria Interfaith Spirituality Center, an organization that trains spiritual directors from the Buddhist, Christian, Jewish, and Muslim traditions. The center was founded by Jeanette Renouf in 1992 and offers retreats and workshops in addition to the spiritual direction training. "Our goal is dedicated to finding a safe oasis to sample the spiritual path and share it with others," says Renouf. "People need support to find their path and follow it" (Messina 2010).

Yet, despite the rich tradition of interreligious learning developing at St. Philip's in the Hills, "it doesn't happen by accident," cautions Greg

Foraker. "There is a continuing need to strengthen and build relationships. We find that we always have to pay attention and be looking for opportunities and connections. We have to be available to invite people in, face our realities, look at what we believe, and live in critical dissonance" (Foraker 2010).

PRINCIPLES OF EFFECTIVE INTERRELIGIOUS PRACTICE

Throughout this chapter we will examine effective interreligious practices as they relate to faith communities and religious organizations. Opportunities for interreligious learning and for building community across religious traditions continue to grow and expand not only in Tucson, but in many other cities and towns, offering faith communities means to learn more about other religious traditions and to forge new friendships. Some of the characteristics of effective interreligious learning in faith communities include:

- It values similarities *and* differences between religious groups.
- It supports participants in finding their "voice."
- It seeks and maintains long-term relationships between members.
- It models dialogical discussions and not religious debates.
- It cultivates mutual respect among all partners.
- It recognizes the diversity within all religious traditions.
- It supports a sense of pride in individual and group identities.
- Participants experience affirmation rather than judgment.
- It teaches religious traditions from the perspective of adherents of those traditions.
- It stresses the need to build relationships within and between religious communities.
- It models compassionate listening.
- It fosters openness and builds capacities in critical thinking.
- It clarifies misinformation learned about other groups.
- It models the belief that disagreements need not fracture community.
- It promotes healing between individuals and groups.
- It emphasizes the practice of interreligious hospitality.

- It assures appropriate food, drink, and space for all participants.

- It structures small groups for nurture and study.

- It invites all partners to shape the experience.

- It adapts as relationships matures and is open to change.

- It emphasizes the need to ask questions as a positive aspect of learning.

- It designs encounters to suit a variety of learning styles, with an emphasis on experiential learning.

- It creates an evolutionary process that cultivates understanding between people as *the* priority.

- Participants trust the educational design and the competence of leaders.

PILGRIMAGE AS A PRACTICE
OF INTERRELIGIOUS LEARNING

Pilgrimage is a spiritual practice of most of the major religions of the world. Traditionally, a pilgrimage refers to a journey of spiritual or religious significance. Some pilgrimages are undertaken physically, while some are internal, in the heart and the imagination. In this way, a pilgrimage is a journey where a divine and human encounter takes place, a visit to a holy site to recall and to pray.

The power of pilgrimage as a means of interreligious learning was the focus of a program sponsored by the Center for Interreligious Understanding in Carlstadt, New Jersey, as a means to combat the rise in Holocaust denial that has surfaced in recent years. In 2010, the pilgrimage visited two Nazi concentration camps, Dachau and Auschwitz, with prominent Jewish and Muslims leaders from the United States. "The best way to convince someone about the truth of something is to let them see it for themselves and experience it for themselves," said Rabbi Jack Bemporad of the Center for Interreligious Understanding. "I feel that it was important to take Muslim leaders who have a really significant following in the American-Muslim community." Of the eight Muslim leaders who made the pilgrimage, some had worked previously with Jewish groups in interreligious dialogue. One group member was on record as doubting the extent of the Holocaust, though he recanted before the trip. The imams were deeply moved by the pilgrimage, especially after speaking to Holocaust survivors, seeing their tattooed numbers, and seeing the victims' hair, suitcases, and belongings. "Almost everybody was in tears," said Imam Muzammil Siddiqi, of the Islamic Society of Orange County in California, a frequent participant in interreligious events. Participants in the pilgrimage agreed that the historical realities of the Holocaust should not be eclipsed by the last sixty years of tensions in the Middle East. "Whatever happened post-Holocaust should not diminish the evil that was the Holocaust. . . . The Israel-Palestinian conflict is very complicated. Let's leave anti-Semitism out of it," said Shaykh Yasir Qadhi, from New Haven, Connecticut, and academic dean of the Al-Maghrib Institute. "It was a very moving experience for all of us imams, in particular myself. I had never seen anything like this. . . . I could not comprehend how much evil could be unleashed" (Diamant 2010, 19).

On their return to the United States, the Muslim leaders who participated in the pilgrimage released a statement citing the six million Jewish deaths, among twelve million Holocaust deaths overall, and condemning any attempts to deny this historical reality as being against the Islamic code of ethics. "We stand united as Muslim American faith and community leaders and recognize that we have shared responsibility to continue to work together with leaders of all faiths and their communities to fight the dehumanization of all people based on their religion, race, or ethnicity," says the imams' statement on Holocaust denial. "With the disturbing rise of anti-Semitism, Islamophobia, and other forms of hatred, rhetoric, and bigotry, now more than ever, people of faith must stand together for truth" (American Imams 2010).

When planning interreligious pilgrimages the trap of "theological tourism," that is, pilgrimage experiences designed solely by members of one religious tradition, without a relationship to those encountered, should be avoided. Some suggested guidelines for interreligious pilgrimages include:

- Begin with an assumption that the Divine is at work in/among all those encountered.
- The pilgrimage is part of a long-term relationship between religious communities.
- If a travel experience, the pilgrimage includes a component that links interreligious learning to the home community.
- The pilgrimage emphasizes mutual and reciprocal relationships among people, rather than one group creating an experience for another.

- The experience requires advance study and an orientation program that incorporates knowledge of one's own tradition as well as of other religions and cultures.

- The design of the pilgrimage allows all partners to play an integral part in the planning process and to determine the parameters of their hospitality.

- Individual and corporate reflection is a central part of the experience.

- The experience is evaluated by all parties.

Although many individuals and faith communities sponsor one-time pilgrimages, such experiences are not as likely to support interreligious learning. Pilgrimages designed to support interreligious learning emphasize mutuality in relationships and the sharing of stories. The importance of honest dialogue during the planning process and the pilgrimage itself contributes to a deeper spiritual encounter among people of different religious traditions. Further, pilgrimage experiences that honor the particularity of differing religious traditions are careful to honor the parameters set by hosts and guests alike. Integral to interreligious pilgrimages is an awareness that the experience needs in some way to be connected to the participants' home communities, and evaluated by all who took part in the experience.

SHARED MEALS AND CONVERSATION

During the month of Ramadan, local mosques often invite interested people from the wider community to an iftar, or break-fast in the evening. The occasion begins with food, dates, and a drink, followed by brief sunset prayer, which guests are either invited to participate in or to observe quietly. Following the prayers, delicious meals of cooked and uncooked food are served. Often, greeters from the mosque are on hand at the door to answer any questions.

Interreligious learning is often facilitated through two of the most basic community-building ingredients of human societies—shared meals and conversation. Building relationships through sharing a common meal is a theme that runs throughout interreligious education efforts in the college town of Bennington, Vermont. "We are learning how a common meal instantly creates bonds of friendship and deep understanding," says Anita Schell-Lambert, the former rector of St. Peter's Episcopal Church in Bennington. "For many in our interreligious circles, a common meal followed by a meditation group or reflection series *is* their religious community,; thus, we were expanding the way we 'worship' here at St. Peter's." Also sponsored by the congregation, a community-wide education series called "Think Global, Eat Local" linked the theme of food with interreligious environmentalism. The five-week series served as a springboard to a variety of community-wide related activities, from communal gardens to a study of the impact of food choice on energy sustainability. Schell-Lambert found that shared goals are key to building interreligious learning. We discovered that we grow and learn more deeply through our diversity." For instance, a recent Lenten series at the church focused on the themes of forgiveness, atonement, and reconciliation, and included Christian, Native American, and Buddhist teachings about the nature of suffering and the need to develop compassion. "Without exception, people felt their own particular faith tradition was enhanced by learning about a tradition very different from their own," says Schell-Lambert (Schell-Lambert 2008).

The need for interreligious learning for families was the concept behind the Families in Conversation program started by Jay L. Kanzler, Jr., an assistant clergyperson at St. Peter's Episcopal Church in St. Louis, Missouri, and a practicing attorney. The idea was to invite families of other faith traditions to have dinner and conversations with families from St. Peter's, a congregation that also includes a "rabbi-in-residence" as a member of its clergy staff. The focus of the encounters is twofold: to develop a better understanding of what others believe and to create an awareness of the similarities and differences between faith traditions. "The initial sessions were very positively received," says Kanzler. One outcome from his own Families in Conversation dinner was the development of a friendship with the imam of the local Bosnian community. When the Bosnian community sought to gain approval for the building of a new community center and mosque, the county government blocked the request. Kanzler believed the denial was due to religious discrimination and agreed to represent the Islamic Community Center in litigation. With the support of many faith groups, the Bosnian Islamic Center was able to reach a settlement and eventually build a new community center and a mosque. "This was a wonderful interreligious effort to bring together rather than to tear apart with ignorance and prejudices," says Kanzler (Kanzler 2008).

Many interreligious encounters begin with the sharing of food and conversation, and it is therefore important for groups to be aware from the start of the dietary needs of persons from other religious traditions. It is good to discuss food issues within your own faith community, and with partners and set an agreed-upon set of basic guidelines. For example, vegetarian or vegan meals (though the definition of "vegetarian" differs across groups) go the furthest in assuring that most will be able to partake of the food. Labeling dishes carefully will help people participate in the hospitality offered without having to be anxious that a particular food will transgress religious observance. It is helpful to provide basic education about the food practices of other religious traditions *before* guests are invited, lest some faith community members be inadvertently inhospitable by expecting the typical fare at an event. It is important that leaders make clear in advance that the food and drink offered at an interreligious gathering are based on the assumption that everyone invited will be able to eat. In all cases, it is important to communicate directly with partners of other religious traditions about issues of food and observance, as well as to provide clarity to food preparers within faith communities. Some general guidelines related to food and drink as part of interreligious learning, include:

- Discuss food and drink issues with all partners while planning interreligious programs and events; share these guidelines with caterers and with all those who prepare food and drink from your congregation.

- Label all food and drink with a list of ingredients as a part of hospitality and as a way to ease anxiety over shared meals. Announce your guidelines for food and drink with the program.

- Fully vegetarian or vegan meals are the most widely accepted menu for all religious groups.

- Fruit juices, mineral water, and herbal teas are the most widely acceptable beverages among religious groups. Alcohol practices vary widely, and alcohol should be avoided in food preparation. Caffeinated coffee and tea are avoided by observant members of some religious groups.

- Avoid cooking with animal fats; for a list of non-vegetarian food additives, see www.vegsoc.org.

- Avoid gelatin products and cheese unless labeled "vegetarian."

- Hindus and Jains avoid eating eggs, garlic, and root vegetables such as onions and potatoes.

- Interpretations of which foods are kosher vary among Jewish groups. Faith communities should check on the interpretation of dietary laws with Jewish partners in advance. Purchased kosher foods are marked with a hechsher (seal). Generally, fully vegetarian foods with disposable dishes and utensils are acceptable.

- Muslims also vary in their interpretations of forbidden foods and food preparation. Most are concerned that any meat be halal, or slaughtered in accordance with Islamic law. Vegetarian or vegan menus without animal by-products are generally acceptable.

- Meat and fish dishes or sandwiches need to be served on separate plates from vegetarian options and should not be mixed.

- Generally, pork, beef, and shellfish should be avoided; chicken and turkey are the most acceptable across religious groups, if meat is to be served at all. Food preparers should be advised that poultry or fish should not be used in fully vegetarian meals.

Related to the issue of appropriate food and drink in showing interreligious hospitality is the issue of religious dress and symbols. Religious dress and symbols are an important expression of religious identity for many people. While the freedom to wear religious dress and symbols is generally accepted in the United States, there are places in the world where this is not the case. Christians should be aware that when visiting religious houses of some traditions it is considered inappropriate to wear religious symbols, such as crosses. Men and women should dress modestly, avoiding shorts and bare shoulders, and in some houses of worship women are expected to cover their heads. In some Jewish congregations, it is expected that all men, and sometimes women, wear kippahs (or yarmulkes) for worship and study, while in others the practice is optional for non-Jewish visitors. While it is not the custom to separate women and men in public worship in the vast majority of Christian institutions, this is not the practice among some other religious traditions. Careful and sensitive preparation of persons participating in interreligious encounters about matters of dress and any other expectations avoids confusion and giving offense.

TEXT STUDY AND CLERGY EXCHANGES

An annual shared Bible study has been the focus of interreligious learning at the Second Church (United Church of Christ) and Temple Shalom in Newton, Massachusetts. The two congregations share a fifty-year friendship dating from the time when Temple Shalom was formed and held its religious school's classes at the Second Church during the construction of its own facilities. The Bible study, which began over a decade ago, focuses on a different theme each year, and has included themes such as, the Song of Songs, the Psalms, and "Jesus and the Talmud." Richard E. Malmberg, pastor of the church, notes that members of his congregation have been "touched and intimidated" by the serious Bible scholarship evident among the laity of the Jewish congregation. Over time the Bible study became a vehicle "to build trust and explore issues and questions on both sides, as well as to go beyond stereotypes of each other," he says (Malmberg 2008).

Malmberg's own interest in interreligious learning stems, in part, from his experience growing up in an interreligious family. He enjoys a good friendship with the rabbi at Temple Shalom, and attends the minyan each Saturday. "These experiences give me a chance to negotiate the boundaries [of my own faith], to learn about my heritage, and to celebrate my vocation at the same time," he says. Because of the religious diversity experienced in the congregation, Malmberg says the Second Church has become known as "a good place for interreligious families to find a home" (Malmberg 2008).

One result of an interreligious discussion group in Stamford, Connecticut, was the First Presbyterian Church's "Rabbi-in-Residence" program. Pastors David van Dyke, Blair Moffett, Mary Thies, Douglass Lind and Rabbi Robert Lennick became friends through the discussion group. When Lennick took a job with an interfaith organization he missed congregational life and was offered a role with the parish, though it was not clear at the time what exactly that role would entail. "We realized it would be that of someone who could speak with a different voice," said Lennick, who began his work at the First Presbyterian Church by co-teaching with one of the pastors courses on social and ideological differences, and on forgiveness, as well as serving as a counselor on interreligious issues (Hirsch 2003, 21).

The close association between the clergy of two different faith traditions at the First Presbyterian Church resulted in increased respect and understanding, although the relationship was not without its discomforts. For instance, at the first Maundy Thursday service with the rabbi-in-residence, the Passion narrative of the gospel of John was read, which speaks of the Jews as those responsible for Jesus' death. The pastors took notice of the rabbi's discomfort, and after the service gathered with him to discuss the text and his understanding of it. "Words I'd always used easily, like *Jew*, suddenly sounded different," said Blair Moffett. "I tried to hear them through

Rob's ears and it made me realize that the words we heard so casually might not be heard the same way." Moffett said that initially there was some discomfort in the church about having a rabbi-in-residence. "When you cross established cultural barriers someone will be disturbed. You never know how or who will take offense. But someone is going to be wounded despite your good intentions. I'm sure there were people who had questions that weren't answered. But there were also people who had questions that were resolved, and that's the measure of the value of this partnership." But you learn you don't get along by 'mushing' people all together. You get along by understanding and appreciating differences" (Hirsch 2003, 21).

Rob Lennick believes that it was his role to encourage the congregation to participate in ongoing interreligious learning: "Whenever you are in an interfaith dialogue, you have to balance honesty with respect for the receiver. In Bible study we read Isaiah 53, one of the 'suffering servant' passages. Jews read that passage as a description of the suffering of Israel. But Christians read it as the suffering of Christ. When I teach that section I want to be able to teach the Jewish perspective without offending Christian understanding. Sometimes the confrontation of ideas is uncomfortable. But for the sake of a successful dialogue I still assert my ideas, not to change anyone's mind, but to share the possibility of understanding," he said. "My goal was not to convert anyone to Judaism. I'm sure there was plenty of tacit disapproval among my fellow Jews that I participated in this group at all! Jewish tradition discourages outreach for conversion. But if you can get a dialogue going, that's the beautiful thing" (Hirsch 2003, 21).

Another congregation which instituted a Rabbi-in-Residence program is St. Peter's Episcopal Church in St. Louis, Missouri. Again, the relationship evolved as clergy from different religious traditions formed friendships, pursued dialogue, and then sought ways to bring the richness of their encounter to an entire congregation. James Purdy, then rector of St. Peter's, says that he started to have lunch and conversations with Joseph R. Rosenbloom, then rabbi of Temple Emmanuel, Frontenac, when he first came to the church in 1998. He eventually asked Rosenbloom to preach at the Good Friday Liturgy in 2000. Rosenbloom is one of the most beloved rabbi's in St. Louis; he retired after forty-two years at Temple Emmanuel. After the Good Friday service, Purdy turned to the rabbi and asked, "Would you like to join our staff someday?" The idea matured into a formal agreement, which included preaching, teaching, and pastoral care. Rosenbloom maintained an office at the church, and at the temple as rabbi emeritus, and served a congregation in Ames, Iowa, once a month. At St. Peter's, the rabbi-in-residence worked with all ages, children through adults, and offered a variety of educational courses. These courses included looking at "difficult" texts, the writings and teachings of Paul, teaching for the every member canvas, and a course on death and dying. In addition, St. Peter's hosted other interreligious opportunities through confirmation classes, observances of Kristallnach, adult discussion groups, and community projects, all with the intention of "informing beliefs, changing attitudes and behavior," said Purdy. "The disease of anti-Semitism lurks virulently beneath a thin veneer, even in civilized Saint Louis" (Purdy 2008).

INTERRELIGIOUS LEARNING WITH YOUNG PEOPLE

Creative interreligious learning includes young people, who bring a curiosity, openness, and energy to their interreligious relationships. Eboo Patel believes that the future of pluralism in America depends on idealistic young people who believe in importance of building relationships across religious traditions (Patel 2012, 101–2). Interreligious learning for children and youth varies in size and complexity. For example, the Church of the Transfiguration, Derry, New Hampshire, along with sister congregation Etz Hayim Synagogue, created the world of first-century Palestine for a summer week-long program designed for preschoolers to fourth graders. Adults from both congregations recreated a first-century village on the grounds. Every day, the students gathered near the well for singing and an introduction to the day's activities. Campers were divided into tribes and each day negotiated the climb up "Awesome Mountain." Each day stories were told from the Hebrew Bible, including David, Esther, and Zipporah. Campers gathered into tribal tents to learn about daily life in biblical times, and walked to the marketplace assembled by members of the synagogue, where the children learned how to grind flour, make tambourines, or compose scrolls. The experience brought together both children and adults from the two congregations to build relationships and engage in interreligious learning (LeSueur 2005, 1, 7).

The Interfaith Youth Initiative (IFYI) sponsored by the Cooperative Metropolitan Ministries (CMM) of Newton, Massachusetts, is an eight-day immersion program, followed by mentoring and gatherings for a full academic year, and is designed for youth fifteen through eighteen years of age as well as college and graduate student staff. Its leadership currently comes from Christian, Jewish, Muslim, and Unitarian Universalist traditions. The curriculum focuses on spiritual formation, dialogue, service, peace and justice, and the arts. The five core values of the program are building bridges, engaging faith, training leaders, making peace, and serving others.

"All too often youth and young adults are both primary victims and chief perpetrators of religiously fueled violence," says the former Cooperative Metropolitan Ministries Executive Director Alexander Levering Kern. "At the same time, the absence of faith—and the hope, community, and opportunity that faith can engineer—breeds cultures of nihilism that prove equally destructive. Like their parents, too many young people in the 21st century seem caught in the pincers of religious extremism and secular materialism" (Kern 2008).

Kern believes interreligious learning is an area where young people can gain skills in dialogue, peacemaking, and public witness that are applicable in many areas of life. Further, young people who participate in interreligious education are equipped to bring positive change not only to their religious communities but to their schools and neighborhoods as well.

"As [Dr. Martin Luther King Jr.] makes clear, what makes community possible is the life-changing discovering of our own true identities and callings as children of God and brothers and sisters to all humanity. Such discoveries often occur in the 'liminal space' of authentic dialogue and exchange with 'the other,' the classic 'step outside of the comfort zone.' When done with conviction and care, interreligious education has the potential, quite literally, to save lives, transform faith communities, and fashion a horizon of hope for our broken world," says Kern (Kern 2008).

The Interfaith Action Youth Leadership Program of Sharon, Massachusetts is another organization that does extensive interreligious education with young people, starting with hosting students from the Open House program in Ramle, Israel. Until that time, the organization hosted monthly meetings with high school seniors from different religious traditions in the regions. Sharon is a town of 17,000 where sixty Christian churches share the religious landscape with eight synagogues, a mosque, and hundreds of Indian, Chinese, Russian and Israeli families. Young people who have worked with the organization have self-described as Jewish, Hindu, Christian, Muslim, Jain, Unitarian, Atheist, and Wiccan. Janet Penn, the executive director, says that interreligious work with adults in congregations in Sharon "is much harder and slower."

Although the organization began by inviting clergy to talk to young people who attended meetings facilitated by adults, over time it became clear that young people were more excited about learning from each other. Penn says that the questions young people had for each other varied. Some were more specifically religious in nature, while others focused on ethnic traditions and cultural identity. "Food was always a big topic of conversation," said Penn (Penn 2008, 2009, 2).

Interfaith Action's Youth Leadership Program is built on a model which incorporates *reflection, connection, and action.* In the fall of a given school year, the program focuses on encouraging young people to reflect on their own religious traditions and practices. As the year progresses, young people make connections across different religious and cultural backgrounds. Lastly, with the support of training and mentoring, young people plan actions that build community, inspire others, and have a positive impact on local issues. Penn says that, while other programs focus almost exclusively on religious literacy, the young people who gravitate to the Interfaith Action Youth Leadership Program are less interested in obtaining information about other religions, than they are keen to understand and share their traditions. Penn attributed this fact to the reality that most students in the district study world religions in ninth grade, so they already have a degree of religious literacy. "While I personally value basic faith literacy, I suspect that once they are friends with a person from another faith tradition, their motivation to learn more about others' religious belief and practice increases," says Penn (Penn 2009, 2).

Janet Penn is appreciative of the action-based emphasis she finds in the interreligious youth movement in the United States, and she has found that young people have the potential to have a far greater impact in their local communities. Rather than designing an interreligious curriculum *for* youth, the Interfaith Action Youth Leadership Program has evolved to a place where young people "actually plan and run programs that create a culture of pluralism." For example, at a time when there was tension between the Orthodox Jewish and observant Muslim young people in the community, the young people met with the local rabbi and imam to plan a program to address the issue. By the end of the resultant youth-facilitated dialogue, young people from the two traditions began to form relationships and gained a sense of their similarities as well as their differences (Penn 2008).

A set of eight core principles guides the work of the Interfaith Action Youth Leadership Programs, primarily through the empowerment of young people to create increased understanding and cooperation among members of different religious and cultural groups. These core principles include:

1. Maintain a profound respect and belief in the wisdom and capabilities of teens.

2. Set the bar high.

3. Don't be afraid of failure.

4. Be prepared to encounter difficulties.

5. Support all youth to be leaders.

6. Plan proactively and don't be afraid to seize opportunities.

7. Be inclusive of all interested youth.

8. Recognize the complexity of adolescent identity (Penn 2008).

Janet Penn believes that these eight core practices, along with the organization's commitment to providing young people with training and mentoring, has allowed the Interfaith Action Youth Leadership Program to continue to expand and deepen its work not only in the local community, but throughout the world. Under the auspices of the organization, young people planned and facilitated interactive sessions and interreligious dialogues at conferences in Atlanta, Chicago, and Amman, Jordan. Two young people associated with the program served as interns for a malaria education program under an initiative of the Tony Blair Faith Foundation to get young people from the various religious traditions involved in the Millennium Development Goals. The young people associated with the Interfaith Action Youth Leadership Program have facilitated dialogues for hundreds of parish groups, following film documentaries, for visiting imams from Uzbekistan, and with local and community leaders. They offered several sessions on interfaith relations at a local synagogue, and they have also worked in schools, for instance, facilitating a day on stereotypes for a Conservative Jewish Day School, and offering a "Global Issues" class at a neighboring high school (Penn 2008).

"I believe the ultimate goal of interfaith youth work is to strengthen the fabric of our civil society, fostering respect and open communication among different religious and ethnic groups," says Janet Penn. "The movement provides teens with opportunities to reflect, connect, and act while in high school and in university. In the process, individuals strengthen their own identities and, as they listen deeply to others, they learn that, in spite of very different religious beliefs, custom, and practices, individuals can treat each other with respect and hope, not fear and mistrust. Talia, a participant in the program said: "Interfaith Action's Youth Leadership Program was by far the most transformative experience of my life. It has shaped my outlook on the value of diversity and dialogue and showed me the value of the youth voice while strengthening my patience, public speaking, and listening skills. It was an honor to be part of a program that brought together different people toward a common goal, and to collaborate with other kids my age to create positive change within our community" (Penn 2008).

Recently the Unitarian Universalist Association's (UUA) Youth Office, in partnership with the Interfaith Youth Core, a Chicago based-organization founded by international interreligious leader Eboo Patel, started an initiative to organize and implement interfaith youth events in communities across the country. Training events were held in Tulsa, Atlanta, and Columbus, Ohio, attracting teams from eighteen congregations. A mother and daughter team, Lauri and Samatha Nandyal of the First Unitarian Universalist Church of Columbus, Ohio, organized 40 Muslim, Presbyterian, and Unitarian Universalist youth to do a spring clean-up day in a local neighborhood. Interestingly, all the groups experienced a lack of participation from conservative Christian congregations in their communities. "Our faith has the most interfaith work to do around Christianity," said Kate Starr, the youth director of All Souls in Tulsa, Oklahoma. "It's easy for us to be open minded and accepting of Hindus, Jews, Muslims, and the liberal Methodists and Catholics who chose to participate in our interfaith event. These aren't the fundamentalists who are condemning our children to hell in school. Our mission as a church is to do more healing work around our own Christian stereotypes. Interfaith work, especially with Christians, helps us really see each other as individual human beings and not as institutions or dogmatic formulas. But for that to happen both parties have to be willing." She added, "Interfaith work is a hands-on way for our youth to experience other faiths who are trying to do the same thing we are—that is: live a moral life, seek insight and ultimate truth, perfect their spiritual nature, live in community and harmony—without trying to convert anyone else or tell them they're wrong. This is, after all, the essential gospel of Jesus" (UUA 2010).

INTERRELIGIOUS LEARNING THROUGH THE ARTS

The arts are a powerful vehicle for interreligious learning. Joyce Herman of the National Coalition Building Institute is a member of Temple Sinai in Rochester, New York, a congregation with historic interreligious relationships with the local Islamic Center and Baber African Methodist Episcopal Zion Church. Herman is involved in interreligious learning, including the development of the documentary on "Prayer in America." The film follows senior religious leaders as they discuss public prayer, the issues that arise in interreligious dialogue, and how prayer relates to the crises of violence in the community. Herman reports that the response to the film brought some "profound interreligious challenges and healing" (Herman 2008). Despite the history of conflict between religious communities, the film uncovers how prayer can promote greater understanding and forge relationships between people of faith.

Another type of interreligious project that involves the arts is the exhibit, entitled "Sacred Origins: An Interfaith Art Project for West Philadelphia," that combines images from forty-five artists. The project was sponsored by the Philadelphia Cathedral, an Episcopal congregation located in West Philadelphia. Creator and public artist Zoe Cohen coordinated the permanent exhibit as part of a one-year residency at the cathedral. "When I started to think about an installation piece, I wanted to create something of my own," said Cohen. "But I had to honor the cathedral's decision to bring people's viewpoints into the space." Cohen took risks as she planned the project, but she was supported by the cathedral council even when it was not immediately apparent what the exhibit was going to look like when completed. She started by contacting a group of other artists representing diverse religious traditions. "I invited them to make a small drawing symbolic of some aspect of their faith practice or background—with an emphasis on origins—the origins of their faith practice in their own life or imagery from stories from their religion," she said. After receiving the individual images, Cohen decided where to place them in relationship with the other images involved in the project. She then created a five-foot by five-foot mixed media wooden panel that incorporated the drawings along with Cohen's own religious images using watercolors, acrylics, gouache (a reflective water-based paint), colored markers, pencils, and wax crayons. The final work reflects the diverse and interconnected interreligious community of West Philadelphia. "It is the creation of people from all walks of life," said Lloyd Casson, then interim dean of the cathedral. "We like it not just because of its artistic beauty, but it goes with the particular place—this is a place of worship for all peoples" (Hames 2009, 16).

THEOLOGICAL EDUCATION
AND INTERRELIGIOUS LEARNING

The need for religious leaders with skills in interreligious learning is central to the mission of a growing number of graduate theological schools and seminaries interested in formation for religious leaders responsive to religious pluralism. In 2009, the Center for Multifaith Education at Auburn Theological Seminary, a research institution that studies theological education, released *Beyond World Religions: The State of Multifaith Education in American Theological Schools*. The authors surveyed 150 Christian, Jewish, Muslim, Buddhist, and multireligious institutions across the United States that train religious leaders. The research indicates that American seminaries are already offering a wide range of courses about other faith traditions, most commonly on Islam and Judaism, and most frequently through the lens of theology. The schools surveyed reported a variety of theological approaches to the subject of religious pluralism, including the belief that learning about other traditions helps students grow in their faith, and that knowledge of other religions is integral to minister effectively in the twenty-first century (Auburn Seminary 2009).

With an interest in preparing religious leaders and scholars steeped in religious pluralism, the Claremont School of Theology in Claremont, California, has launched a "university project," with the intent of training religious leaders from a variety of religious traditions under one roof. The school has a 125-year United Methodist tradition, has operated ecumenically, and now has a growing interreligious presence among faculty and students. In partnership with the Academy for Jewish Religion, a transdenominational, pluralistic Jewish institution, and Bayan Claremont, a college founded by the Islamic Center of Southern California (ICSC) where Islamic religious leaders, scholars, and educators are educated, the newly formed Claremont Lincoln University now also has Hindu, Buddhist, Jain, and Sikh partners involved in the project. "We are trying to catch up with the practical reality of how congregations, synagogues, and mosques are already trying to create some rapport among themselves," says Jerry Campbell, president of Claremont School of Theology. Claremont School of Theology launched the project to improve relationships across faith traditions. "Dialogue takes place among friends—people who know each other," says Jerry Campbell "There will be peace in the world when religious leaders decide to make peace. Our hope is that there will be less mistrust and conflict between the religions if their future leaders interact as they pursue their education," he says. "We want our students to learn how to cooperate across religious boundaries to diminish conflict." 'It is not enough to speak in God's name while ignoring the fundamental teachings of our traditions to love our neighbors as ourselves, or to treat others as we would like to be treated," says Rabbi Mel Gottlieb, former president of the Academy of Jewish Religion. "How can this love develop if we have no relationship with our brothers and sisters in different religious traditions?" (Dias 2010)

Jihad Turk, director of religious affairs for the Islamic Center of Southern California, acknowledges that some will find the interreligious partnership challenging. "There are always going to be those who are uninterested and mistrustful of working with other institutions, and so we don't expect participation from those." Key to the university project is the belief that all the religious traditions involved need to be represented in their particularity. The project is not about watering down religious traditions or creating a "food court" of religions. Rather, the intent is to create an environment that challenges all to become educated in their own traditions, as well as those of others, to promote mutual respect, and to work together on common concerns and issues (Lipman 2010; Lansdburg 2010, A13).

Interreligious theological learning is also integral to the mission of Andover Newton Theological school and Hebrew College and rabbinical school in Newton Centre, Massachusetts, where the two schools share adjoining campuses. In 2008 they launched a new joint initiative called CIRCLE, the Center for Interreligious and Communal Leadership Education which is co-directed by Jennifer Peace, professor of interfaith studies at Andover Newton and Or Rose, a rabbi and Director of the Center for Global Judaism at Hebrew College. Peace believes that it is imperative for theological schools to create "multiple access points" or opportunities for students from differing religious traditions to get to know each other both inside and outside the classroom. "We need to create new ways for our students to bump into each other and begin to form the relationships that are foundational to interreligious understanding." Students can participate in single events, such as an annual joint Community Day held every spring, celebrations of moments in the sacred calendars of the two communities or various special lectures offered throughout the semester. Students can also join a year-long peer group that focuses on a range of topics of mutual interest like text study or social justice issues such as prison justice and environmental concerns. In addition Hebrew College and Andover Newton offer joint courses co-taught by faculty from each school. Students with a particular aptitude in the area can become

CIRCLE fellows and spend a year developing their interfaith leadership skills with a cohort of students from each school. The CIRCLE fellowship program expanded in 2012 to include Muslim community fellows as well. To foster and support all of this shared work, the two faculties have spent time together in joint faculty meetings and retreats to consider new ways that the school can work together. Jennifer Peace is clear of the importance for the Christian community of reaching seminary students from as many points on the theological spectrum as possible, including the evangelical community, which has the fastest growing number of seminary students. "This work needs to speak to people of conviction," says Peace. (Peace 2009)

THE PROCESS OF INTERRELIGIOUS LEARNING

Interreligious learning in faith communities is an opportunity for people to learn about and experience religious traditions other than their own while building deep relationships with persons of different religious backgrounds. Most importantly, ongoing interreligious learning values *relationships* in *community*. Ongoing interreligious learning, in contrast to single events, is most effective because it gives participants the opportunity to build relationships over time. Bilateral encounters, those experiences designed for two distinct religious traditions, or, at the most, trilateral encounters, those experiences shaped through the encounter of three separate religious groups at one time, provide the most opportunity for participants to build interreligious relationships. Such relationships allow participants to deepen their understanding of their own tradition, discover similarities with other traditions, and acknowledge that which makes each religious group distinct. Educational programs with the participation of more than three religious groups at one time are inspiring, but for those with limited knowledge of other religions, or with little experience interacting with people from other traditions, the experience can be overwhelming or confusing.

To establish ongoing interreligious learning in a faith community, it is helpful to begin by forming alliances with one or two other religious groups in the local community, chosen either through shared history, or because they, too, would like to develop ongoing relationships with people from another religious tradition. If the interreligious relationships between two or more religious traditions in a local community begin to bloom, it is likely that other traditions will also want to participate. Once people have an authentic experience of interreligious learning, they will want to do more for their own sake, and others will be attracted to the process. Faith communities of all sizes and geographical locations have the local resources needed to develop transformative interreligious learning experiences based in the religious diversity of their own communities.

The shape of interreligious learning in faith communities may be adapted to many different formats, depending on the faith communities' location, partners of other religious traditions, and learning goals. Overall, the most effective interreligious learning in faith communities includes a five-stage inter-related process:

1. *Prepare Leaders.* The first-stage process is for faith community leaders to prepare themselves for further interreligious learning through study and reflection. Before engaging a faith community in interreligious learning, leaders should be able fully to articulate their own religious traditions and practices and be informed about the traditions and practices of interreligious partners. Inherent in this first stage of the process is a leader's ability to understand the distinctiveness of their faith tradition, as well as that of others, to ensure that the religions studied are viewed from the perspectives of their own merit.

2. *Prepare the Community.* The second stage of the interreligious learning process is to prepare members of the faith community for interreligious encounter through study and reflection. Participants who have a firm foundation in their own religious traditions and practices, are more able to encounter others with confidence and mutual respect. Similar to stage one of the process, participants should also have opportunities to study the traditions and practices of religious partners before encounter.

3. *Share Stories.* Stages one and two pave the way for the third stage, when leaders and participants alike engage in interreligious learning through the sharing of stories. As the various formats portrayed in this chapter suggest, interreligious learning is most effective when based in ongoing interaction among participants from different traditions. Begin by sharing stories and sharing spiritual reflections on these stories. The relationships formed through sharing stories shape interreligious learning in ways content-driven learning alone does not.

4. *Shared Reflection.* Stage four of the process involves reflection on the experience of religious pluralism from the perspective of one's own faith tradition. What did we learn about our own religious tradition from this interreligious experience? What is the value of religious

pluralism? How might our interreligious encounters be deepened in the future? Shared reflection as a stage in interreligious learning allows leaders and participants alike to deepen relationships and to evoke future possibilities.

5. *Discern Resources for Further Action.* As interreligious groups reflect on future possibilities, they also begin to identify common issues and resources for future action. What are the shared concerns of the members of the community? How might we work together for the common good? What are some of the skills and resources we have to contribute to the project?

6. *Evaluate and Celebrate.* Lastly, all interreligious learning should include a comprehensive evaluation, including all partners, as well as ample opportunities for celebration. Interreligious learning is supported through frequent assessment to ensure that all voices are heard as part of the conversation. Community celebrations allow interreligious communities opportunities to deepen relationships and to get to know each other beyond religious traditions.

There are a wide variety of ways to shape interreligious learning, and those featured in this chapter are just a few of the possibilities. Interreligious learning is a means for faith communities to enrich their members, to challenge ignorance and oppression, and to explore forgiveness and reconciliation. Through an ongoing commitment to interreligious learning, spirits are enriched, minds are expanded, and communities are transformed.

REFLECTION QUESTIONS

1. Reflect on your own interreligious activities. In what ways did you learn about other religious traditions? What types of learning were most effective?

2. As you read through the stories of interreligious learning in chapter 3, what are some of the possibilities from your own faith community? Who are your likely partners?

3. How might you integrate interreligious learning into the religious education of different age groups within your faith community?

4

Sharing Sacred Spaces

I dreamed
That stone by stone I reared a sacred fane,
A temple, neither Pagod, Mosque, nor Church,
But loftier, simpler, always open-doored
To every breath from heaven; and Truth and Peace
And Love and Justice came and dwelt therein. . . .

ALFRED LORD TENNYSON, *AKBAR'S DREAM* (1892)

THE CATHEDRAL CHURCH OF St. Paul on Tremont Street in downtown Boston was founded as the city's fourth Episcopal Church in 1818, established by a group of patriots who wanted a church that was wholly American. Two earlier established Anglican parishes had been founded in Boston by the British before the American Revolution, and one other became Unitarian. When the Church of St. Paul was designated as the cathedral for the Episcopal Diocese of Massachusetts in 1912, the bishop chose to symbolize that it was "a house of prayer for all people" by removing the doors to the boxed pews. Since August 2000, the Cathedral Church of St. Paul has hosted a growing Muslim community for prayers every Friday afternoon.

The relationship between downtown Boston's Muslim community and the cathedral began when the cathedral staff and a local Muslim business owner got to know each other as neighbors. The Muslim owner of the café next door to the cathedral got to talking with Jep Steit, the dean of the cathedral, about the need for a place to pray on Fridays. The Muslim men in the area typically prayed in a space provided by an adjoining university, but they were outgrowing that space and looking for a location near their businesses. Streit thought that a large renovated space underneath the cathedral sanctuary, Sproat Hall, might fill the need. Sproat Hall was typically used by the cathedral congregation on Sundays and for cathedral programs, but it was available from 12:30 to 1:30 on Fridays, when the Muslim community prayed. Moreover, the room had space for prayer rugs and adjacent restrooms for washing before prayers. Since the Muslim community moved into the cathedral, numbers at Friday prayers have grown; now hundreds of men attend. A small number of Muslim women pray separately, in a smaller area above the space used by the men.

Although a few cathedral staff members had concerns about the shared space arrangement, due primarily to the increased traffic in the building, overall the arrangement has brought the communities closer. Jep Streit recalls hearing the vibrations from the prayers of the Muslim community through the floor during one particular Good Friday service at the cathedral. "All I could think of during that service was that what we are doing is really important and good," he says. Over the years of the relationship, Streit has made it his business to visit the Muslim community on occasion and to reiterate the cathedral's welcome to its neighbors. He remembers one such visit, shortly after the attacks of September 11, 2001, that was particularly poignant. Streit felt, given the anti-Muslim furor fueled by the attacks, that he wanted to let the community know not only that they were still welcome, but that the cathedral prayed with and for the Muslim community. "Those events in 2001 were for many American Muslims a time of deep spiritual crisis," says Streit. "I don't know any Arabic, yet I could tell how those men were grappling with the events. They prayed fiercely. For me, it was one of those times I felt closest to God" (Streit 2010).

Mawdudur Rahman, a professor at Suffolk University, located down the street from the Cathedral Church of St. Paul, started the Muslim prayer group in downtown Boston over 20 years ago. As an observant Muslim, Rahman was forced to travel to outlying towns for prayers when he first arrived at Suffolk University. Eventually the university provided the use of a basement room to Muslim faculty and staff to use for prayers, but the group soon outgrew that accommodation. For several years the group prayed at another church on the other side of Beacon Hill. As the prayer group continued to grow, Rahman and other leaders began to look for a place adjacent to Boston Common, and they contacted the cathedral. "They were very open, and very respectful," said Rahman about the people of the cathedral. For his part, Rahman was clear that the respect between the two communities needed to be reciprocated for the relationship to flourish. "From the beginning my goal was to honor the host, and I made that clear to those who prayed there" (Rahman 2010).

Professor Mawdudur Rahman has been a leader in the Boston Muslim community for many years and is active in civic affairs, institutional boards, and with religious organizations across the region, and yet he believes that the relationship between his community and the cathedral is "a very unique" association. "Our people respect him [Jep Streit, dean of the cathedral] in the way they respect their own religious leaders. They would come to him in a crisis. The people at the cathedral not only know our needs, they come up with accommodations before we even need to ask." For instance, Rahman and the Mulsim community were impressed when the cathedral consulted them about the renovation of one of the bathrooms so it might be better suited to meet the needs of the Muslims who must do ablutions before prayers. One of Rahman's dreams is to have an open access interreligious library available for people who are interested in learning more about other religions. This same library would have tea and coffee available for informal conversations and would host monthly interreligious community meetings to encourage interreligious and intercultural understanding. "You cannot respect people you do not know," he says. "We need to find ways that people who want to do something, who want to work together, can understand other religions, receive respect and give it back" (Rahman 2010).

Over the course of sharing sacred space, the Cathedral Church of St. Paul and their Muslim neighbors have grown together to serve the larger community. A few years after the relationship began, the Muslim community offered to help with the cathedral's Thanksgiving dinner for the homeless. The Muslim community donated the turkeys, cooked them, and helped feed those who came to the dinner. On another occasion, after an Anglican hospital in Gaza was bombed and the Episcopal diocese asked local congregations to contribute funds, the Muslim community donated to the cause, actually more than every other church in the diocese combined. It was later discovered that one of the Muslim men who regularly prays at the cathedral was born in the hospital that was bombed. More recently, as news media across the country reported on the church that had decided to burn the Qur'an, the cathedral staff decided that their response would be to *distribute* copies of the Qur'an, in an effort to offer interreligious education to the wider community and to support the Muslim community. Not only did the Muslim community like the idea, they decided that they would pay for the copies of the Qur'an and choose the edition made available at the front desk of the cathedral! "The ripples of this relationship are always interesting," says Jep Streit. "When you are neighborly with your neighbors there are opportunities to respond as things come up" (Streit 2010).

Jep Streit feels that the relationship between the cathedral and the Muslim community is a justification for their chosen designation of "a house of prayer for all people." "It makes sense, fills a need, and is really so easy for us to do," he says about the hospitality the Cathedral Church of St. Paul offers its Muslim neighbors. "When I think about how we spend so much time on projects without a definable result, yet it is so easy to have them [the Muslim community] here. They often say how grateful they are to us—that there are times when it would have been easy for us to ask them to leave. But I am grateful that they are here" (Streit 2010).

Sacred spaces are an inherent part of the religious traditions of the world, and in sharing them, we are in a very real way welcoming others into our home. "The ache for Home lies in all of us," writes poet Maya Angelou, "the safe place where we can go as we are and not be questioned" (Angelou 2010). We live in a global age, where people operate in a way disconnected from a sense of place or a spiritual home, writes John Inge, a bishop in the Church of England. "The skyscrapers, airports, freeways, and other stereotypical components of modern landscapes—are they not the sacred symbols of a civilization that has defied reach and derided home?" (Inge 1993, 17) In a spiritual sense, the idea of "home" means more than a place to sleep; it is also a place of belonging, a place where you go and are automatically taken in and accepted. French mystic and social philosopher Simone Weil writes about the human hunger for a sense of home as a "need for roots." "To be rooted is perhaps the most important need of the human soul. It is one of the hardest to define. A human being has roots by virtue of [their] real, active, and natural participation in the life of a community, which preserves in living shape certain particular treasures of the past and certain particular expectations of the future" (Weil, 1952, 43).

PRINCIPLES OF SHARING SACRED SPACES

The purpose of this chapter is to reflect on the resources of sacred spaces for interreligious learning, specifically through shared physical spaces and shared prayer experiences. The realities of sacred spaces, our choices of venues, dates, and times, have a major impact on interreligious encounters. In is important to find spaces to gather that put our neighbors at ease and nurture the nascent community in formation. Often, in the early stages of interreligious relationships, before members have a strong sense of each other's sensitivities, it can be helpful to meet in more "neutral" spaces, such as community centers, schools, and education centers, or even town buildings. When local interreligious groups choose to meet at houses of worship, they often rotate the location in an effort to avoid identification with one tradition and to encourage a wider sense of ownership among religious participants. When holding interreligious gatherings in houses of worship, it is important to discuss among all participants which areas of a particular building are considered sacred space, which areas are open to other sorts of activities, and what religious customs are prevalent. For instance, where should shoes be removed and/or heads covered? Where is silence practiced? Ordinarily, it is good to assume that our interreligious neighbors might have more reservations than they feel comfortable about articulating, for fear of giving offense, for example, about being offered blessed food at a place not part of their own tradition, or on entering a sacred space where the custom is to offer respect to the symbols of another tradition. In all cases, it is important for neighbors and hosts to be clear about needs and expectations in advance of any encounter. Here are some suggested guidelines for visiting sacred sites in conjunction with interreligious learning:

- Consult the calendar and site schedule to make sure that your visit does not conflict with worship or other events. If visiting with a group, always call in advance and schedule the visit. Confirm a day in advance—often sacred sites accommodate unexpected events, such as funerals, etc.

- Most publicly accessible sacred sites have a website, and these should be consulted.

- Avoid visiting while worship is in session unless you have consulted with your hosts, and you have a clear sense of the purpose of the visit. Would you like to observe worship? Would you like to participate? Would you rather view the space during downtime?

- Make sure when visiting sacred sites that you are aware of which areas are open to the public, and which are reserved for members or particular occasions.

- Decide whether you want to visit on your own, or whether it might be mutually enriching to go with other interreligious partners.

- Consult a religious etiquette book in advance for advice on dress and codes of conduct for individual faith communities. Generally, modest dress in muted colors for men and women; no shorts or bare shoulders. In some sacred spaces visitors might be expected to cover their heads and/or remove shoes.

- Learn about the religious tradition in advance of your visit, and if you are bringing a group, ensure their orientation as well.

- If you have a specific contact person at a sacred site, confirm how they would like to be addressed by yourself and your group.

- Check with the sacred site about the use of photography.

- Turn off your phone or put it in silent mode.

- Do not eat, drink, or bring food and drink into sacred spaces.

- Always be quiet and respectful when you visit sacred spaces. Be aware of your impact on other visitors, as well as members, including those present for prayer, and take care not to disturb. Avoid loud conversations.

- Once inside a sacred space, take time to acclimate yourself and tune in to your environment. Before rushing to take photographs (if allowed), peruse the subtle characteristics of the interior. Why is this space sacred? Look at the structure, shapes, colors, materials, light, symbols of the space. How does this space relate to its tradition? Its environment?

- If visiting with young people, advise parents in advance about the intention and scope of the visit. Parents have the right to remove their children from such visits, although sometimes what they most want is clarity about the visit's purpose. Encourage interested parents to go along. They may then be better equipped to assist you with follow-up.

- Provide all with a time of reflection, feedback, and follow-up on the visit.

TYPES OF SACRED SPACES

Early Celtic Christians used to describe sacred spaces as "thin places" in the veil between heaven and earth. Throughout history and across religious traditions, the definition of those spaces that "touch heaven" is expansive, including the use of buildings and natural environments. Sacred spaces are linked to historical memory, or those places where events of special significance between God and humanity have occurred. Solitary spaces, both external and those within the human psyche and spirit, are also considered sacred, as they free us from distractions and invite prayer and meditation. Those of us who go on retreat or visit the houses of religious communities often experience the prayer-soaked spaces as part of monastic hospitality. Just as sacred spaces are found in stillness and solitude, so too, they are found where God is experienced as active and alive amidst humankind in celebration, dance, or song. Religious groups conceive of and use sacred space differently. An operational knowledge of these differences is an important aspect in planning interreligious encounters and in sharing sacred space across religious traditions. Some basic considerations include:

- Some groups sit in rows in pews; some stand or sit in circles.

- Some groups meet indoors; some prefer outdoors.

- Some groups require sacred images; others forbid sacred images.

- Many groups orient toward particular directions and are assisted when the directions are marked in some way; some require space that can accommodate different orientations.

- Many groups incorporate concepts of sacred geometry and number that are not necessarily obvious to the eye into sacred spaces.

Baha'i Faith—No special needs for interreligious space; prefer to have nine sides and a dome in their temples.

Buddhism—Cannot have fixed seating; need a Buddha image and an altar, to burn incense, and room to bow, sit and process.

Chinese Religions—Must orient north-south.

Christianity—Many need access to a water source. Many need the ability to display a cross in churches.

Hinduism and South Asian Religions—Must have a place for shoes; need a water source and the ability to use an open flame and burn incense.

Indigenous/Tribal Religions—Some tribes need access to nature and knowledge of cardinal direction; prefer to gather in circles.

Islam, including Sufism—Must have a place to wash and leave shoes, and must have the direction to Mecca indicated. Space should not have representational art that cannot be removed.

Judaism—Cannot have religious symbols of other faiths that cannot be removed. Some branches of Judaism allow such symbols to be covered and thereby made invisible.

Neopaganism—Must have access to nature, the ability to meet in a circle, and an indication of the cardinal directions. When inside, prefer environmentally friendly designs without fixed seating.

Shinto and Japanese Religions—Must have a place to wash; prefer access to nature.

Sikhism—Must have a place to leave shoes and to wash feet; cannot have representational art that cannot be moved.

Zoroastrianism—Must have access to water and have an open flame; prefer to sit on the floor.[1]

Today, opportunities to share sacred spaces for prayer and reflection across traditions and cultures include elements of all these historic models of sacred space. Some interreligious relationships, such as that between the Cathedral Church of St. Paul and the Muslim community in downtown Boston, involve a congregation with a building extending hospitality to a group of another religious tradition. With intentionality, these space sharing partnerships can grow beyond landlord relationships into vibrant interreligious partnerships extending throughout the larger region. The significance of sacred space extends beyond the physical reality of a building. Buildings are metaphors for the religious experience of those who inhabit them, those who pray, sing, grieve, and experience joy there. Through light, color, stone, fabric, wood, and art, sacred spaces support the spiritual lives of individuals and communities. Sacred spaces are integral to building interreligious communities as they educate and inspire generations of believers and offer hospitality to their neighbors. In doing so, sacred spaces also become places of memory. Like the prayer and ritual they host, sacred spaces are places where the realities of human life are remembered. Even traditions that do not typically attach significance to houses of worship and

1. Adapted from Frew, *Sacred Spaces.*

prefer to pray in nature settings share with other religious traditions the desire for spiritual experience and to make the world a better place.

James Ingo Freed, the designer of the Holocaust Memorial Museum, said that he conceived of the museum as a "resonator," or a space to recall the horrible reality of those events. "In many ways, that is the purpose of religious architecture. On one hand, worship spaces are crucibles of memories. On the other hand, they can help the worshiper imagine how things might be. This combination of memory and imagination can help some people survive." Within our sacred spaces, religious communities come together to pray, read, sing, and eat in ways that for many are a source of sustenance. Sharing sacred spaces, bringing people together to understand their different faiths and to build a better world, is a form of religious dialogue. Creating holy space where all can practice their religions involves interreligious dialogue and is about both spiritual and design issues. In the past, many intentionally interreligious spaces, such as airport chapels, appeared barren or sterile. Today's new sacred architecture suggests that intentionally interreligious spaces, such as college or hospital chapels, link innovation with spiritual consciousness in an effort to embrace the richness of religious diversity. Events of religious significance happen in spaces. They are the intersection of all humanity. "A life that is, in some way, holy and wholly other than what is experienced now. This is the tremendous burden placed on religious architecture—to serve as a firm foundation of faith and a platform for courage and creativity" (Crosbie 2000, 9).

INTERRELIGIOUS SACRED SPACE:
TRI-FAITH INITIATIVE, OMAHA, NEBRASKA

Creating permanent shared sacred spaces makes a strong statement about interreligious commitment and is a long-term investment in the community. Such partnerships not only enhance relationships between religious groups, but also generate opportunities which emerge when space is shared in a mutual way. The Tri-Faith Initiative in Omaha, Nebraska, is an interreligious project that includes Temple Israel, the Episcopal Diocese of Nebraska, and the American Institute of Islamic Studies. The group intends to build a multifaith campus in west Omaha that will include three separate houses of worship—a mosque, a synagogue, and a church, as well as a fourth building for interreligious education and collaboration. The design will include a separate kitchen for each of the groups. The concept behind the project is that co-locating facilities will maximize the resources of all the groups involved and foster respect and greater mutual understanding among the participating religious traditions. The group obtained a plot of land in West Omaha large enough to accommodate the four buildings and the necessary parking. The three faith groups of the Tri-Faith Initiative agreed to use the same architect to give the campus design elements in common, while at the same time preserving the distinctiveness of each faith. The initiative is currently governed by a board of directors comprised of representatives from each of the founding religious groups. While each faith group conducts its own planning process for its house of worship, the board of the initiative is involved in a long-range planning process to define the programs of the interfaith education center.

The vision of the Tri-Faith Initiative was born out of the need for a parking lot. About six years ago, Temple Israel in Omaha, a congregation very active in the interreligious community of the city, began to outgrow their building. Since many congregants lived in the area of West Omaha, they began to look there. Parking in the area was expensive, so the temple began to look for partners. Several churches were approached but not interested. But The American Institute of Islamic Studies and Culture was interested in sharing property, realizing that their times of worship and holy days were not in conflict with those of the Jewish community. The Episcopal Diocese of Nebraska was also interested in possibly planting a congregation in the area and signed on to the initiative. The three religious organizations formed a partnership, and four years ago the Tri-Faith Initiative obtained its nonprofit (501c3) status.

Ernesto Medina, an Episcopal priest, was with the Tri-Faith Initiative from its beginning and feels that the relationships formed through the project are unique and more intense than other interreligious relationships he has experienced before, "because we know we are going to literally be neighbors. We have been pushed to be open and honest with each other." Medina envisions the initiative as "a picnic table" and says that project members gather frequently around food-related events, such as dinners in each other's homes, for meals and conversations. The initiative also sponsors picnics and programs to allow members of the different faith groups to share meals and conversation as well. "The closest relationships I have here (in Omaha) are my colleagues in Tri-Faith. We know each other's children," says Medina. Project colleagues further bonded as bids on three separate properties failed, until the initiative obtained its twenty-five acres. "I am sure we will have challenges as we begin to build the buildings and campus. But our faith is stronger because we can share it," says Medina (Medina 2009).

The Episcopal Diocese of Nebraska envisions the new church that will be built on the shared campus in west Omaha as "a gathering place for all Christians to come into the Tri-Faith Initiative," says Medina. While a church in the Episcopal tradition, and governed through the diocese and local vestry, "they will need to go to the edges, to be defined by hospitality, welcome all, and be open to input from diverse voices," he says. Medina is also excited by the possibilities for the fourth building on the campus, the one slated to be an interreligious educational center. "It will be the place where we share moral and religious authority," he says. "It will also be the place where we provide a model for the reconciliation that we live together" (Medina 2009).

HISTORIC CHURCH-SYNAGOGUE PARTNERSHIPS

One of the oldest known church-synagogue partnerships in the United States is between Bradley Hills Presbyterian Church and Bethesda Jewish Congregation in Bethesda, Maryland. The two congregations began formally sharing a building in 1967 when a rabbi and 20 families in Montgomery County began to rent space from the church; eventually the independent Jewish congregation began to share more facilities and to worship in the main sanctuary. On some Friday nights, the Jewish congregation worshipped in the hospitality lounge of the church, and on special occasions when they worshipped in the main sanctuary, such as the High Holy Days, members of the synagogue would cover the church's suspended cross and other Christian symbols with banners featuring Hebrew scripture and art. By 2001 the two congregations pledged to raise the funds to construct together a new building, Covenant Hall, which provides the synagogue with dedicated worship space, and gives the church additional space for education and informal worship. "The idea of sharing our space is so logical and practical that I can see our partnership becoming a recognized role model for the successful coexistence and connections of two faiths," said church member Susan McVay at the time of the joint building project (Mizejewski 2001). Sunny Schnitzer, the rabbi of the Bethesda Jewish Congregation, believes that the relationship between the two congregations is "a model of interfaith appreciation and tolerance" (Schreiber 2005, 13).

In contrast to other congregations from a many religious traditions, Bethesda Jewish Congregation has never pursued constructing its own building. From its inception, the Jewish congregation believed money used on construction would be better used to serve human needs. The Jewish congregation now pays a percentage of the costs for Covenant Hall as well as an annual fee to cover part of the mortgage and the finance charges. "I think we were very wise to beat the 'edifice complex,'" says Sunny Schnitzer. "Religious groups tend to feel that having their own building somehow ties a permanence and gravitas to the congregation's existence. Our congregation doesn't feel that way. Rather than building funds or campaigns to renovate and expand every few years, we're able to focus our dollars and energy on the community. Even when we built Covenant Hall with the church, 10 percent of the money we raised went toward the National Center for Children and Families, a homeless center up the road" (Schreiber 2005, 13). The hexagon-shaped Covenant Hall is named after a quote from Jeremiah 31:33 and refers to the following covenant signed between the two congregations:

COVENANT BETWEEN BETHESDA JEWISH CONGREGATION AND BRADLEY HILLS PRESBYTERIAN CHURCH

We, the members of Bradley Hills Presbyterian Church and the Bethesda Jewish Congregation, form together this covenant to honor the Intimate and Infinite God of Creation, the One God we both worship. Taking to heart the biblical charge to be a light to the nations, we seek to offer a prophetic vision of interfaith partnership in a pluralistic world. Continuing a relationship begun in 1967, as spiritual siblings sharing sacred space, we commit ourselves to:

> Acknowledge and celebrate our commonalities and differences; Foster appreciation for the richness of our respective traditions; Encourage curiosity and dialogues between our two communities of faith; Bear witness to our faith in cooperative activity in the world; Create with each other what we cannot create separately.
>
> Recognizing the word of our great teachers, we commit ourselves to fulfill the Great Commandment: You shall love the Lord your God with all your heart, with all your soul, with all your mind, and with all your might. With deepest gratitude, we pledge

to continue to celebrate the light bestowed upon us. May this
union of spirit and space spark a flame of respect and understanding throughout the world. (Used with Permission)

Covenant Hall includes two sanctuaries and incorporates a Star of
David pattern formed by diagonally connected vertices also replicated in
the angles of the roof. The sanctuary used by Bethesda Jewish Congregation in Covenant Hall no longer requires that worshippers cover Christian
symbols or roll a portable ark in and out of storage. When the doors are
open, the permanent ark at the east end of the room reveals the Torah;
closed, the blond maple doors blend into the wall. A light fixture above
the ark represents Judaism's eternal light. "A Jew walking into this room
immediately recognizes it as an ark," said Schnitzer. "A non-Jew sees it as a
blank wall" (Broadway 2010).

It is important to note that, when Bradley Hills Presbyterian Church
proposed collaboration with Bethesda Jewish Congregation on the multi-
million dollar building project, not all members were enthusiastic. "We
didn't have 100 percent affirmed cheerleaders," said Susan Andrews, former pastor at Bradley Hills. She said that some of her congregation were
not sure that they wanted "to get that close" to the Jewish Congregations;
others felt that the Jewish Congregation "not only was invited to participate but they'd better." Eventually, most of the congregation supported the
partnership in a spirit of respect and inclusiveness, through some members
were not as active after the agreement was reached. For the Bethesda Jewish Congregation it took "a great leap of faith" in committing funds to the
project, as well as wrestling with the philosophical issues of being tied to
a building. "We were letting go of a piece of our identity, but we agreed to
help the church work it out," said Sunny Schnitzer. Susan Andrews saw
the two congregations as "spiritual siblings with shared sacred space." At
the same time, the two faith communities are separate and distinct, strive
to learn from each other, and celebrate common ethical commitments.
"It is clear we are Christian and they are Jewish," said Andrews. In addition to a traditional joint Thanksgiving Service, which, starting in 2006,
also includes Jaferia Islamic Center, the congregations share in other joint
educational offerings, social justice projects in the community, and pulpit
exchanges and have travelled together to the Holocaust Memorial Museum
(Schreiber 2005, 13).

Another long-term church-synagogue partnership is found in Ann
Arbor, Michigan, where the Cross and a Star of David stand side-by-side

on Packard Road, symbolic of St. Clare of Assisi Episcopal Church and Temple Beth Emeth, a Reform Jewish congregation. At first, Temple Beth Emeth met in homes and rented facilities, but in 1969, after the congregation grew to sixty families, they were invited by St. Clare's to rent space. As the story goes, one secretary worked for both congregations, and on her desk sat two phones. She answered one, "Shalom, Temple Beth Emeth," and she answered the other, "Hello, St. Clare of Assisi." The demographics of the two congregations are similar in the town that is home to the University of Michigan. About 85 percent of both congregations are academics, with the remaining membership represented by other professionals. Bruce Warshal, a former civil rights lawyer and the rabbi who led Temple Beth Emeth during its initial years with St. Clare's, said that both were "highly sophisticated, highly educated congregations. Also, not overly rich." The congregations stood together against poverty, discrimination, and the Vietnam War (Schreiber 2005, 13).

In 1975, the two congregations together founded Genesis of Ann Arbor, a corporation to own, operate, and maintain their common property. At the time the church proposed making the relationship between the two congregations permanent, Temple Beth Emeth was interested in a building but concerned about the costs. Marilyn Scott, a longtime member and former president of Temple Beth Emeth, was among those who felt that the relationship with St. Clare's was a step toward changing the world for the better. "There were Holocaust survivors and others in the congregation who felt that, given the way the world had treated the Jews, it isn't safe to trust Christians," said Scott. "I felt it was important to try. In a world that had experienced the Holocaust, it was necessary to show that Jews and Christians could trust each other in this profound way." To form the permanent partnership, Temple Beth Emeth purchased half of St. Clare's building. "It was helpful to us that there was no Christian iconography in the building's design," said Scott. "It was a physical space that could just as easily be used as a synagogue." The relationship continues to work for both congregations. "Our rubbing shoulders with them made us more Jewish and made them more Christian," said Bruce Warshal (Schreiber 2005, 13).

Today, each congregation maintains its own distinctive religious identity and separate program. They share classrooms, the social hall, the kitchen, and the custodial staff. Each congregation has its own offices and maintains a religious space of its own, consisting of a Jewish chapel and St. Clare's chapel. Although intermarried families feel comfortable there, they live their Jewish or Christian lives separately. Neither Robert Levy, the rabbi at Temple Beth Emeth, nor James Rhodenhiser, the rector of St Clare's, will co-officiate at marriage ceremonies or encourage families to attend both services. Youth groups and social gatherings remain separate. Together the congregations host a Thanksgiving Eve service, a joint Passover Seder, and an annual pulpit exchange and sponsor outreach to homeless families. The two congregations continue to fight for social justice together. For instance, in 2004 when marriage equality for gay and lesbian couples was on the ballot in Michigan, Temple Beth Emeth and St. Clare of Assisi Episcopal Church agreed to show their support. A billboard with the message, "Be Just, Love Decency," was displayed on the grounds (Schreiber, 2005, 13).

In the city of Ann Arbor, with its five Episcopal churches, St. Clare's is the smaller of the two congregations, as Temple Beth Emeth's membership continues to grow to over three times that of the church. Scheduling building use can at times be a challenge when holy days overlap or during wedding season. Yet, despite the challenges of sharing space as the temple continues to expand, St. Clare's remains committed to the partnership. James Rhoden-hiser believes that sharing worship space is "a good American spiritual gift to the world. Maybe God's done something to America that He hasn't done any-where else. Americans don't want to write off their neighbor's faith. I think it is a very deep thing to be affirming of your neighbor's faith and see good in it." Rodenhiser also affirms, "St. Clare parishioners wouldn't know who they were without Temple Beth Emeth. It's a key piece to our identity as a church. Part of a being a Christian is honoring Judaism. If you get to that point, you feel less defensive. There is no reason that any Christian church couldn't have a relationship like this" (Rhodenhiser 2009).

Given the long history of persecution and forced conversions the Jewish people have experienced at the hands of Christians, the reality of these long-term interreligious partnerships is significant. For some Jews, the prohibition against praying in churches, or for some, even walking past churches, is difficult to overcome. Although Christians benefit from inter-religious encounters with many traditions, acknowledgment of the unique history shared with Judaism makes the relationship critical to deeper inter-religious learning. Although the sharing of sacred space between Chris-tians and Jews may first originate out of practical needs, such partnerships do have a major impact on the members of the organizations involved and the communities they serve.

Overall, Christians and Jews who support such partnerships find themselves on the social and theologically liberal side of their religious traditions. Space sharing arrangements tend to be the most prevalent among mainline Christian denominations. Although more conservative Jews and evangelical Christians do share alliances because of shared values, they are less likely to share sacred space. There are notable exceptions to this trend, however. Rabbi Irving Greenberg, an Orthodox leader and author, believes that, as Roman Catholicism and other major Christian denominations recognize the validity of Judaism after Vatican II, the relationship between the more conservative members of the two faiths will also change. "Socially and culturally, Orthodoxy has the strongest memory," he says. "Ironically, though, many Orthodox Jews are now the ones forming the closest connections with traditional Christians, seeing eye-to-eye with them on issues such as abortion or support for parochial schools. Our whole relationship with Christianity is in the process of changing, theologically as well as humanly" (Schreiber 2005, 13). While many Jews, even the non-Orthodox, are uncomfortable praying in spaces with Christian iconography, many are also in favor of sharing sacred spaces where such symbols are not on permanent display. "Indeed, in view of a Jewish tradition that commands us Jews to feed and clothe our Christian neighbors, and to pay respect to their dead through proper burial, I am delighted that Jews and Christians can show one another mutual care by sharing a sacred space in this manner," says David Ellison, a Reform rabbi and president of the Hebrew Union College—Jewish Institute of Religion, who attends a Jewish congregation that shares sacred space with a Christian congregation in New York. City (Schreiber 2005, 13). As with many Jewish questions, there is more than one way to interpret the subject of synagogues, or houses of assembly, that share sacred space with congregations of other religious traditions.

Christian congregations also practice space sharing with religious groups beyond the Abrahamic faith traditions. Christ Episcopal Church in Roanoke, Virginia, shares space with Stone Mountain Zendo, a Soto Zen Buddhist group that meets on Wednesday evenings and Saturday mornings in the church's basement room. The Buddhist group was founded in 1979 and originally met in the home of its founders. Though a Zen Buddhist group, it is open to all people, regardless of religious affiliation. The group gives the church a nominal yearly donation, and accommodates church members during Lent and other times when they need full use of the building. "We're deeply grateful for the space," said Richard Normand, the group's leader. "This is so central, and it's easy for people to get here" (Wrey 2004). "It opens people up to new things in their own spiritual practice," said Deborah Hentz Hunley, the rector of Christ Church (Podger 2006).

INTENTIONALLY INTERRELIGIOUS SACRED SPACES

A Bedouin tent in the garden of St Ethelburga's Centre for Reconciliation and Peace sits in the middle of London, and has brought together more than 25,000 people for dialogue on almost every issue that divides the human communities—religious extremism, gang culture, sexual morality, generational tensions, racism, Islamaphobia, anti-Semitism, poverty, and education, to name a few. St. Ethelburga's Centre for Reconciliation and Peace was built on the ruins of a church devastated by an Irish Republican Army bomb in 1993 and was dedicated "to encourage and enable people to practice reconciliation and peace-making in their communities and lives." The tent is a place for people from all faiths to meet as equals (Binyon 2009).

While opportunities to construct intentional interreligious spaces are limited, the creators of the tent believe that providing shared space for cultivating interreligious relationships is central to the task. The creators of the tent avoided the use of explicitly religious symbols, basing the overall design on the principles of sacred geometry. The tent is made of goat's hair in a traditional Bedouin style; the windows bear the word for peace in seven languages. Inside, lined with carpets, there is space for visitors to sit in a circle on chairs or on cushions. The tent is set in an Andalusian-style peace garden, and it was created as a sacred space of hospitality. It is a new type of space for new types of conversations across religious boundaries. The conferences and conversations hosted by the Reconciliation Centre bring together Muslims, Jews, Sikhs, Christian fundamentalists and liberals, students, poets, pastors, and professors. With fabric woven in Saudi Arabia and strong enough to withstand the London climate, the tent has been in use almost every day since it was officially opened by the Prince of Wales in 2006. All participants in the dialogues leave their shoes outside and come in to sit in a circle, with all books and pamphlets left on a central table. "People come in the tent angry and confrontational," writes one London newspaper reporter on the tent and its purpose. "They argue and negotiate, sometimes shout, and sometimes break down. But gradually the tent works its magic. It encloses an intimate space. It calms. It forces people to listen. It prompts admissions, concessions and confidence" (Binyon 2009).

"We've developed a technique that works," said Simon Keyes, the director of St. Ethelburga's. 'The element of surprise is important: It's romantic but simple, an unexpected space—two steps away from the street. People are not expecting a Bedouin tent in the middle of London. They aren't sure where they are—it is a 'liminal space' outside most people's experience. They have to leave their shoes outside and enter somewhere quiet, dignified. It seems almost religious—but there are no religious symbols or imagery here. The normal rules do not apply." The conversations in the tent at St. Ethelburga's Centre for Reconciliation and Peace in London are usually limited to fourteen to twenty people, and require enough time for participants to become less formal with each other. There are no lectures in the tent—it is a "powerpoint free zone"—and no one religious group controls the conversations or outcomes. Organizers believe that, if the tent can work in London, it can also work in Jerusalem and Northern Ireland and many other locations throughout the world that are embroiled with religious strife. "The value is that often we do not come to conclusions," says Keyes. "The tent is a place where people can change their minds" (Binyon 2009).

The demands of religious architecture are such that sacred spaces are not only required to provide shelter, comfort, and beauty to the groups who live and pray there, but are expected to encourage a sense of spirituality as well. What sets sacred spaces apart from secular buildings is their ability to bespeak the deepest yearnings of the human soul and to express tangibly the beliefs of religious communities. The designs of physical spaces have an impact on the kinds of activities that take place there and the capacity of groups to build interreligious community in a particular location. Issues such as building accessibility, the use of religious symbols or images in the design, the layout of rooms, rules and regulations related to the space, are all factors to be considered when planning interreligious space. While creating new buildings or renovating existing ones may be beyond the means of many interreligious groups, explicit attention to making existing space hospitable to partners from other religious groups not only builds community but has the potential to become spiritual practice as well. The desire to create interreligious sacred spaces is becoming increasingly common, for instance, through school, university, and hospital chapels. Similarly, rooms set aside for interreligious prayer and meditation are appearing in workplaces and shopping centers.

In 2008 the new Wilson Chapel at the Andover Newton Theological School of Newton Centre, Massachusetts, was recognized with an award of merit by the American Institute of Architects' Interfaith Forum on Religion, Art, and Architecture and *Faith & Form Magazine*. In keeping with the interreligious commitments of the theological school, the chapel combines the architectural elements of the New England meeting house with religious pluralism. The chapel contains a glass wall that faces the global south, and thus the Christian future, and its inner walls are made of Jerusalem stone. Like historic meeting houses, the chapel can be used for religious and secular events. Crosses and a pulpit, which are set up for Christian services, are entirely movable. There are no fixed pews; rather, the space is designed to be responsive to more communal and participatory ceremonies. The floor of the lobby is paved with African slate. At night, the main windows of the chapel glow dramatically. The chapel shares the hilltop with the campus of Hebrew College. "Each of these faiths has its own architectural history, its own architectural traditions, markers, and expectations," said Brett Donham, the architect of Wilson Chapel and an Episcopalian, in relation to the many religious groups on the campus (Paulson 2008). The design of the space should not be confined to one religion exclusively, but at the same time it should not appear bland or compromised.

Chapels in hospital settings and similar institutions are charged with providing spiritual care to persons of a wide range of religious backgrounds. While many hospital prayer rooms and chapels appear devoid of decoration, they are important examples of interreligious sacred space sharing. Such sacred spaces are sites of spiritual encounter and interreligious learning where regular staff, along with new visitors, drop by to pray on their way to work or in the midst of spiritual crisis. Through supporting interreligious chapels and prayer rooms in healthcare institutions, faith communities provide spiritual care and hospitable spaces for interreligious learning, encouraging healing and wholeness.

SHARED PRAYER AND INTERRELIGIOUS LEARNING

Every day billions of people throughout the world raise their voices in prayer, and, while the forms and languages differ, the human desire to communicate with the divine is constant. Shared prayer and worship is often included in the activities of local interreligious groups. Perhaps the most commonly held forms of shared worship shared silent prayer and meditation or prayers said in a pattern of sequential offerings by members of different religious traditions, where others listen but do not actively participate. Typically, interreligious worship services take one of three forms. The first is a service from one tradition, such as a community Seder, in which members of other religious traditions are invited to participate in a Jewish ritual.

A second format is that of an interreligious service with an agreed-upon order that borrows from a variety of traditions. Community-wide interreligious Thanksgiving services are frequently of this format. That is, representatives of local religious traditions work together on a shared format, and the occasion is hosted on rotation by different religious communities or is scheduled at some "neutral" site, such as a school or city hall.

The third type of interreligious service has a "serial" format where each religious tradition involved plans and executes a defined segment of the overall experience. Many civic religious observances utilize this format, for instance, when Jewish, Christian, Muslim, Buddhist, and other leaders each in turn share prayers, music and ritual from their own tradition for an interreligious gathering. The serial form of worship is advantageous for interreligious gatherings for a variety of reasons. First, each faith community selects and presents its own material. Those in attendance are left free to participate in whatever ways they feel comfortable and able to do so. In such gatherings we respect and support the prayers of other faith traditions, yet we are not technically worshipping together. Rather than referring to such gatherings as "worship," more inclusive terminology can be used, such as "interreligious gathering," or "interreligious celebration," or "interreligious day of remembrance," depending on the character of the assembly. Some general considerations for interreligious shared prayer include:

- The representatives of all religious traditions in the experience should be included in planning from the outset.

- Each faith tradition will choose its own representatives to participate in the planning.

- It is always a good idea to plan interreligious prayer jointly, or to consult those of other religious traditions who will be in attendance, even in cases where persons of other faiths are invited to a Christian worship service.

- Be clear about the reason, intent, and scope of the shared prayer, as well as how the event will be publicized. The term "worship" may be problematic for some, and the group may instead prefer other terms, like "celebration," "event," etc.

- Before planning shared prayer, learn about the other faith traditions in your community, and your expected behavior.

- Before participating in shared prayer with another faith community, be clear about the meaning of doing so for you and for them; avoid participation that violates your integrity or that of the other communities, and at the same time maintain a respectful presence; always allow all participants to choose their own level of participation.

- Agree in advance with all groups that interreligious shared prayer is not an occasion for proselytizing.

- Offer opportunities for dialogue and hospitality after interreligious shared prayer to help build interreligious community.

- At the beginning of interreligious gatherings, participants should be advised about what is going to happen and the options for participation.

- In addition to spoken prayers, readings, and song, planners should be mindful of the importance of silence and meditation in the shared experience.

- Provide translations for those parts of the shared prayer experience said or sung in other than the primary language of the community.

- Possible venues should be discussed as part of the planning, including the benefits or challenges of meeting in religious sites, such as churches, synagogues, or mosques, or in public venues, such as city buildings, schools, etc. Using multiple venues is also an option.

Joint spoken prayers, known in Christian terms as worship services, are not encouraged by all interreligious partnerships because there is a danger of participants' feeling pressured to join in what appears to be worship of a divinity not recognizably of their own tradition, or in contradiction of their own religious truth. Some groups are particularly sensitive to the appearance of religious syncretism or idolatry, for example. Other groups are wary of religious assimilation. Religious leaders of some traditions do not participate in public prayer with religious groups other than their own; other groups feel it is generally inappropriate to have visitors participate in worship. Non-theistic religious groups, such as Buddhists, may have difficulty with prayer and worship that assumes a divine being. Others may feel awkward or alienated by religious images in prayer or song which are not a part of their own tradition. Similarly, members of some traditions find the terms "worship" and "service" challenging. Given the opportunities for fracturing rather than building interreligious community through shared prayer and worship, it is important to define clearly the goals of such experiences as well as to involve members of the various religious communities in the planning of the events (Australian Consultation on Liturgy, 2009).

However, there are occasions where interreligious observance is appropriate and valuable, as, for example, for interreligious groups and partnerships which have formed a deep community, share a common purpose, or are acting in response to a community event. In 2009 Barack Obama became the first president of the United States to attend a White House Seder. In addition to the celebration of Passover, the gathering commemorated the Seder in Harrisburg, Pennsylvania, held a year before in the basement of a hotel when campaign staffers were unable to return home for the holiday (Vecsey, 2009). The White House Seder was not only a celebration of a major religious holiday; it also marked a milestone in the interreligious community of the campaign staff. Interreligious communities also unite for prayer in the midst of international, national, and local tragedies and disasters. For instance, when a freeway bridge collapsed during rush hour in the Twin Cities in 2007, community religious leaders pulled together for shared prayer and action. Four days after the tragedy, St. Mark's Episcopal Cathedral hosted 1400 people for a service of healing that included prayer leaders from the Jewish, Christian, Muslim, Hindu, Native American, and Hispanic communities. "Our city has suddenly become small," said Rabbi Sim Glaser of Temple Israel, Minneapolis. "When tragedy strikes, there is only one way to turn, and that is to each other, because [God] is in all of us" (Barksdale, 2007).

Online interreligious communities frequently offer resources that link civic events with opportunities for interreligious shared prayer. For instance, A Season of Prayer for Peace is an interreligious organization designed to support local faith communities and groups interested in organizing joint events that witness for peace in the community. The organization also encourages prayer in local communities for peace in the Middle East and posts on its website prayers, litanies, texts, hymns, and other resources for shared prayer. Similarly, The Network of Spiritual Progressives, a network led by Rabbi Michael Lerner, offers suggestions on ways to bring prayer into civic holidays, such as the Fourth of July, as well as socially responsible Passover and Easter celebrations. Congregations interested in resources for interreligious civic events should also consult their local interreligious organizations.

The dedications of sacred spaces become civic occasions of shared prayer. One such civic celebration of shared prayer was the dedication of the new Buddhist worship site in Wellford, South Carolina, on July 4, 2010. The three-day celebration was open to local Buddhists and non-Buddhists and attracted pilgrims from throughout the world. Buddhist monks processed around the site carrying relics to be placed in the stupa. The first Cambodian Buddhist stupa in the United States, its dedication ceremony designated Spartanburg County, South Carolina, as a holy site. Maya Men, a Buddhist and the organizer of the celebration, deliberately chose the Fourth of July weekend for the celebration. "It's Independence Day for the United States and also independence for the stupa and the Buddhist relics," said Men (Rutz 2010).

Other common examples of interreligious worship, though not often acknowledged as such, are interreligious marriages and funerals. Different cultures and faith traditions have diverse traditions to honor these occasions as well as other rites of passage. Such occasions are often times of high emotions for the families of those involved as well as for visitors. Although religious customs surrounding marriages and funeral vary, most people can identify with the joy and sorrow involved in these occasions. Wrote one Anglican priest of her experience with a multifaith funeral, "It is such situations that make us all realize that within our own culture and tradition we are all trying to do our best to bring up our families, earn a living, worship our God, to the best of our abilities. It is when unity is seen in action that I believe we receive a glimpse of God's Kingdom. However, having a watered-down religion in order to keep everyone happy, with the hope of not offending anyone, is not right. The way forward, in my view, is that as Christians we need to be clear what it is that makes up our integrity and what it is to which we must hold firmly. That is how we will gain the respect of people who practice another faith, for usually they are very clear about what they believe and why" (Torry and Thorley 2008, 70).

INTERRELIGIOUS WORSHIP—PLURALISM SUNDAY

One example of interreligious learning through shared prayer is the annual "Pluralism Sunday" initiative of The Center for Progressive Christianity. The date is designated as the first Sunday in May, but it can occur other times during the year. The intention of the day is to encourage a more intimate awareness of the religions of the world through worship. The Center for Progressive Christianity provides resources through its website, and congregations are encouraged to adapt the celebration to their own communities and to include existing interreligious relationships.

Pluralism Sunday began the first Sunday of May in 2007 with participation from sixty-five congregations in the United States, Canada, Australia, and England, and continues to expand annually. The celebration points to the second tenet of The Center for Progressive Christianity's Welcome Statement: "By calling ourselves progressive, we mean we are Christians who recognize the faithfulness of other people who have other names for the way to God's realm, and acknowledge that their ways are true for them, as our ways are true for us." Since its inception, the many ways Christian congregations celebrate religious pluralism have grown. For instance, University Christian in Enid, Oklahoma, observed Pluralism Sunday with readings on peace from the Qur'an, Hebrew Scriptures, Bhagavad Gita, and Christian Scriptures (Galbreath 2007). On Pluralism Sunday in 2007, which was also Pentecost Sunday, St. Mark's Episcopal Church in Penn Yann, New York, had a Jewish, Muslim, and Christian "trialogue" sermon where the religious leaders of the participating faith communities spoke to their own faith traditions' approaches to religious pluralism. A Jewish cantor read from the Hebrew Bible in Hebrew and led some congregational singing. Readings also included Muslim (read in Arabic) and Baha'i texts, and a member of the congregation wrote a special prayer about religious pluralism. During the exchange of peace in the service, the cantor taught the congregation a song of peace in Hebrew and Arabic. The service ended with a blessing in Hebrew, English, and Arabic. After the service, guests and congregation members continued the discussion (Yarbrough 2007).

STRATEGIES FOR SHARING SACRED SPACES

Sharing sacred space contributes to interreligious learning and serves the practical needs of religious communities. Through the sharing of sacred spaces, members of religious traditions build lasting relationships and learn about religious traditions other than their own. Some considerations when sharing sacred space include:

- As a way of encouraging interreligious relationships, hold "open days" to encourage visitors to visit your sacred space and invite other faith communities to visit.

- Before sharing your facilities, you need an estimate of the total cost of running it—repairs, maintenance, insurance, security, utilities, supplies, etc. Keep in mind that these costs will go up with increased use of the building, whether or not a partner contributes financially.

- Be aware of the types of programs or groups which require special licenses, additional insurance, etc.

- Determine the lines of communication among all sharing groups.

- To the fullest extent possible, groups interested in potentially sharing sacred spaces should enter into frank discussions at the beginning of the relationship about the assumptions and expectations that each group is bringing to the partnership. As interreligious relationships change over time, clear and direct communication is essential.

- If you are considering sharing sacred spaces with another religious group, consider what areas of your buildings and property are the most welcoming. How might you become more welcoming? How might existing buildings better accommodate the wider community? What spaces need to be maintained for the exclusive use (or near exclusive use) of one religious group? What spaces can be shared?

- Clear guidelines that govern behavior in your buildings are imperative and should be shared with all in a space-sharing partnership. Policies which take into account the use of utilities, security, damage to the physical plant, cleanliness, kitchen standards, food and alcohol consumption, noise regulation, are all matters to consider.

- Scheduling is a major component of sharing sacred spaces and should be discussed in advance. Who uses shared spaces and the daily and weekly schedules are important, as are considerations for holy days, festivals, weddings and funerals, use of the parking lot, etc.

- In addition to spaces used for worship and prayer, what other spaces will be shared? Education space, kitchen(s), parking, offices, restrooms, grounds, and their care and upkeep all need to be negotiated clearly.

- If planning changes or there are renovations to existing buildings, how might spaces become more hospitable to interreligious partners? If your space sharing partnership is long-term, are there more costly projects that could be undertaken together, such as making the building handicapped accessible, or replacing organs and sound systems, etc.

- When designing and building interreligious spaces, every stage of the process from initial ideals, to engaging architects and builders, through to planning, design, and management needs to be shared among the partners in the project.

Human beings in every age and across traditions have a deep yearning for a spiritual home, and that is no less true today. We live in a time when our capacity to share sacred spaces, physically and materially through our religious centers and psychologically and spiritually through shared prayer and meditation, are critical for many people who yearn to find a home, a place where they can belong. "Did you know you had a true home?" asks Thich Nhat Hahn. "No one can take it away from you. Other people can occupy your country, they can even put you in prison, but they cannot take away your true home and your freedom" (2010, 67). Sharon Daloz Parks, a scholar of spiritual development, critiques the notion of "journey" as the controlling metaphor for the spiritual life, arguing that the future of our planet is dependent upon the renewed connection of the metaphors of journey *and* home, detachment *and* connection, pilgrims *and* home-makers. "For the primary task before us, both women and men, is not of becoming a fulfilled *self* (or a faithful nation) but rather to become a faithful *people*, members of a whole human family, dwelling together in our planet home, guests to each other in 'the household of God.'" (Parks, 1989, 315) Sharing sacred spaces, by using them to further interreligious learning, is critical to deepening encounters across religious differences, and to widening our limited experience, to a more diverse perspective on what is holy, and of the shape of our religious landscape.

REFLECTION QUESTIONS

1. Reflect on the "sacred spaces" in your own life experience. What did they look like? How did they feel? What qualities made them sacred or holy?

2. How might your faith community best utilize your facilities to support interreligious learning? What are ways your faith community can express interreligious welcome?

3. Weddings, funerals, and Thanksgiving Services are some of the common interreligious shared prayer events for families and faith communities. How might these occasions become opportunities for interreligious learning?

5

Compassionate Action
as Interreligious Learning

All faiths insist that compassion is the test of true spirituality and that it brings us into relation with the transcendence we call God, Brahman, Nirvana, or Dao. Each has formulated its own version of the Golden Rule, "Do not treat others as you would not like them to treat you," or in its positive form, "Always treat others as you would wish to be treated yourself." Further, they all insist that you cannot confine your benevolence to your own group; you must have concern for everybody—even your enemies.

KAREN ARMSTRONG, *TWELVE STEPS TO A COMPASSIONATE LIFE* (2010)

THE INTERRELIGIOUS RELATIONSHIPS OF First Christian Church in Falls Church, Virginia, were built through a shared parking lot. In the early 1990s, the Muslim community needed to secure parking in the area for their Friday prayer service in order for construction plans for the mosque to be approved, and they approached the people of First Christian Church. Located only one-half mile from the proposed site for the mosque, the church agreed that its parking lot could easily be shared, thus opening the door for a deeper relationships with its Muslim neighbors.

Blessed with the rich racial, ethnic, and religious diversity of northern Virginia, First Christian Church, Dar Al-Hijrah Mosque, and other partner congregations have created a rich interreligious mosaic that serves all in the wider community. Not long after the shared parking lot, the partners joined with other community congregations to create a Memorial Peace Garden on the grounds of St. Anthony's Roman Catholic Parish. The Memorial Peace Garden, graced by thirteen Peace Poles created by different faith communities and school groups, is a burial ground for the ashes of the poor of the wider community. It was at the Memorial Peace Garden where the minister of First Christian Church, the imam of Dar Al-Hijrah mosque, and the priest of St. Anthony's prayed together with members of the community on September 11, 2001. Not far away, on the front grounds of First Christian Church, members of the community are invited for "Neighborhood Nights" during the summer months. With no agenda other than the opportunity for neighbors to meet neighbors, the church offers free ice cream, blood pressure checks, face painting, and a moon bouncer for children of the Hispanic, Muslim, and Anglo communities (Chesson 2010).

Kathleen Kline Chesson, senior minister at First Christian Church in Falls Church, marvels at all that has developed in the intervening decade. The warm and respectful relationships among the members of the interreligious community have served as foundation for a wide range of shared community action that serves the whole community. Unlike programs that are interreligious in name only, where there is little relationship among the faith communities, relationships in the Falls Church interreligious community are built on all levels of interaction. For instance, First Christian Church founded the Safe Haven day shelter program for the homeless and unemployed, which serves breakfast and lunch to 125 guests each Tuesday and Thursday, as well as providing the services of a psychiatric and general nurse practitioner and a social worker. Safe Haven volunteers include Buddhists, Christians, Jews, Muslims, and members of the multicultural community surrounding the church. Former homeless guests of the program organize a clothing ministry, and members of other faith communities cook and serve. Since most of the guests of the program are non-English-speaking, the day shelter also offers an English-As-A-Second Language (ESL) program. "It is important to us that the volunteers for our programs reflect the many religious and cultural communities that we serve," says Kathleen Kline Chesson. Dar Al-Hijrah mosque down the road sponsors one of the largest meal programs in the area, also providing clothing and other services to all in the community. During Ramadan the mosque offers food to all who come, sometimes for as many as 800 guests at a time. Members of other faith communities are always invited to iftar dinners, including members of First Christian Church, who continue to lend their parking lot for Friday prayers (Chesson 2010).

Beyond providing for the basic needs of people from all religious traditions in the region, in 2007 the interreligious community of the Falls Church area founded VOICE—Virginians Organized for Interfaith Community Engagement—an organization of sixty religious congregations that engages with power structures that can be lobbied for changes for the common good. "We take seriously the charge to love our neighbors and respond to their needs as we find them," says Kline. First Christian Church in Falls Church was one of the founding members of VOICE. "Disciples' [Christian Church (Disciples of Christ)] polity emphasizes how God lives in different cultures, and the need to nurture wholeness in a fragmented world, and that for us extends to those of other faith communities," says Chesson. Chesson believes that faith communities need to "bloom where they are planted" and interreligious action within the wider community is a response to God's love where it is found. "We are uniquely situated for direct interfaith community engagement. We are mostly, however, a congregation that worships, teaches, has a great traditional music program, teaches Sunday school, and visits the sick" (Chesson 2010).

In addition to interreligious action and advocacy, First Christian Church has also allied itself with national and international organizations. The congregation hosts dialogues sponsored through the Rumi Forum, a non-partisan organization founded by Turkish Muslims in 1999 to foster interfaith and intercultural dialogue, stimulate thinking and an exchange of opinions on supporting and fostering common ground and peace all over the world, and provide education and information exchange. Named after thirteenth-century Sufi poet and philosopher Mawlana Jaladdin Rumi, the organization sponsors activities that support all of humanity and life on the planet. First Christian Church has sponsored a number of interreligious dialogues through the Rumi Forum. Also resident in the congregation is a Buddhist group called the Compassionate Services Society that teaches Tai Chi at no cost two evenings per week in order to contribute to the health of the wider community. In an era when many congregations fear diminishment, First Christian Church is "striving mightily to speak the language of love in bold and visibly active ways" (Chesson 2010).

PRINCIPLES OF COMPASSIONATE ACTION

The chapter explores the rich connections between interreligious learning, and practical action for the common good, most notably through local faith communities and religious organizations. One of the opportunities resulting from interreligious learning is that faith communities come together to care for the wider community. Religious communities that discover the power of the values and visions they hold in common and that work together for the good of all humanity and the planet are themselves transformed. The Fourteenth Dalai Lama, Tenzin Gyatso, says that compassion and love are two aspects of the same thing and give rise to such qualities as hope, courage, determination, and inner strength. Compassion is the wish for another to be free of suffering, while love is the desire for them to have happiness. "Genuine compassion is based not on our own projections and expectations, but rather on the needs of the other; irrespective of whether another person is a close friend or an enemy, as long as that person wishes for peace and happiness and wishes to overcome suffering, then on that basis we develop genuine compassion for their problem," he writes. "This is genuine compassion. For the Buddhist practitioner, the goal is to develop this genuine compassion, this genuine wish for the well being of another, in fact for every living bring throughout the universe" (Tenzin Gyatso 2010, 26).

Scholar Karen Armstrong, the author of twenty best-selling books, suggests that practical compassion action for others, or living the Golden Rule, is the defining value of all religions:

THE GOLDEN RULE AND THE WORLD'S RELIGIONS

Baha'i Faith

Lay not on any soul a load that you would not wish to be laid upon you, and desire not for anyone the things you would not desire for yourself.
Baha'u'liah, Gleanings

Buddhism

Hurt not others with that which pains yourself.
The Buddha, Udanavarga 5.18

Christianity

In everything, do to others as you would have them do to you, for this is the law and the prophets.
Jesus, Matthew 7:12, NRSV

Confucianism

One word which sums up the basis of all good conduct . . . loving kindness. Do not do to others what you do not want done to yourself.
Confucius, Analects 15.23

Hinduism

Do naught to others which if done to thee would cause thee pain.
From the Mahabharata 5.1517

Islam

No one of you is a believer until he desires for his brother that which he desires for himself.
Sunnab

Jainism

One should treat all creatures in the world as one would like to be treated.
Lord Mahavir, 24th Tirthankara

Judaism

What is hateful to you, do not do to your neighbor. This is the whole Torah: all the rest is commentary. Go and learn it.
Hillel, Talmud, Shabbath 31a

Native Spiritual Traditions—Squamish Tribe

Humankind had not woven the web of life. We are but one thread within it. Whatever we do to the web, we do to ourselves.
Chief Seattle

Shintoism

Be charitable to all beings, love is the representative of God.
Ko-ji-ki Hachiman Kasuga

Sikhism

I am a stranger to no one; and no one is a stranger to me. Indeed, I am a friend to all.
Guru Granth Sahib, p.1299

Taoism

Regard your neighbor's gainas your own gain; and regard your neighbor's loss as your own loss.
Lao Tzu, T'ai Shang Kan Ying P'len, 213–18

Unitarianism

We affirm and promote respect for the interdependent web of all existence of which we are a part.
Unitarian principle

Zoroastrianism

Do not do unto others whatever is injurious to yourself.
Shayast-na-Shayast 13.29

Karen Armstrong believes that, with the rise of fundamentalist forms of all major religions in the world, religious leaders have failed to challenge intolerance and promote the compassionate message of their faiths. "This is what the world needs from religion right now. We do not need more certainty—we have seen too much certainty recently—but we need greater respect for the rights of others, including our enemies. She believes that religious people who fan the flames of hatred are not only dangerous, but have religion all wrong. "We cannot afford these polarities anymore because we live in one world—that was the revelation of 9/11 [September 11, 2001]. We are all members of one another, as St. Paul said, and what happens in Iraq or Afghanistan today will have repercussions in New York and London tomorrow." Armstrong believes that forms of spirituality focused on self-fulfillment that do not lead to practical compassionate action are value-less. Rather, the purpose of spiritual practice is to help us put ourselves to one side and to learn *to feel with others.* "Without compassion, there is no religious life at all" (Armstrong 2010, 150). With the support of the Fetzer Institute, Karen Armstrong developed the "Charter for Compassion" as a means to promote compassionate action in the world:

CHARTER FOR COMPASSION[1]

The principle of compassion lies at the heart of all religious, ethical and spiritual traditions, calling us always to treat all others as we wish to be treated ourselves. Compassion impels us to work tirelessly to alleviate the suffering of our fellow creatures, to dethrone ourselves from the centre of our world and put another there, and to honor the inviolable sanctity of every single human being, treating everybody, without exception, with absolute justice, equity and respect.

It is also necessary in both public and private life to refrain consistently and empathically from inflicting pain. To act or speak violently out of spite, chauvinism, or self-interest, to impoverish, exploit or deny basic rights to anybody, and to incite hatred by denigrating others—even our enemies—is a denial of our common humanity. We acknowledge that we have failed to live compassionately and that some have even increased the sum of human misery in the name of religion.

We therefore call upon all men and women ~ to restore compassion to the centre of morality and religion ~ to return to the ancient principle that any interpretation of scripture that breeds violence, hatred or disdain is illegitimate ~ to ensure that youth are given accurate and respectful information about other traditions, religions and cultures ~ to encourage a positive appreciation of cultural and religious diversity ~ to cultivate an informed empathy with the suffering of all human beings—even those regarded as enemies.

We urgently need to make compassion a clear, luminous and dynamic force in our polarized world. Rooted in a principled determination to transcend selfishness, compassion can break down political, dogmatic, ideological and religious boundaries. Born of our deep interdependence, compassion is essential to human relationships and to a fulfilled humanity. It is the path to enlightenment, and indispensible to the creation of a just economy and a peaceful global community.

While religious traditions vary in terms of the degree of pluralism they embrace, all make the point of directing adherents to show compassion to others—neighbors, strangers, and even enemies. Karen Armstrong suggests the spiritual practice of "looking behind the headlines" to the ordinary people who are affected by a crisis. "Remember that they did not

1. Copyright © 2010 Charter for Compassion. A Project of the TED Prize, Fetzer Institute. Used with Permission.TED Prize The Fetzer Institute.

choose to be born into that part of the world. Like you, they simply found themselves in a particular situation and may have been forced to conduct their whole lives in a context of violence, deprivation, and despair." Through developing an emphatic outlook and a greater understanding of our neighbors, we begin to recognize their suffering and to feel it as intensely as our own, allowing it to change our hearts. The last step, according to Armstrong, loving our enemies, makes clear that practicing compassionate action is not about pity or sentimentality, but about taking risks to envision the world anew. Practicing compassionate action is a life-long process of learning about ourselves and our neighbors. "A truly compassionate person touches a cord in us that resonates with some of our deepest yearnings. People flock to such individuals because they seem to offer a haven of peace in a violent, angry world. . . . But even if we achieve only a fraction of this enlightenment and leave the world marginally better because we have lived in it, our lives will have been worthwhile," writes Karen Armstrong. Truly compassionate religious communities also touch the hearts of the communities they serve, through the practice of practical compassionate action (Armstrong 2010, 193).

LOCAL ACTION AND INTERRELIGIOUS LEARNING

In her article on the application of the work of Brazilian educator Paulo Freire on interfaith education in Australia, Cathy Byrne of the Center on Social Inclusion, Macquarie University, in Sydney, argues that Freire's contribution to religious education and interreligious learning is his idea that the exploration of otherness is an essential part of the journey of knowing the self. For Paulo Freire, the purpose of all education was to liberate, and that can only occur within a culture committed to critical reflection and praxis. As a Christian, Bryne writes out of concern for Christians trained only from Christian-centric perspectives in Christian systems, and suggests that if the goal of religious education is to contribute to peace and the common good, that it is impossible to achieve those goals without interreligious learning. If interreligious learning is going to *re-create* rather than *replicate* existing society, it must challenge entrenched values and consciously expand its knowledge base, moving people to better know "the other" and seek cooperation across social groups (Byrne 2011, 48–51, 57).

There are many practical reasons for local faith communities to come together for interreligious action. Such work ensures that faith community leaders come to know each other and develop relationships of trust and friendship; it enables members of congregations and religious communities to improve local life and address issues of common concern; it is educational and provides an opportunity for those who participate to learn more about their neighbors' faiths as well as their own; it allows for joint projects that are more sustainable than individual efforts; it contributes to a sense of cohesion in the wider community; it provides a means to address prejudice, injustice, and religious discord; it encourages the religious community to speak out for the voiceless; and it provides a safeguard against the use of religion as a tool of intolerance, division, and conflict. In any given community, there are likely to be different understandings and motivations behind interreligious action, rooted in the teachings of each religious tradition's culture and experiences. Motivations and attitudes toward interreligious cooperation will differ; unity in this regard is less important than a sense of openness and goodwill that leads to healthy collaborations and friendships.

The Parliament of the World's Religions believes that now "sustained encounters between people of different religious, spiritual, and cultural traditions have created heightened momentum toward actualizing our many visions of a better world, as well as stronger possibilities for establishing ethical common ground." Faith communities can do what economic plans and political programs cannot attain: That is, an inner change, a change of heart, a conversion to a new vision of humanity in relationship with others. The hope of the Parliament of the World's Religions is that local religious institutions and communities will creatively engage each other and cooperate on behalf of the peoples of the world to address disintegrating community, the unrelenting demands on the earth's resources, growing injustices and divisions, and spiritual indirection. According to the Parliament, the common critical issues for local faith communities to address today include building community in diversity, and thus restoring respect and mutuality in place of tension, hostility, and violence; finding sustainable and peaceful ways to meet the needs of people while preserving the integrity of all life on the planet; alleviating the suffering of the majority of the human community through economic, political, and social reform; identifying compassionately with others and building solidarity among peoples; and seeking spiritual grounding from the wisdom of the religious traditions of the world to move beyond self-interest, building community in the spirit of hospitality, and expressing compassion through service" (Council for the Parliament of the World's Religions 1999, 5, 7–9).

In addition to the Parliament of World Religions, other global organizations, such as the United Nations, have outlined issues of critical concern for religious leaders and faith communities today. In the year 2000, the 189 member states of the United Nations pledged to eradicate extreme poverty by 2015 through implementation of the Millennium Development Goals (MDGs). The eight MDGs speak to the value of all life as represented by the world's religious traditions and address the critical needs of the most vulnerable in our midst: 1) Eradicate extreme poverty and hunger; 2) Achieve universal primary education; 3) Promote gender equality and empower women; 4) Reduce child mortality; 5) Improve maternal health; 6) Combat HIV/AIDS, malaria, and other diseases; 7) Ensure environmental sustainability; and, 8) Develop a Global Partnership for Development.

Local faith communities and religious organizations use the Millennium Development Goals as a source for interreligious action, for religious education of all ages, for organizing religious women's organizations, for organizing interreligious youth events, and for linking interreligious organizations in a region. The MDGs are also the platform for the organization Religions for Peace, the largest global coalition of representatives from the world's religions (www.wcrp.org 2010).

Overall, the combination of building trusted interreligious encounters, along with the introduction of critical thinking and shared analysis of problems, results in the type of interreligious learning which best supports long-term positive change. The benefits of interreligious action in local communities differ widely according to context, but most faith communities and religious organizations engaged report positive changes on a variety of levels. At a basic level, interreligious action is a form of dialogue. Just as some individuals and groups dialogue most effectively through conversation, others dialogue best through shared interreligious action. As such faith communities and religious organizations work to alleviate suffering and improve their regions and the wider world, they, too, are transformed. They discover the power of a group of people from different religious traditions working together to forge a shared future for their community. Many interreligious groups across the country provide basic human services such as food, housing, fuel, and work. Many also engage with civic institutions and government to address the root causes of poverty. Most interreligious action presumes that a key aspect of the work is to promote relationships within a local community. Spiritually, making people feel that they are part of something that contributes to the common good has a deep impact. As

Jonah Pesner, rabbi of Temple Israel in Boston, notes, "[It is not only about] healing the world, but also bringing together this congregation and making people feel like they are part of something. No one should show up to a synagogue and feel like they don't belong or have a part" (Interfaith Funders n.d., 7). Some of the benefits of interreligious action in faith communities include:

- Deeper relationships within the faith community and with members of other religious traditions.

- Enlivened faith through a more thorough knowledge of one's own tradition, as well as the religious traditions of neighbors.

- Transferable skills that are not only valuable in interreligious action but are also valuable in other congregational contexts, including listening skills, dialogue skills, hospitality skills, collaboration skills, small group skills, media skills, etc.

- Increased participation and leadership by members (laity) in interreligious relationships.

- Increased confidence in public action and in the faith communities' ability to tackle larger questions and issues in the community.

- A more visible public profile for the faith community within the wider community and a growing sense of the positive impact of the faith community from beyond its membership.

- A deeper understanding of the connection between the inner dimensions of spirituality and practical compassionate action in the world.

- Growth—for some faith communities, new members; for others, spiritual growth, growth in connections to the wider community, growth in a sense of mission or purpose.

In many faith communities, there are many demands competing for a finite amount of time and material resources. Clergy frequently mention the many rewards of interreligious relationships and at the same decry the limited amount of time they are able to devote to them. In some faith communities, interreligious and ecumenical relationships are considered to have a lower priority than those efforts that are directed to internal activities or direct care of members. In times when many faith communities feel diminishing memberships acutely, religious leaders often feel implicit and sometimes explicit pressures first to accomplish what is believed to bring in new members. Sometimes religious leaders feel they must choose between doing the work the faith community prioritizes and forming deeper relationships with the wider community and with those of other religious traditions. Key for faith communities and religious organizations is to discern with interreligious neighbors what issues or concerns are mutually shared, the most urgent, and the most suitable for collective action. "Open your heart to the agony of the world and listen to what comes to you," suggests spiritual activist Andrew Harvey (Palmer 2006, 91).

FOOD AND FUEL

The underlying purpose of interreligious environmentalism and eco-justice initiatives is to support life-sustaining societies that "think globally and act locally." Through interreligious action and spiritual practices, such initiatives reinforce ways of living which stress the interconnectedness of all creatures and a more livable world. One such interreligious initiative is active in the town of Bennington, in southwestern Vermont. While there is minimal racial and ethnic diversity in the rural community, there is economic diversity and considerable poverty in the region. Like many New England rural communities, there is significant underemployment and many of the available jobs are part-time and do not pay a living wage. Though the region once supported manufacturing jobs, the erosion of those positions over the last several decades has contributed to the growing sense of desperation among people living there. It is not unusual for people to have several jobs at one time in order to survive economically. Based on the receipt of food stamps, it is estimated that approximately 23.1% of children ages 0–18 live in poverty (Community Profile 2008, 13). As is the case in other communities, people who live in poverty in Bennington experience its impact in a variety of ways, including limited access to housing, fuel, and food. There is little affordable housing in the town. The escalating fuel costs in recent years means that the cost of utilities is high, as is the cost of running inefficient vehicles. High fuel costs also mean that food costs increase. Over the past few decades, many families in the region have received public assistance on a regular or emergency basis. As Anita Schell-Lambert, former rector of St. Peter's Episcopal Church in Bennington, notes, "Religious leaders, social workers, and school teachers, for example, daily observe a segregation of opportunity as played out in education and jobs; evidence of uneven access to housing, nutritious food, medical care, and heating fuels;

and social isolation characterized by fear, anxiety, and lack of meaningful relationships" (Schell-Lambert 2008, 13).

The Bennington Interfaith Council represents sixteen faith communities and nine religious traditions in the greater region. Members of the council meet monthly to strengthen relationships and to plan joint projects. The Interfaith Council manages a local Food and Fuel Fund (FFF) with strong links to health and human services in the area. The focus of the FFF is on developing food and other energy resources locally through a commitment to interreligious environmentalism while acknowledging the diversity of religious traditions present. "Here a common creed is not found in prayer books," says Schell-Lambert, who now serves a congregation in Rhode Island, "but rather in a passion for earth care so that we can continue to decrease our ecological footprint, living more simply so others live" (Schell-Lambert 2008).

The Food and Fuel Fund of the Bennington Interfaith Council was created as an emergency fund in 1973 as a response to the oil embargo at that time. Local faith communities decided to pool their resources to help those in need in the community. "We're talking about the most basic fundamental human needs," says Joshua Boettiger, rabbi of Congregation Beth El in Bennington. "We're talking about the Food and Fuel Fund being the last safety net for people who fall through the cracks with the other social agencies in town. It's always tight, and so we are gearing up. People have been using the word 'crisis' and anticipating a crisis." Bain Davis, of the Bennington Society of Friends (Quakers), says, "Every one of our faith communities has a self-story that we are not only about being faithful people, but also a serving people. And that self-story needs to sometimes be pushed a little further to the surface" (Rondeau, 2008).

Typically, 60 percent of the FFF goes for housing costs, including rent, mortgage payments, security deposits, and utility bills. Another 25 percent goes for emergency items such as food, prescriptions, and household items. A small portion of the FFF goes to transitional housing for the homeless, and the remainder covers administrative costs. Although the FFF was initially run by a volunteer clergy manager, the Bennington Interfaith Council made the decision to employ a part-time manager to build the capacity of the fund, along with a professional grant manager, actively involved in one of the faith communities and with skills in health and human services. These structural changes marked a paradigm shift in the philosophy of the work of the fund from "alms giving" to using assets-based community development in an effort to more effectively to involve the people the fund serves. As the Robert Wood Johnson Foundation suggests, "Justice can be achieved only when people gain the political and economic power to make key decisions about their futures and the future of their communities." To that end, the FFF encourages clients to conserve, to change behaviors, and to prepare for the hard winters that are part of living in New England. Religious leaders there are concerned every winter with people dying in their homes without fuel. In many cases people are at risk the entire winter, not just due to a sudden cold snap. "We can do more together than we can do individually," says Anita Schell-Lambert, "but it does not mean only more money but sacrifices on every person's part, and it also means pooling resources, and not just financial resources, but places to stay" (Schell-Lambert 2008). For example, the FFF sponsors weatherization workshops to teach people to insulate their homes better so that available funding will stretch to fill more need. The fund also pairs adult mentors who have experience with the practical and financial management of a household with those at risk to help people gain the skills to problem-solve their situations.

The FFF works with other community agencies, including Efficiency Vermont, the Bennington Energy Committee, and the New England Grassroots Environment Fund, in efforts to lower the electric bills of the region's poorest residents. The main constituencies of the FFF include members of the faith communities of the Bennington Interfaith Council, as well as those in the wider area who have historically received assistance from the fund. Most of the people served by the fund are single women with incomes of less than $10,000 per year who have multiple children at home. Other groups with significant challenges are male single parents, persons with disabilities, and the elderly. The FFF has gained a reputation in the region as a source of concrete help to people in need and as a caring presence in the community. New clergy in the region have noticed that participation in the FFF has not only heightened the public profile of their congregations, but has, in part, brought people to them, not because of their religious affiliation but because of what they are doing in the community. Through building interreligious community focused on environmentalism and eco-justice, the religious communities of Bennington, Vermont, are providing much needed assistance to those living in poverty and at the same time using their voice to support legislation that addresses climate change and the possibility of a sustainable future. Rather than getting stuck in generational poverty, the interreligious community of Bennington is hoping to work with the wider community to envision an alternative future. "When we face the harsh reality of global warming and commit ourselves to drastic reform, we can have a vision of a cleaner world and local community for our children," writes Schell-Lambert (Schell-Lambert 2009, 37).

• The Bennington Interfaith Council has a direct impact on local congregations through community action committed to building local sustainable religious communities. At St. Peter's Episcopal Church, the living out of this commitment took several forms, including an energy audit, a course on environmentalism, an additional course on local foods, and setting up a locavore (an organization dedicated to eating foods grown locally), the development of a community garden, participation in an interfaith energy service alliance, an annual convention on sustainability, a partnership with the local school district, and spiritual practices and liturgies which support the evolution of the community. Integral to the spirit of the work is the commitment on the part of St. Peter's Episcopal Church and the other faith communities to make drastic reforms. St. Peter's underwent an energy audit in late 2005 conducted by Vermont Interfaith Power and Light. The congregation then integrated the three-fold pattern of *reduce, reuse,* and *recycle* into every aspect of its common life, from conserving heat to re-cycling cell phones and computers, buying renewable energy, using water, planting trees, turning off lights, holding rummage sales, using non-toxic cleaning supplies, double-sided photo-copying, banning Styrofoam, and selecting religious education curricula for children and adults. "We have made significant changes to our lifestyles as we continue to explore what it means to be a steward of God's creation," said Schell-Lambert (Schell-Lambert 2009, 30).

COMMUNITY GARDENS

As part of their commitment "to think globally, act (and eat) locally," St Peter's Episcopal Church in Bennington established a communal vegetable garden. The garden is open to all those in congregations and neighbors who wish to work in it. The congregation provides space, training, and a team to manage it using organic gardening and composting methods. The food produced is shared among the gardeners, the congregation, and local agencies. "The garden is the latest example of how interreligious relationships are strengthening and deepening our ties to Bennington and to one another as members of the interreligious community," says Anita Schell-Lambert.

All the interreligious action programs at St. Peter's are coordinated through collaborative planning and implementation throughout the town. "The real staying power of them is rooted in many faith traditions and new ways of doing business," says Schell-Lambert. "Caring for the planet and all its inhabitants is also integrally related to peace-building in best spiritual practices. These programs always include a shared meal—with food grown locally, if possible," she says. "In Bennington it is such environmental and economic justice initiatives that to date have found the most common ground for interreligious collaboration. They have profoundly changed St Peter's" (Schell-Lambert 2008).

David Haberman, a scholar and professor of Hinduism and Ecology at Indiana University sees the profound connection between spiritual practice and community gardens. "The best environmental practice for every con-gregation to embrace is, quite simply, to plant a garden," he says (Haberman 2008). Many of the major religions of the world set stories in gardens, and share tales of planting and reaping the harvest. The image of the garden also underscores the interdependence of all living things. Faith commu-nities, commonly known for the spiritual food they offer, also contribute to physical sustenance through food grown in communal gardens. Faith communities with communal gardens build wider and deeper community relationships through planning, planting, harvesting, cooking, eating, and sharing communally grown food. In addition, opportunities to share food and food practices build cultural competency across religious and cultural groups in the community.

To support the communal garden, members of St. Peter's eco-team hosted two master composters for a workshop on indoor (vermiculture) and outdoor composting techniques. After the workshop, participants commit-ted to composting at home, as well at their workplaces, where possible. Five families also left with starter worm bins. The harvest from the communal garden is an important part of the congregation's shared meals, and the eco-team worked with local food banks in an effort to grow organic food for and with the families served by the garden (Schell-Lambert 2009–23).

St. Peter's Episcopal Church is also the site of the Blooming Chefs program, a youth initiative of the Quantum Leap Project of Bennington College and the local school district. The Quantum Leap Project supports at risk young people from the wider community. The Blooming Chefs pro-gram trains young people from the community in food preparation, nutri-tion, and local ecosystems, helping them make the connections between food and building a better local community and world. Students also gain a greater sense of the connections between nutrition, health and education, and the role of the garden and kitchen in the local community. A primary goal of the Blooming Chefs project is "eco-literacy," or providing young people with an understanding of the biological, cultural, historical, geographical, and agricultural systems in which they live. In addition, students delve into environmental stewardship through gardening, the culinary arts, creative writing, and the visual arts. Through participation in the communal garden, students gain hands-on experience in planning, planting, cultivation, and harvesting organic food. Overall, the project offers children, youth, and families new skills, a deeper sense of purpose, and a more profound connection with the greater community (Schell-Lambert 2009, 30–38).

INTERRELIGIOUS PEACEMAKING INITIATIVES

Another focus of local, national, and international interreligious action are peacemaking initiatives. Local expressions of interreligious peacemaking (or peace-building in some locations,) include festivals, workshops, conferences, and interreligious centers all dedicated to supporting efforts among members of faith communities and beyond. Glen Stassen, professor of Christian ethics at Fuller Theological Seminary, is the author of several books that focus directly on what he terms *just peace-making practices* to abolish war. Frustrated by religious discussions of peace as a general ideal, Stassen's interest is to go a step further and identity specific and concrete practices that individuals and groups can utilize in actual conflicts. His work is about Christians learning to practice peace, not just talk about it. In developing just peace-making practices, Stassen has worked with other ethicists and experts in international relations. They hope that other faith traditions will also develop their own just peace-making ethic. "We are addressing all persons of various faiths and no claimed faith who are concerned about peacemaking, or who could become concerned if they had a map that would make sense of events and of peacemaking trends for them and that would indicate directions their participation can take" (Stassen 2009, 77).

As an evangelical Christian, Stassen is concerned with the biblical basis of peacemaking, particularly the way of Jesus. He writes, "Thirty-seven times Jesus confronted the ruling authorities in Jerusalem and their supporters for their injustices, including oppression of the poor, domination of the powerless, exclusion of the outcasts, and the violence against victims. . . . Scriptures are full of warnings that injustice is a major cause of war."

Stassen finds that focusing on the following peacemaking *practices* is an effective way to unite people despite differing religious traditions, faith perspectives, and methodologies:

Support nonviolent direct action; take independent initiatives to reduce hostility; use cooperative conflict resolution; acknowledge responsibility for conflict and injustice; seek repentance and forgiveness; promote democracy, human rights, and religious liberty; foster just and sustainable economic development; recognize emerging cooperative forces in the international system, and work with them; strengthen the United Nations and international efforts for cooperation and human rights; reduce offensive weapons and weapons trade, and, encourage grassroots peacemaking groups and voluntary associations (Stassen 2009, 65–77).

It is the belief of Stassen and his colleagues that people of faith have an obligation to support peacemaking practices and to work for conditions that will foster peace. A transnational network of grassroots groups, including local faith groups, to do the practices of peacemaking in their families and neighborhoods, and religious communities is integral to making this work effectively. Not only are such peacemaking groups able to transcend narrow national and ideological perspectives, they also serve as a voice for the voiceless and support the long-term commitment needed for peacemaking. "They can criticize injustice and initiate repentance and forgiveness. They can nurture a spirituality that sustains courage when just peacemaking is unpopular, hope when despair or criticism is tempting, and grace and forgiveness when just peacemaking fails" (Stassen 2009, 77).

Many other groups and organizations across the world and within different religious traditions also focus on peacemaking. For example, the Abrahamic Faiths Peace Initiative (AFPI), http://abrahamicfaithspeacemaking.com, is a group of Jewish, Christian, and Muslim activists in Southern California united in the belief that peacemaking is an essential and defining mandate of the three faith traditions. The group grew out of the relationships and trust built by religious leaders active in the peace movement over several decades in Los Angeles through anti-nuclear campaigns and rallies protesting the Vietnam War and the first Gulf War. As committed Jews, Christians, and Muslims, the members of the group make their wrestling with their own respective faith traditions an important focus of the group's, and they actively support theological justifications for peace in each tradition. Activist as well as educational in nature, the AFPI supports justice and peace efforts in the region and in the wider world. Concerned that religion is often used as a means to justify violence and warfare, the group makes available for download an extensive list of educational resources, along with an interreligious peace-making curriculum, *For One Great Peace* (2012), grounded in scripture and the traditions of the Abrahamic faiths. These resources address a range of congregational situations, such as preaching, worship, and religious education for young people and adults. Participants in AFPI bring the dialogue into their own faith communities and organizations as part of the educational process.

HOW DO WE BEGIN?

Discerning interreligious action in faith communities and religious organizations benefits from intentional discernment which includes members from as many of the stakeholders in the project as possible. The excitement of interreligious encounters and the vastness of human need in our communities often lead congregations to jump into action before the group has adequately discerned whether it has the resources and the leadership to pursue a particular path. For this reason, it is wise for leaders to spend adequate time in discernment, building relationships within the group, discerning what the group hopes to do together and the resources needed, before jumping into interreligious action. The amount of time spent on strengthening relationships is a sound investment toward the time when conflicts ensue, as will most certainly occur in interreligious situations. It is better to invest in relationships at the beginning of a shared project than to have it derail later. Three to six months of regular community building and discernment is not too long for interreligious congregations and religious organizations interested in practical compassionate action to work together before projects are chosen.

The processes interreligious projects utilize to discern shared action vary, but many long-term partnerships benefit from participation in an intentional action-reflection that guides the work they do together. The concept of an action-reflection process is taken from the work of the Paulo Freire, who believed that learning through dialogue was in itself liberating. Action-reflection processes are transformational because people feel empowered when they act and reflect on their own experience. Rather than delegating action to outside experts, the assumption in action-reflection is that the knowledge and skills for change lie within the group itself.

Although some action-reflection groups may have a designated convenor or facilitator, the assumption is that leadership is shared and that everyone in the group is responsible for what happens. An action-reflection process could be structured in response to an interreligious incident in a community. The model could also be used as a method for bringing different religious groups together for a period of time to establish relationships and to examine common issues and concerns. Some groups utilize a form of the action-reflection process on an ongoing basis, as a continuing way to transform and renew the purpose of the group. The action-reflection process is most effective with small groups of approximately a dozen people, although some interreligious groups have more participants, and other much larger congregations or religious organizations facilitate several groups concurrently. A basic format for an action–reflection process in a congregation or among several religious communities includes the following phases:

Covenant—The group agrees to form a community, decides on guidelines for conversations, logistics, frequency of meetings, membership, etc.

Community—Spiritually and relationally, the group builds the community.

Sharing Stories—Participants share their stories and listen to the stories of others, naming the issues and concerns prevalent in their own experience.

Framing the Issues—Participants compare and analyze their stories with the wider community and extract issues and concerns, prioritize, and assess resources available.

Theological Reflection—Participants reflect on what they have heard from the perspective of their own religious tradition.

Taking Effective Action—The group participates in shared action.

Evaluation—The group participates in ongoing evaluation of their process and the project.

Celebration—The group builds community through shared celebrations, such as prayer, worship, festivals, etc.

Whether your faith community or religious organization hopes to start a new interreligious action project, or whether you are part of an existing initiative, the following checklist may be helpful. Some questions may be more relevant to congregations and organizations with a formal structure than they are to informal or ad hoc groups:

INTERRELIGIOUS ACTION CHECKLIST FOR FAITH COMMUNITIES AND RELIGIOUS ORGANIZATIONS

1. What are the prevailing opinions about religious diversity in your congregation? What is the general level of religious literacy of your own tradition, and of other religious traditions?

2. What is the history of interreligious engagement in your congregation? Who is reflected in that history and who is excluded? What did you learn from that history?

3. What is the actual religious pluralism of your community? What is the religious diversity *within* your congregation? What houses of worship are within a ten-mile radius of your congregation? What are the demographics? What relationships do you already have ecumenically or with other religious traditions? Who is your audience?

4. What kind of interreligious initiatives or projects already exist locally? Is a new project needed or would energies be better focused in joining an existing effort?

5. Who are key interreligious religious leaders of your community? How diverse is the group? How might additional leaders be inspired and recruited? How cohesive is the group?

6. How representative is the group? Are any religious communities excluded intentionally or unintentionally? How will membership be determined?

7. Who participates? In addition to clergy (religious leaders) how do other people in the community participate? How will you mobilize volunteers?

8. What kind of relationships does the group have with other related organizations?

9. How will you record and publicize what you do?

10. What resources do you have to support this work? (For example, time, money, space, etc.)

11. How will you make decisions? Who speaks for the group?

12. Who will make this project their *top* priority?

Take Note. Point number 12 on the checklist is particularly important. Even in the case of shared leadership, most effective and on-going community-based interreligious organizations have leaders, sometimes as few as one or two, who have made the commitment to make the project a priority in their work. Without consistency in leadership, interreligious projects may easily get lost in the midst of the many competing needs in most congregations.

The late Rabbi Abraham Joshua Heschel, a friend and colleague of Dr. Martin Luther King, Jr., declared during the march from Selma that "our feet are praying" (Kaiser 2010, 30). So, too, do those who participate in interreligious action pray with their feet while working for a better world. Interreligious learning is a powerful tool for equipping people in local communities with skills and resources in order to contribute more effectively to the common good.

REFLECTION QUESTIONS

1. Reflect on the Golden Rule from the perspective of various religious traditions. What resonates with you? Surprises you? How might you best live the Golden Rule in your own life? In your congregation?

2. Reflect on your congregation's experience by using the Interreligious Action Checklist. Is your congregation currently involved in interreligious action? How might this experience be enriched? What are the opportunities for interreligious action in your own community?

3. Abraham Joshua Heschel uses the image of "our feet are praying." As you pray and reflect on interreligious action of your community, what images and metaphors come to mind?

6

Initiating Intentional Interreligious Learning Communities

The sacrament of human life is the sacrament that supersedes our religions. We live before we believe, and we are human before we are religious. Our life together is a temple where we all meet.

SAMIR SELMANOVIC (2009, 58)

BEN SCHNELL LEARNED ABOUT Faith House in Manhattan after reading the book *It's Really All About God*, written by the community's co-founder, Samir Selmanovic, a Seventh Day Adventist pastor from a Muslim-Atheist-Jewish-Christian religious heritage. Schnell wanted to check out one of the Faith House programs, but he lived in Portland, Maine, with a Honda Scooter as his only mode of transportation. Despite the chilly two-day commute to New York City, Schnell participated in a community holiday craft event at Faith House where he learned about Hanukkah, Islamic prayer beads, and Eastern Orthodox icons. He was drawn to the urban interreligious community out of a desire to meet people from other religious traditions and learn something about their experience in a warm and intimate gathering. "With so much religiously motivated violence in the world today, people getting together in a living room setting to celebrate each other's faith, now that's worth seeing, even if it means a long, chilly commute," he writes (Schnell, 2010).

Faith House in Manhattan is an experiential and intentional interreligious community of people who come together to deepen their personal and spiritual journeys through shared rituals and a commitment to social justice. A non-residential community of "people of all faiths and no faith at all," Faith House hosts "Living Room Gatherings" twice a month as a means of building interreligious community among people of deep faith in a world of many faiths. The purpose of the Living Room Gatherings is to share the ritual practices and holy days of different religious traditions with those who are not of that tradition, or those from the same tradition who want to delve deeper into the meaning of the practices. For instance, a Living Room Gathering for the Jewish festival of Purim was organized as a celebration for an interreligious group, including non-Jews and observant Jews who had never heard the Book of Esther read in English before. Christian Living Room Gatherings included celebrations of Advent, Lent, a service for Holy Saturday, and one for the Feast of St. Francis. Muslim Living Room Gatherings have included a Ramadan iftar, the meal where Muslims break their fast in Ramadan, and an invitation to experience salat, or the practice of Muslim prayer. "That invitation to try salat, to experience it with my body and offer prayers to God and Jesus alongside my Muslim friends, opened my heart," writes Bowie Snodgrass, co-founder of Faith House and an Episcopalian. "There was no attempt to convert me to Islam, but I was converted in that instant to the profound beauty and humility of salat, of submitting before God with my forehead upon the ground, this faith practice of my neighbors" (Snodgrass 2010, 43).

Bowie Snodgrass stresses that the spirit of the Living Room Gatherings is not "universalism," nor do they "mix and match" ritual practices from different traditions together. Rather, practices are shared by adherents of the particular religious traditions. "We ask people to share what they most treasure about a particular practice for an interreligious audience, what it is they would most like other people to know about and to understand," says Snodgrass (Snodgrass 2010). Snodgrass suggests that in most interreligious relationships there is a degree of awkwardness at first encounter, whether we are guest, host, or on more neutral ground. Through the shared ritual life and devotional practice of Faith House, participants embrace the gift of encountering God in the other as "holy awkwardness," a spiritual discipline critical to survival in the twenty-first century (Snodgrass, ATR, 2010, 175–76).

Although the Faith House community attracts seekers and people with little or no religious background, the majority of those who attend have a primary religious affiliation and are members of faith communities or other religious organizations. The leadership sees participation in Faith House as supplemental to participation in faith communities, though for some people it is their primary religious community. A multi-generational community, participants in Faith House gatherings range in age from twenty to seventy, and they come from many walks of life. In addition to the Living Room gatherings, the community takes field trips to participate in services, lectures, concerts, and other interreligious offerings throughout the city. One series began with a special focus on "food and faith." Samir Selmanovic shared his experience growing up in a Croatian atheist family where the sacred was communicated through food. Authors of a book on mealtime blessings shared food blessings from different religious traditions. Others were asked to share their own sacred dishes and stories. Another program featured a seder for Tu BeShvat, the only Jewish celebration ordained by the kabbalists. The meal featured fruits, wine, mystical teachings, and meditations from a storyteller who specializes in mysticism and Hasidic tales. Faith House also sponsors annual interreligious Passover Seders.

"We have come to appreciate that a faith that is lived in isolation is not a very deep faith," says Snodgrass. "Faith is meant to be a public thing. As you move out, you can build more trust, and you can include more people. Religions just can't function in isolation. We are interested in building bridges and tunnels and organizing people through the internet, not building great walls." She continues, "We believe that practicing religious people can *get* other religions through spiritual practices in a way that explaining them on a white board doesn't touch." Snodgrass has experience with the emergent church movement and is a member of the congregation of the Cathedral of St. John the Divine. She stresses that Faith House is most interested in partnerships with those individuals and organizations that are looking for ways to embrace a vision of interdependence between people of different religious backgrounds. "We are not interested in a vision limited to religious tolerance, and we are not reaching out to intolerant people, either," she says. "Even when people openly embrace our vision, we realize that we will still have surprises. We might rock their world a little bit" (Snodgrass 2010).

Intentional interreligious communities such as Faith House have sprung up across North America. The Pluralist Project at Harvard University reported in 2008 that there were more than 500 such groups, with the largest numbers in New York, California, Massachusetts and Illinois. Samir Selmanovic said that he founded Faith House out of an interest to "build a church where Christians are not in charge." He explains, "We wanted to include all the people who have a right to belong and be partners in the discussion, not as outsiders that need to be converted, but as insiders that we need to be interdependent with." Selmanovic believes that communities like Faith House are urgently needed in this world, and that, through shared study and spiritual practices, people from different religious traditions will *"actually learn to need one another."* Selmanovic says "we can't wait for the two to three billion Christians and Muslims in the world to become secular to have world peace" (Neroulias 2008).

PRINCIPLES OF INTENTIONAL INTERRELIGIOUS COMMUNITIES

The intentional interreligious communities detailed in this chapter put into practice the idea that shared values and a desire for interreligious encounter can unite people across religious and ideological lines, and build on these commitments to enhance the wider community. Although the intentional interreligious communities detailed here achieve this goal by a variety of means, all strive to create a strong sense of mutual trust, respect, and understanding within their membership, listen to the needs of their community, and strive to meet those needs. Many of these communities strive to *compliment*, rather than to compete with, faith communities, and often work in partnership with multiple religious organizations. The following principles are characteristic of these intentional interreligious communities:

- Regardless of the specific activity, cultivating healthy relationships is a high priority in intentional interreligious communities.

- Attention is given to creating space where all have access to participation, and where mutual respect is the expectation.

- Intentional interreligious communities seek to preserve the distinctiveness and authenticity of religious traditions, at the same time upholding shared values.

- The focus of community life is ongoing growth and learning; people are encouraged to bring their deepest selves to the encounter.

- Open and respectful dialogue about differences is encouraged, with the understanding that in the midst of strong differences, it is possible for people to remain in relationship and to work together for the common good.

- Networking is a high priority in intentional interreligious communities, as both a way to further learning, and as a creative extension of community life.

- Generally, intentional interreligious communities actively seek to engage a wide range of religious and philosophical traditions, not just those that typically participate in local activities.

INTERRELIGIOUS CONGREGATIONS

The West Cummington Congregation in rural Massachusetts burned to the ground in January 2010, mourned by many in its surrounding community. The 171-year-old structure was home to a congregation affiliated with the United Church of Christ and was a spiritual home to many more in the community. On any given Sunday, the congregation of 60 or so would include Jews, Roman Catholics, Buddhists, spiritualists, agnostics, and atheists—as well as Congregationalists. "We are not constrained by any tradition," says Stephen Philbrick, who was a sheep farmer and a poet before the congregation called him as minister over fifteen years ago (Filiprov 2010). Philbrick draws on members' own poetry, literature, sacred texts from a variety of faith traditions, as well philosophy for his messages that are more focused on building the community than on doctrine. "I don't believe God stopped talking 2,000 years ago says Philbrick (Contrade 2010).

"It feels cool to pray, even if you don't believe something," says Sandy Elia, a member of the congregation who was raised as a secular Jew. "When you live in the middle of nowhere, community becomes more important, especially in winter," she says (Filiprov 2010). Joy Chipman, the church clerk, does not consider herself particularly religious, but she came to the church to meet people when she moved to the community, met her fiancé there and was helped by members of the congregation when she battled a serious illness. "As my beliefs changed, it allowed that," says Laura A. Sheridan, a member of the congregation for fifteen years. "Everyone else seemed to be on their journey, too." The people in the town of less than 1,000 residents are determined to rebuild, but, until that is possible, they will meet at the parish house down the street. On the day that fire destroyed their building, the congregation gathered not far from the ruins and collected $900 to send to the people of Haiti for relief of the devastation there. Due to the increasingly interreligious nature of our cities and towns, some congregations are building interreligious communities from within. "We wanted to be an open and warm place to fill every Sunday with our expressions of warmth and prayer," Philbrick says (Contrade 2010).

Other intentionally interreligious congregations are also forming locally, some linked together through organizations such as the Council of Interfaith Congregations, and others independently. For example, the Interfaith Community Church in the Ballard area of Seattle, Washington, is an intentional interfaith community focused on healing and education. Grounded in the spirit of openness, welcome, and mutual respect, the congregation welcomes individuals and families from all faiths and spiritual traditions.

Steven Greenebaum is an interfaith minister who served the Interfaith Community Church as an associate minister for four years and is now starting another interreligious congregation in Lynnwood, Washington. Greenebaum, a Jewish Unitarian Universalist in background, says he grew more interested in "interfaith" as his spiritual orientation and less interested in his Unitarian Universalist affiliation. He is interested in gathering people of many different religious traditions together, including Muslims, Christians, Jews, and humanists, all covenanting to respect the spiritual paths of others while keeping their own. "I want our church to be a place of love where we do not expect people to leave their religious beliefs at the door. Which path is right is not important; what is important is that we are on the path to a better world" (Greenebaum 2009).

A major theme in Greenebaum's teaching is the idea of "living interfaith." Rather than coming together occasionally for interreligious events or projects, "living interfaith" is a commitment to come together weekly to form community and to work for the common good. Greenebaum does not seen "living interfaith" as the "right" way for people to come together, but he does believe it is a viable way to live in love and peace. "Religious people invest a great deal of energy, emotion, and blood in who is right, and I believe that we are living in the wrong paradigm when we do that," he says. Greenebaum believes that a paradigm shift requires that we ask different questions, such as, "How does worship bring us closer to the kingdom of God? To love our earth? How can we model ways to live with each other and love each other?" (Greenebaum 2009)

INTERRELIGIOUS FAMILIES

When Methodist-raised Chelsea Clinton, the daughter of former President Bill Clinton and Secretary of State Hillary Clinton, married Jewish investment banker Marc Mezvinsky in 2010, the media once again brought to the attention of the public what many local religious leaders already knew. That is, that the number of interreligious marriages continues to grow. Statistical studies have attempted to document this trend. Ten years ago the American Religious Identification Survey found that 22 percent of Americans married outside their own religious tradition (ARIS 2001). A 2008 survey by the Pew Forum on Religion and Public Life found that more than one-quarter of married Americans have a spouse of a different faith (Pew Forum 2010). Author Kate McCarthy, who considers these marriages and families as a form of interreligious encounter and the most intimate form of interreligious dialogue possible, argues that all existing studies agree that intermarriage is a growing phenomenon in American society, though more for some groups than for others. She suggests that while the number of interreligious unions is on the rise, such marriages and families have been present in the United States since its inception, perhaps as one indicator of a religious culture that is "committed to pluralism in principle but uneasy about it in practice" (McCarthy 2007, 136).

Anxiety and prohibitions in regard to interreligious marriage vary considerably across religious traditions and cultural groups. McCarthy notes that even religious groups which emphasize the need for mutual understanding between religious groups and which advocate for dialogue do not necessarily extend the same degree of openness to the idea of intermarriage. "When it comes to interfaith marriages, however, the rhetoric of openness and tolerance often changes sharply," she writes. "Interfaith partnering presses religious institutions to the limits of their interest in dialogue, because it takes place at the heart of religious identity and propagation: the family" (McCarthy 2007, 128). What is at stake is a range of culturally-embedded factors that are part of family life, including values, sexuality, religious education, language, child-rearing practices, family relationships, gender roles, dietary codes, home-based practices, holiday celebrations, and emotional styles.

In 2008 the Berkley Center for Religion, Peace, and World Affairs of Georgetown University published a report, *A Leap of Faith: Interreligious Marriage in the United States*. In the United States, where 78 percent of the population self-identifies as Christian, the report specifically examines the challenges and benefits of Jewish-Christian, Muslim-Christian, Hindu-Christian, and Buddhist-Christian couples. Researchers examined the lives of forty-five couples seeking ways that interreligious families can create mutually satisfying religious lives. Many of the couples interviewed emphasized the key themes of communication, balance, tolerance, and appreciation. Similarly, researchers found that issues around how to raise children are important for interreligious couples to discuss early in their relationships. Though the interreligious couples interviewed reported challenges, they also shared that spiritual growth and growth in understanding and tolerance were some of the benefits of their relationships. Finding common ground in prayer and shared values helped these interreligious couples resolve differences and remain optimistic about their futures. "You need to know that there are going to be conflicts because religion can tug at your heart; however, such conflicts will give you the opportunity to sit down, discuss, and bridge the gaps," said one respondent. The report further advises interreligious couples to get educated about each other's traditions and go to each other's religious services; to expose children to both faiths and to find a community of support; to go on spiritual retreats and/or do community service together; to value differences; and to compromise, giving a little to take a little and to keep things together (Berkeley Center for Religion 2008, 41).

Jewish-Christian marriages are the most commonly documented interreligious family types in the United States today, and both religious traditions have reflected seriously on the repercussions of such pairings. Among Jews, a stigma is attached to intermarriage, although all branches of Judaism express interest in outreach to interreligious families. The Jewish Outreach Institute estimates there are about 1,000,000 intermarried couples, and the rate of intermarriage is approximately 52%. Some Jews see intermarriage as a fact of life and outreach to interreligious families as imperative for cultural transmission. Other commentators are concerned that what genocide did not accomplish in the twentieth century, assimilation into a predominately Christian culture will—bringing about the extinction of the Jewish people. Given the dominant status of Christianity in the United States, intermarriage is generally seen as less of a threat among Christian groups in terms of religious survival, though some denominations may consider it a threat to personal faith. Among major Christian groups in the United States, only the Southern Baptist denomination actively opposes interreligious marriage (Jewish Outreach Institute 2009).

The transmission of religion, race, culture, and language characteristic of interreligious marriages is also a concern among some American Buddhists and Hindus, particularly among first-generation Asian immigrant families. Although both Buddhism and Hinduism as traditions are very open to other religions, the commitment to preserve cultural identities as minorities in a dominant culture can outweigh more spiritual considerations. "At the level of family and community, especially among recent immigrants, members of typically pluralism-affirming religions often experience considerable resistance to marrying someone outside their tradition, a resistance reinforced, of course, by the wariness or outright hostility of surrounding groups," writes McCarthy (McCarthy 2007, 130).

Unlike Buddhism and Hinduism, Islam offers clear guidance in the case of intermarriage: a Muslim man may marry a Christian or a Jew, while a woman may not marry a non-Muslim unless the man converts. Given the traditional understanding of marriage in Islam as the highest calling and the union between two families, there are enormous pressures to marry within the religious community. Although the inequality in the prohibitions against intermarriage stems from the fear that a woman and her children could be subsumed into her husband's religion, there is a tension between this practice and the gender equality articulated in the Qur'an for some Muslim women. As with other religious groups, the rate of intermarriage among immigrant Muslims has increased with every generation (McCarthy 2007, 133–34).

Many faith communities are not even fully aware of the extent to which interreligious families are present. Families that traditionally shared a single faith tradition are more commonly finding themselves in interreligious relationships as sons or daughters form relationships and marry partners of other religious groups. As wider communities grow increasingly diverse, it is also more and more common for members of faith communities to encounter people from other religious groups at school or in the workplace. Although not discussed in some faith communities as recently as the 1950s, growth in international and domestic adoptions are further diversifying religious communities.

Religious conversions from one faith tradition to another also contribute to the formation of interreligious families. Although marriage is a common motivator for conversions, the rich diversity of spiritual paths today suggests that people convert for many other reasons. A 2009 article on new converts in *Moment* magazine, shares the conversion stories of an African American hip-hop artist, a Mormon, a Baptist minister, an

Iranian-born Muslim, a Chinese-American, and a Mexican-American, all of whom had recently converted to Judaism ("The New Jewish Convert," 2009, 30–39). Interreligious families generally meet the challenges of raising their families amongst multiple religious traditions. Particularly within the Abrahamic traditions, a popular approach is to raise children within one or another faith exclusively. This approach is popular in monotheistic traditions, particularly for those who hold absolute truths and believe that these truths are to be transmitted to children through teaching and tradition. In these families, the couple chooses one religious tradition, and the other partner either converts, acquiesces, or continues to be observant in their own faith tradition while the family officially celebrates holidays and celebrations in the other tradition. In some cases, one member of the couple was more active in their faith tradition from the beginning; in other cases, the choice was more difficult. Another common option for interreligious couples, largely in an effort to avoid the tensions inherent in choosing one tradition over another, has been to raise children in no particular faith tradition whatsoever, with the idea that offspring will find their own spiritual path in the future. Other families take a more syncretistic approach and try to merge religious traditions based in the belief that religions share common core values. This approach is challenged, however, when trying to celebrate certain religious holidays, such as Christmas and Hanukkah, that really are distinct and have different meanings and symbols.

Within the past twenty years there has been an increasing shift among interreligious couples to find ways to share two faiths in one household that are respectful of the values and limitations of both traditions. In this alternative way, both parents teach children the different belief systems and give them the space eventually to decide for themselves. Rather than providing no religious education to children until they seek it themselves, this way of being an interreligious family seeks to portray different religious traditions in a balanced way so that young people will be able to make an informed choice. The goal of this style of interreligious parenting is to teach children to be proud of both traditions. The challenge of interreligious parenting is open communication and healthy respect between partners, including support of each other's religious observance (Comfort 2004, 21–22).

"The idea is that the children will have information so that they can make good informed choices," said Clay Dockery of the Interfaith Community, an organization which offers Jewish-Christian couples and their children a welcome place for holiday celebrations, religious instruction, and community (Wiener 2008). Interfaith Community founder Sheila

Gordon, a Jew married to an Episcopalian, started the organization with a small group of families in 1987, has one adult daughter who identifies as Jewish and one who leans more toward Christianity. Gordon believes that pressuring couples to choose one religion rather than another is the wrong approach and can lead to one parent feeling marginalized. "Kids will recognize if one parent is not happy or the grandparents are not being respected," she says. "We think that's not a good way to raise children" (Wiener 2008).

Perhaps most of all, interreligious families appreciate respectful welcome and open learning environments when seeking a spiritual home. Typically, congregations sensitive to intermarried families actively encourage full participation in family and adult activities and, when possible, integrate family members into committees and service organizations.

MULTIPLE RELIGIOUS BELONGING

More controversial for members of monotheistic faith traditions than the idea of learning from and respecting other religious traditions is the reality of those who claim multiple religious identities, that is, those who identify with and participate in more than one religious tradition fully and simultaneously. Although persons who identify as Hindu-Christians or Buddhists-Christians are more prevalent in Asian contexts, growing religious pluralism in the West has brought issues related to multiple religious identities into discussions of faith and practice. For some, the notion of multiple religious identities suggests a form of syncretism, viewed negatively as the mixing of religious beliefs and practices. Other scholars believe that a certain degree of syncretism exists in many religious contexts and most religious beliefs and practices are drawn from a variety of sources. Still others do not believe it is possible to hold multiple religious identities equally, and that one identity is likely dominant. Yet others associate multiple religious identities with "cafeteria religion" characteristic of New Age seekers or those who have difficulty fully committing to one religious tradition or another. Interestingly, in Asian contexts, it is not uncommon for people to frequent temples of different religious traditions, depending upon the circumstances. As younger generations grow to perceive religion as fluid rather than fixed and static, and as larger numbers of children from interreligious families grow into adulthood having shared in the religious practice of both parents, the topic of people with multiple religious identities will continue as an issue within faith communities (Kwok 2006, 540–44).

INTERRELIGIOUS CLERGY GROUPS

The Three Interfaith Amigos of Seattle, Rabbi Ted Falcon, Pastor Don MacKenzie and Brother Jamal Rahman, host the Interfaith Talk Radio Show and meet weekly for mutual spiritual direction. They gained an international following as their friendship grew and as their home congregations became closer as well. "When we first started, the three of us were like three circles touching," said Falcon, "but, over time, our circles have become more interlocked. We are still distinct circles, but we share more and more together" (Frykholm 2008, 22).

As religious leaders of the Jewish, Christian, and Muslim traditions, the Three Amigos are one popular example of the growing number of clergy groups that inspire interreligious learning in their home locales and beyond. The most effective of such groups provide opportunities for friendships and mutual support to develop among members and their congregations, as well as providing opportunities for interreligious learning and hospitality to the wider community. Flexibility in membership to allow for a variety of religious leaders, as well as a committed leadership core that keep the momentum going, are also characteristic of vibrant interfaith clergy groups. Interreligious clergy groups are one way of building interreligious community as local religious leaders develop working relationships and work for the common good. Although the scope, focus, and membership of local clergy groups vary greatly from community to community, the groups most often share the common goal of building mutuality and respect among members of different religious traditions in a particular locale, and in this goal concentrate on including both clergy and laity in their work.

One example of a clergy group gathered to build interreligious community in a local town is the Wayland Interfaith Clergy Association in Wayland, Massachusetts. A collegial association of ten Christian, Jewish, Muslim, and Unitarian Universalist religious leaders, the association has a long history of collaboration in the community. Located half-way between Boston and Worcester, Massachusetts, Wayland is a suburban, semi-rural community with a population of approximately 13,000 in 2000. With an excellent school system and access to the city, the affluent and professional community continues to grow in cultural and religious diversity. Notably, Wayland's houses of worship are in near proximity to each other in a small geographical area that allows easy access between faith communities. The faith communities included in the Wayland Interfaith Clergy Association are First Parish Unitarian Universalist, Trinitarian Congregationalist Church, St. Ann Roman Catholic Church, St. Zepherin Roman Catholic Church, Community United Methodist Church, Temple Shir Tikva (Reform), Congregation Or Atid (Conservative), the Islamic Center of Boston, Peace Lutheran Church, and the Episcopal Church of the Holy Spirit.

The Wayland Interfaith Clergy Association meets every four to six weeks for fellowship and planning at a different venue each time and, with the assistance of a seminary intern, sponsors a wide range of annual programs for people of all ages in the community. Aware that the designation "clergy" is not a term used in all religious traditions, the association broadened its membership to include religious leaders from all the religious communities in the town. Members of the association pool resources for a stipend for the intern, making it possible to continue quality programs amid busy clergy schedules. In addition to encouraging collegiality among religious leaders in Wayland, the clergy association also supports social services and strives to design its initiatives to address local religious and ethical issues in a timely manner. Past initiatives include a reflection group on ministerial practice, a concern for Darfur, an interfaith dialogue series, advocacy on local issues such as low and moderate income housing and domestic violence, and support for Hurricane Katrina relief. Because of its deep roots in the local community, the Wayland Interfaith Clergy Association is represented on town boards and organizations, particularly those dealing with housing and youth services, and works with safety officials and the public schools. In addition, the Wayland Interfaith Clergy Association collaborates with another local interreligious group, the Wayland/Weston Interfaith Action Group to support its local initiatives.

Frederick Moser, rector of the Episcopal Church of the Holy Spirit, is the convenor of the Wayland Interfaith Clergy Association and the formal supervisor of the seminary intern for the project. "What we do is provide opportunities for people to get to know their neighbors better," he says. "We found that we were all living in this diverse community, but that there were not many formal ways people could get to know each other. Otherwise, we all stayed within our own congregations, and basically got to know only those of our own religious tradition." Moser believes that, while not all the people of faith in Wayland are interested in interreligious learning, many are, and the experiences bring deep rewards to those who do participate. Among those in his own congregation, Moser finds that "we have a group of die-hards that participate in many of the interreligious programs, and other groups of people who participate more selectively but remain supportive." For Moser, his colleagues in the Wayland Interfaith Clergy Association are some of his closest professional relationships, "a real resource as well as a forum to discuss what is going on in our community and in our own traditions. We seek a common ground and we focus on that, he says." As a clergyperson with a passion for building ecumenical and interreligious relationships, Moser is also the ecumenical officer of the Episcopal Diocese of Massachusetts and the moderator of the Commission on Christian Unity of the Massachusetts Council of Churches, where he sees the need for developing a stronger sense of ecumenism among churches engaged in interreligious conversations. "The divisions among Christian groups and our ability to have conversations with other Christians is an important consideration in interfaith conversations," he says (Moser 2010).

The meeting format of the Wayland Interfaith Clergy Association varies, using a range of approaches designed to respond flexibly to the interests of the group. For instance, the group has worked on case studies together and studied sacred texts together. Recent concerns have included homelessness, hunger, and bullying in schools. In a community where the religious education of youth is an important focus of all faith communities, the Wayland Interfaith Clergy Association addressed a need by providing a six-session course on different religious traditions for young people called the "Wayland World Religions Course," which became a required part of Confirmation preparation for several of the local churches. A similar course on prayer across religious traditions was designed for adults in the community. Interfaith spirituality and ritual practices are celebrated through community events, as, for example, a workshop entitled "Holy Water" about water rituals in Christianity, Islam, Judaism, and Unitarian Universalism. The workshop focused on transformative practices from the perspectives of the various traditions. Other offerings of the Wayland Interfaith Clergy Association have focused on practices related to grief and dying from the perspectives of different religious traditions and women's spiritualities from an interfaith perspective.

"During my interfaith work, I frequently encountered misconceptions about Islam and Muslims. This saddened me and I decided to make a difference. I wanted people to know the true face of Islam and the message of the Qur'an," writes Shaheen Akhtar, of the Islamic Center of Boston, and a member of the Wayland Interfaith Clergy Association. Akhtar is passionate about interreligious work and has devoted significant time to the study of the Qur'an and other religious traditions. Born and raised in India, Akhtar came to the United States in the 1970s with his family. As a practicing Muslim living in a new culture, he felt he needed to understand his own religion on a deeper level. His own involvement in building interreligious community dates from over a decade ago when his daughter participated in an interfaith youth leadership program. Since then, Akhtar has worked with young people in a variety of community settings. He is an advisor to an interfaith education program designed to recognize the impact of stereotyping and prejudice in all its forms and to help young people develop strategies for confronting oppression in their daily lives. He is active as an educator at the Islamic Center of Boston, where he runs the Qur'an study group for adults, including both converts and those interested in learning more about Islam. He also coordinates the Interfaith Book Club for the Wayland Interfaith Clergy Association. The club has a dedicated and enthusiastic following of participants from throughout the community and meets at the Boston Islamic Center and Temple Shir Tikva, which are across the street from each other. The two locations help to create a welcoming and inclusive environment for participants (Akhtar 2010).

Akhtar says his interreligious work is inspired by one of the verses in the Qur'an, in which God says, "Humankind is naught but a single nation" (2.213). "The Qur'an teaches that, regardless of our religious affiliation and practice, we are all creations of God. This is a universal bond that ties us together as part of one human family. Our differences should not be a cause of hatred but should serve as a catalyst for beginning to know and understand each other," he says. "Through the book group I have been able to coordinate programs for the benefit of the community at large," he adds. "I believe that it is important for us to come together with honesty and without judgment to share what our faith means to us. I believe that it is important to listen to what others have to say and to work together for the good of humanity" (Akhtar 2010).

MULTIFAITH CHAPLAINCIES

The multifaith character of many college and university campuses and healthcare institutions is partially discussed in chapter 4 in of this book in regard to sharing, and in some cases constructing, sacred spaces. These spatial and architectural changes reflect the religious diversity in these contexts and the creative responses among chaplains of many traditions to celebrate and build these communities. In many areas, long before faith communities began to build interreligious relationships, healthcare chaplains and chaplains in higher education settings were already heavily involved in working with many religious traditions. While such chaplaincies were at one time filled with clergy focused on a specific tradition, the understanding of these roles has expanded to include the need for multifaith competency and sensitivity in addition to one's own spiritual tradition.

Institutions of higher education are some of the most religiously diverse communities in North America, requiring a deeper look at the role of spirituality and moral development within the context of learning and professional development. A recent spirituality study of 112,000 college students supported the notion that college is a time for students to develop spirituality in ways that can last after they have finished their formal education (Rojas 2010). Chaplaincies related to schools, colleges, and universities bring together students, faculty, administrators, and the wider religious networks they serve into religiously pluralistic communities. Academic communities are a microcosm of our larger societies and have negotiated issues that also emerge in congregational interreligious communities, such as religious conflicts on campus, balancing fundamentalism, food practices, the celebration of holy days, multifaith worship, decisions about which religious groups to recognize or include, gender roles, and representative religious leadership. Many such campus organizations have partnered with congregations or have provided resources to faith communities interested in building interreligious community, such as event speakers, joint programs, or shared community action.

For example, the Campus Ministry at Boston College holds a Commonground Interfaith Retreat to bring together people from a variety of religious traditions and of no religious background to experience different spiritual practices and to dialogue and build community. The 2010 retreat day featured a series of dialogues about interreligious life through "Food, Faith & Fellowship." Also in fall 2010, Northeastern University celebrated a "Spiritual Wellness Week" with a guided Labyrinth meditation, a demonstration of the healing power of bowing in Islam, a workshop on the Zen art of Japanese calligraphy, a workshop on mandalas, and a yoga demonstration, among other activities. The various faith communities on campus also participated in a progressive dinner where participants ate a different course of a shared meal at the different religious centers on campus (Stuart 2010).

Eboo Patel, founder and director of the Interfaith Youth Core (IFYC), believes that building bridges between faith communities on campus will equip students with important skills they can use as the next generation of leaders in all sectors of society. Further, Patel sees campuses as social laboratories where models of interreligious dialogue and service based in cooperation rather than conflict can be tested. Colleges and universities have the resources and opportunity to engage religious diversity and form interreligious communities in ways not easily found through other social institutions (Patel 2010, 14).

Chaplains at prisons and other correctional institutions are also addressing religious pluralism and striving to foster interreligious learning. For example, the Milwaukee prison system has added a Buddhist chaplain to serve inmates, staff, and families, along with Jewish and Christian colleagues. At a minimum-security prison in California, inmates have designated a "holy ground" where those from diverse traditions might worship together (McCarthy 2007, 205). In the same state, a recent study of inmates who participated in a religious book group found that violent incidents were reduced by a third. Chaplains in prisons and other correctional facilities not only provide for the religious needs of the inmates, staff, and families, but also connect these institutions with faith communities outside, who work in partnership as volunteers and provide crucial places of hospitality and resettlement to those inmates eventually released (Thompson 2004).

ONLINE INTERRELIGIOUS COMMUNITIES

A factor that should not be ignored in any examination of building interreligious learning is the reality that religion-oriented websites abound, and that millions of people encounter religious diversity in cyberspace. Although past generations traditionally found religious encounters in physical gathering places, such as congregations, the internet has changed the way many people think about and form communities. This does not mean that faith communities are not important as centers for community building, but many are declining in numbers while the numbers of interreligious websites are growing. More and more people participate in interreligious learning in cyberspace, as they share key beliefs or purposes with others who are geographically out of reach. The internet now brings more religious information to more people than ever before, and the numbers will continue to grow in the future. Most religious traditions, as well as all major and most minor Christian denominations, have an online presence and seek to establish their control and authority in this developing sphere of religious activity. Most religious traditions are also represented by "official" and "unofficial" sites, allowing for a great diversity of participation in interreligious learning practically anywhere in the world. People can join a completely virtual church or cyber-sangha, they can pray and receive spiritual guidance online, and they are able to visit virtual sacred spaces.

According to a 2004 study of the Pew Internet and American Life Project, 64 percent of Americans who were on the internet used it for spiritual or religious purposes. A year later, the same study found that two-thirds of American adults are now online (Pew Internet and American Life Project 2004). Religious websites reveal that participation is not limited to one type of opinion, and that exclusivist, pluralistic, and a wide variety of perspectives in between are present. In this way, the internet is seen as a tool to advance interreligious learning, because it provides access for many voices, even among the marginalized and those not institutionally affiliated. Given that the internet transcends the borders of physical space, it brings individuals together who otherwise would not be in contact, or at least where physically proximity would involve huge obstacles. On the other hand, it is this lack of physical "embodiment" which is also a source of criticism of online religion. As Kate McCarthy asks, "Aren't the veil, the turban, the yarmulke, the bindi part of what draws people to interfaith dialogue? Such marks of difference, invisible in internet dialogues, are part of the precious particularity of religious identity that is sometimes jeopardized online" (McCarthy 2007, 192–93). In other words, does the internet mask social and material differences that are integral to the learning process? Is it even possible to have authentic interreligious learning if differences are not recognized or valued? McCarthy's analysis of online religious dialogue sites such as *Belief.net* suggests that while such sites nourish personal spirituality, people largely participate in them as individuals, and there is therefore little connection with social transformation. "It may be that the kind of soft pluralism fostered by this and other dialogue forums is not after all the best sustenance for committed social action, though it may be deeply personally enriching" (McCarthy 2007, 193).

The need to be media savvy is an important consideration for all faith communities today, lest we reinforce the polarization between those who affiliate with more traditional religious institutions and those who express their spirituality and seek meaning and community in more popular and amorphous ways (Helland 2004, 34). The many examples of interreligious learning featured in this book could not be supplanted in their entirety by virtual communities, nor are all participants looking for that type of encounter. Yet, in terms of communications, outreach, and education, technology has a great deal to offer to those interested in interreligious learning and is an important avenue to be explored as part of local interfaith communities.

INITIATING INTERRELIGIOUS COMMUNITIES THROUGH HOSPITALITY

"Don't neglect to show hospitality to strangers, for by doing so some people have entertained angels without knowing it" (Hebrews 13:2). Hospitality is a spiritual practice of most religious traditions. For example, the Sufi mystic Jelaluddin Rumi celebrated the world's religions; when he died, his funeral was attended by Muslims, Christians, Hindus, Buddhists, and Jews. Rumi writes, "This being human is a guest house," entreating us to welcome and entertain all. "Even if they are a crowd of sorrows, who violently sweep your house empty of its furniture, still, treat each guest honorably. . . . Be grateful for whatever comes, because each has been sent as a guide from beyond" (Rumi 1997, 24). Mahatma Gandhi's sense of the importance of the practice of hospitality was evident in his ashram family, which included woman and men, young and old, Christians, Muslims, and Jews, untouchables and Brahmins. He believed that the spiritual practice of hospitality was a suitable model for Indian society, and he lived out his vision of a house where all windows and doors were open to people of good will (Eck 1991, 88).

Through interreligious learning, faith communities participate in providing hospitality and care to their neighbors. Interestingly, the words "hostility" and "hospitality" share the same root, despite their different meanings. Hostility thrives on turning intra- and intergroup differences into conflicts, while hospitality is about remaining open to persons and insights different from our own. One meaning focuses on seeing outsiders as potential enemies, while the other stresses willingness to take risks and offer welcome (Brussat and Brussat 2010).

Pentecostal scholar Amos Yong, in his book on hospitality and the religious other, points to Jesus as both the recipient and the conduit of God's hospitality. As a "journeying prophet," Jesus was the guest of many during his public ministry—Peter, Levi, Martha, Zacchaeus, various Pharisees, and unnamed homeowners—only to realize that he who eats at the table of others at the same time proclaim the banquet of God to all willing to participate. We know from the gospels that Jesus ate and drank with people beyond his own tradition; he also touched and listened to and cared for people in ways beyond the boundaries of the social hierarchies of his day. Jesus modeled an inclusive hospitality that involved women, children, slaves, the poor, the blind, those with physical disabilities, essentially the marginalized of his world (Yong 2008, 101–2).

Episcopal theologian Fredrica Harris Thompsett views hospitality as a radical form of mutuality in which each brings to the relationship what they have to offer. "This ministry of hospitality was more radical than toleration of difference—Jesus challenged and reversed widely accepted religious convention" (Thompsett 1989, 129). Theologian Miroslav Volf uses the image of the "mutual embrace" as a way to envision welcome and hospitality. In the act of reaching beyond ourselves to connect with another, in waiting at the border to see if they are open to us, in holding them close to ourselves, and finally in letting go, both are transformed (Volf 1996, 140–45).

Today, interreligious hospitality includes providing appropriate food and drink to our guests, a challenge for some faith communities, but hospitality in the spiritual sense means even more. Not only is the stranger to be genuinely welcomed, but we are to listen to their stories along the way. This welcome integrates respect with care as well as a refusal to judge those within our midst. To Jesus, hospitality was so basic, so important, that it was one of the practices which separated the sheep from the goats (Matthew 25:35). In interreligious learning, the practice of hospitality is about making space within our lives and in our communities by extending care to those from other religious traditions as our own family, and to attend openly and respectfully to their stories and experiences (Smith 2000, 117–18).

There is no single recipe for interreligious hospitality. Some suggested guidelines are provided here in an effort to address common issues involved in extending welcome to persons from other religious traditions. Ideally, faith communities and religious organizations engaged in interreligious hospitality will develop their own guidelines over time. Here are some guidelines to consider when building interreligious community:

- Be clear about roles and expectations. Is the encounter about individuals sharing their own experience? Is it a more formal situation, where participants in the dialogue are expected to represent their religious tradition or community?

- Approach others with the same respect that we expect, as equals. Remember that dialogue includes listening as well as speaking. Practice openness, honesty, and compassionate listening. Remember that all religious traditions include saintly adherents and unsavory characters; all traditions have histories marked by nobility and by evil. Participants in interreligious learning must be prepared to challenge as well as affirm their own tradition as well as those of others.

- Invite and extend hospitality as if it were your own home. Receive hospitality from those of other traditions on their own terms. Study the customs of other religious traditions, so you can plan appropriately in terms of calendar, accommodations, seating, social etiquette, food, and drink. Label food and drink. A vegetarian menu without alcohol or caffeinated beverages is the safest when in doubt.

- Optimally, interreligious learning should be planned with the involvement of all parties. Clear communication among all parties is about expectations. Is the encounter designed to be informal or for a designated purpose?

- Persons participating in interreligious learning have a right not to be subjected to proselytizing. Rather, dialogue is for mutual sharing and growth in understanding.

- Dialogue partners should be free to define themselves and their religious traditions in their own terms.

- Opportunities for interreligious learning are often the most vital when participants have a chance to meet each other as people and grow in relationship as well as to pursue other learning and action.

- Dialogue partners should be aware of the diversity *within* religious traditions and of the theological and ideological assumptions behind these differences.

- Shared ritual, worship, meditation, and festivals should grow from shared relationships and understanding. This is a controversial area for some individuals and traditions, and it should be considered with sensitivity to the religious traditions present.

- Issues of separation and disunity must be addressed, as well as areas of agreement and unity. Interreligious learning is not served by avoiding pain and conflict. Rather, understanding and relationships are built by coming to terms with what divides us and choosing to remain in relationship despite that reality. This includes respecting the right to disagree.

• Interreligious learning is enhanced through participation in local and regional projects as well as through relationships with global organizations.

There are many forms of intentional interreligious learning communities both related to and distinct from faith communities and formal religious organizations. They provide opportunities for deeper exploration of our own religious identities and those of others. Some of them reach people otherwise not connected to faith communities, and thus serve wider humanity. Intentional interreligious communities challenge faith communities by keeping conversations about religious pluralism alive, and by actively demonstrating that ongoing encounters across differences are not only possible, but generative resources for deepening relationships and serving the wider community. Intentional interreligious communities are a growing segment of the American religious landscape and potential partners for faith communities interested in deeper learning and creative partnerships.

REFLECTION QUESTIONS

1. What intentional interreligious communities are part of your religious practice? The practice of your faith community?

2. One of the Living Room themes at Faith House in Manhattan is "food and faith," referring to the many ways food communicates the sacred in our religious and cultural traditions. What is the relationship between "food and faith" in your own experience? In the experience of your faith community?

3. Research online resources and virtual communities from the perspective of a religious tradition that interests you. How might your faith community better use technology to enhance interreligious learning?

7

Interreligious Learning and the Future

What's the final possibility? I think it's the bridge. I think it is the bridge between church and world, between Christian and Muslim, even between believer and secularist. . . . It is a bridge that builds civil society where people from different backgrounds live in equal dignity and mutual loyalty. Build a bridge and say, "I do this because I am Christian." . . . My highest hope is that Muslims in America can situate themselves as a stone in this bridge, just one stone. We are next to a Jewish stone and a Christian stone, each of us together forming an arch for humanity to cross this bridge from a time of crisis to a time of cooperation (2009, 32, 40).

Eboo Patel

Interreligious learning emanates from the collective belief that we are all, despite religious differences, part of one human community; if life is improved for just one person due to our efforts, all benefit. "My humanity is bound up in yours," said Desmond Tutu, archbishop emeritus of Cape Town, "for we can only be human together" (Tutu Foundation, UK 2010). Many of the religious leaders of the world have supported the notion that, while there are many differences between peoples, we also share in the common work of peace and reconciliation for the sake of a better world and preserving our planet. Mahatma Gandhi famously said, "My wisdom flows from the Highest Source. I salute that Source in you. Let us work together for unity and love" (Satyagraha 2010). This last chapter looks at interreligious learning from the perspective of the future. What role does interreligious learning have to play in the future of faith communities? How can more widespread interreligious learning contribute to the vision of greater unity and love?

The Jewish tradition refers to the practice of *tikkun olam,* or the healing and the repair of the world. People of good will, people of faith, are knit together in a global and interdependent world and have the opportunity through interreligious learning to be transformed for the sake of one another and for the world. Of course, some choose to ignore the realities of people of other religious traditions living in our midst. Eboo Patel works with young people and groups across the country to encourage them to actively and positively engage with religious diversity. He delineates seven responses made by religious communities to the realities of pluralism. The first is to build a "bubble," in the belief that their particular tradition is to be followed so closely that adherents need to be closed off from others. There are traditions that have succeeded in doing this in ways that are respectful of others, such as Amish communities. For those communities who have neither the commitment nor the resources to exist in a bubble, Patel explores other options, including "the barrier," for those who accentuate the differences between their religious tradition and others; and "the bomb," for those who seek to kill those of other religious traditions. Bigotry, the fourth option, goes beyond the option of the barrier in that it not only opposes other religious traditions, but denigrates them. The fifth option is bifurcation, for those who live two different lives, a faith life and a church life; the sixth option, blasé, is for those so confused by religious diversity that they opt out altogether. The last option, the bridge, embraces Patel's image for faith communities interested in interreligious learning. "I think the theology of the bridge, the practice of the bridge, the faith formation of the bridge is going to be key not only to civic life in the 21st century but to maintaining faith identity," he says (Patel 2009, 37–39).

In the introduction of this book it was noted that interreligious learning is critical for human survival. Watching the daily news reinforces the argument that the need for interreligious learning is growing in the twenty-first century, and that without it human catastrophe ensues. If faith communities are going to help people maintain healthy religious identities, and if they intend to participate in civic life, then they need to become bridges to religious diversity (and other forms of diversity as well) that are beneficial to the common good. Interreligious learning a bridge between current religious conflicts and the peaceful human community we strive for in the future. Eboo Patel believes that religious communities interested in building bridges need to break out of the clash of civilizations mentality prevalent in many media approaches to religious pluralism. Instead of starting with the assumption that different traditions are locked in adversarial relationships, a position that supports extremists of all religious groups, Patel proposes that we begin with the assumption of interreligious cooperation. "We live in a world of Jews, Muslims, Christians, Hindus, Secularists, Buddhists, Baha'is, who want to live in equal dignity and mutual loyalty with each other in a world in which extremists want to dominate all of us," he says. "We do not honor extremists by giving them the title 'Muslim,' 'Jewish,' 'Christian,' 'Secularist,' or 'Hindu.' We call them what they are: the extremists of all traditions belong to one tradition, the tradition of extremism" (Patel 2009, 40).

The challenges of interreligious learning rest not solely within Christianity, Islam, Judaism, Buddhism, Hinduism, or other religious traditions per se, but rather within the conflicts which arise among their adherents. In other words, the knowledge of other religious traditions, as important as it is, cannot build bridges alone. Eboo Patel emphasizes the need for both the knowledge, including teaching our children about their own tradition and those of their neighbors, and the skills needed fully to appreciate religious diversity and to engage creatively with those of traditions and cultures different from our own. "It's the way we put these stones together that creates a bridge that people can walk over," he says (Patel 2009, 40).

Sociologist of religion Robert Wuthnow believes that one of the impacts of globalization is that American Christianities, as well as other religions, are involved in an increasing global engagement, and caused in part by the shrinkage of distances between North America and other parts of the world. The greater ease of transportation, communication, migration, and integration with other parts of the world is inextricably linked with the various cultures of which we are a part, including religious culture. While there is no single world culture, local communities find themselves now more connected with people in other parts of the world than ever. The overall global shift in world Christianities to the Southern Hemisphere has also brought Christians into close encounter with other religions. One positive result of globalization is the growth in religious and humanitarian aid and relief organizations, many of which are interreligious in character. These organizations have created new alliances for the betterment of humanity and the planet. In local faith communities, as several of the stories in this book attest, preaching and teaching about the common bonds between people and the responsibility to be engaged with people of other religious traditions will continue to be a recurring theme. The faith communities featured in this book, and many others beyond it, have spent thousands of hours engaged in interreligious learning. "The challenge for congregations large or small will nevertheless be one of striking an appropriate balance between the needs of the congregation itself and people of other countries [and other religious groups]," says Wuthnow. "Because of the tendency to emphasize local concerns, effort will be required to motivate involvement in global activities" (Wuthnow 2010, 140).

Faith communities are rooted in their local context, and it is therefore not possible to suggest one model for interreligious learning. Faith communities of all sizes, locations, and economic levels are capable of engaging in interreligious learning. What is most important is that a faith community view interreligious learning as central to its mission and to its own self-interest rather than as a special program or an "add-on." As the stories featured throughout this book suggest, individuals and faith communities are transformed through interreligious learning, although each has had its own encouragements and struggles along the way, and each has to discern its own pathway into the future. It is a basic premise of this book that all faith communities, no matter the location or the resources available, have the capacity to embrace interreligious learning in some way and that they are enriched by their efforts. Here is a list of ten things faith communities can do to support interreligious learning. Can you think of others?

TEN THINGS FAITH COMMUNITIES AND RELIGIOUS ORGANIZATIONS CAN DO TO SUPPORT INTERRELIGIOUS LEARNING

1. Investigate the "religious landscape" of your community. What religious groups are present? Do you have a contact list for the various groups?

2. Reflect on the religious pluralism *within* your faith community or organization. Are there any interreligious families? Staff members or volunteers from other religious groups? How might your faith

community or organization better serve those from other religious groups in your midst?

3. Ask people from other religious traditions to tell you about their communities, as a part of religious education, a worship service, etc. If your faith community or organization already has formed some interreligious relationships, are there ways they might be deepened or expanded?

4. Visit another religious group in your community when they hold an open day or offer a community program. Hold a visiting day and invite the wider community for hospitality.

5. Find ways to work with other religious groups in your town on common issues, such as poverty, homelessness, education, etc.

6. Study. In your own faith community or religious organization or with another religious group, design an educational experience or share in a book group.

7. Intentionally do business with businesses run by members of other religious groups.

8. Support efforts against religious hate crimes and discrimination in your community.

9. Support local, national, and global interreligious organizations with your time, ideas, and material resources.

10. Pray that God may empower you to support interreligious relationships and learning through your faith community or organization.

STRATEGIES FOR SUPPORTING INTERRELIGIOUS LEARNING IN FAITH COMMUNITIES

Without minimizing the distinctiveness of each faith community, it is possible to point to some characteristics of interreligious learning that are applicable in a variety of contexts. There is no one way to support interreligious learning, and yet there are values held and experiences shared by many different faith communities along the way. These characteristics offer faith communities, religious organizations, and other groups interested in interreligious learning some guidance and opportunities for further reflection (Kujawa-Holbrook 2002).

1. *Build on Health.* Faith communities or religious organizations that are self-involved, riddled with unresolved internal conflicts, lacking skilled leadership, without coherent management, failing to provide spiritual care to members, or avoidant and hostile to the surrounding neighbors are not in a good position to begin to build healthy relationships across religious differences. Although the term "health" is a relative one, building relationships across religious differences requires that those involved have the capacity to trust and have some positive experience of community for support and nurture. Healthy communities are those where people interact with each other in respectful and appropriate ways, where feelings and ideas are expressed directly and openly, where the gifts of all are welcomed, where leadership is exercised for the common good, where there is an openness to ongoing learning and issues in the community, and where people feel their pastoral needs are addressed. Stories in this book attest to the importance of the bonds of friendship in order for interreligious learning to withstand the bigotry, threats, natural disasters, and international incidents that can undermine them. In short, interreligious relationships will not be any deeper or more respectful than the relationships felt within the faith community itself.

2. *Practice Hospitality.* One of the key skills of the faith communities featured in this book is the practice of hospitality that extends beyond membership into the wider community and the world. Many of the leaders interviewed for this book attest to the belief that their faith community is there for *all* people, adherents of their own faith or not, and they make this belief a cornerstone of their mission. Many interreligious encounters are enhanced through simple acts of hospitality, such as good food that all can eat, sensitive scheduling, and the appropriateness of the site. Besides a commitment to hospitality, these faith communities intentionally value members' skills in welcoming others. Hospitality need not be lavish or expensive, but it must come from open hearts. Tenzin Gyatso, the 14th Dalai Lama, once said, "My religion is kindness." Most of the religions of the world urge adherents to practice hospitality, and some promise followers rewards in the afterlife for showing kindness to a neighbor (Amin, 2001).

3. *Commit to Lifelong Learning.* Faith communities and religious organizations destined to be more than museums often have a deep commitment to lifelong learning for all ages. This formation reveals

(and at times challenges) both the heritage and the traditions of a given religious group and leads to further investigation of other religions. Members of faith communities and other religious organizations throughout this book committed to interreligious learning are deeply grounded in their own faith, have a high degree of religious literacy, and are willing to examine critically their religious beliefs from the perspective of other religious groups. Denial of negative history prevents the formation of authentic interreligious relationships and maintains divisions between religious groups. Transformational learning is always reciprocal; that is, just as we learn from our own religious tradition, we learn equally from those of other religious traditions with whom we have engaged. Through compassionate listening and critical reflection, and through the challenge of presenting our own faith to others, interreligious learning offers opportunities to gain fresh insights about our own faith and to learn new things about God from each other.

4. *Foster Multicultural Competency.* The stories in this book suggest that faith communities and religious organizations interested in interreligious learning have skills in navigating diverse expressions of religion, ethnicity, race, language, and culture as they manifest in human communities. They are also aware of the dynamics of cross-cultural encounters and strive more deeply to understand and welcome "the other." The experience of interreligious encounters, whether in public forums or in family homes, presents a range of varying cultural customs and practices, including food-related practices, domestic customs, sacred rituals, gender roles, linguistic differences, communication differences, the use of space, etc. Some of these differences emanate from particular religious traditions; some are attributable to a group within a religious tradition; still others are due to the part of the world from which the group comes, or from historical or environmental factors. Multicultural competency stresses the need to differentiate between what is religious tradition or religious teaching and what is cultural and/or ethnic custom, as well as the importance of not comparing religious groups without understanding these distinctions. Cultural differences are often magnified in *intra-religious* dialogue where groups share in a particular religious tradition but express that tradition across a variety of cultural contexts. Religious communities throughout the world, such as Buddhists, Jews, Muslims, and others,

live out their beliefs within the context of a variety of cultures. Similarly, different branches of the same religious traditions often meet within interreligious contexts, when otherwise they might not. Multicultural competency helps faith communities recognize cultural differences between groups and equips members with skills to appreciate differences and form relationships across differences.

5. *Support Visionary Leaders.* Leadership is a key variable among faith communities and other religious organizations that are concerned with interreligious learning long-term. The stories from the faith communities and religious organizations here indicate that leaders for interreligious learning come from many different religious traditions; they are clergy and laity, women and men, some employed by religious organizations and some not. Yet a characteristic many share is their capacity to see interreligious learning in terms of a long-term *process* rather than a *program* or *product*. Many of the leaders interviewed for this book have an abiding belief in the importance of interreligious learning and a vision of people from all religious traditions united for the common good. Leaders committed to interreligious learning tend to share a sacrificial commitment. They come from many different backgrounds, but they share common experience in that they most express some "turning point" or "conversion" resulting from a direct and personal encounter across the boundaries of religious difference that dramatically shifted the way they view the world. Grounded and nourished through spiritual practice, these leaders tend to envision their work as a "partnership" and hence tend to be non-dominant, preferring to lead through example, support, encouragement, and participation. Interreligious leaders have a tested yet optimistic view of humanity and fundamentally believe in the capacity for transformation through the agency of people of good will. Moreover, they tend to view interreligious learning as an integral part of their purpose in the world, rather than a distinct or segmented activity. On the skill level, committed interreligious leaders tend to be compassionate, reflective teachers and risk takers open to failure, knowledgeable in group process and institutional change, multi-culturally competent, media savvy, and, perhaps most importantly, *persistent*. At the same time, many interreligious leaders find joy in their work and are supported and nurtured through the process of working for positive change in their local communities and the wider world.

6. *Emphasize Prayer.* While there are differences of opinion about the efficacy of shared worship, it is also the case that interreligious learning recognizes the power of prayer in the myriad forms in which it takes place. Among the characteristics of interreligious learning are its rich symbolic life and its attention to the ritual and aesthetic needs of a wide variety of religious cultures. One of the common "entry points" for many faith communities is the sharing of sacred spaces. The promises and challenges of space sharing partnerships often lead to increasing interreligious relationships and other joint learning and initiatives among those involved. For many, the task of including symbols, texts, language, images, and rituals of other traditions into an experience of shared prayer with integrity is challenging, but it is also an opportunity for deep learning. How does the prayer life of a faith community depict other religious traditions? Those faith communities and religious organizations committed to interreligious learning stress the importance of prayer in this work and share a commitment to cultivate and expand their spiritual lives on an ongoing basis. All the faith communities interviewed for this book have had to reexamine their worship, music, education, and other aspects of congregational life from an interreligious perspective.

7. *Develop Networks and Democratic Partnerships.* Most interreligious leaders attest to the importance of building and participating in networks from a variety of sources—local communities, denominations, official interreligious groups, global organizations, ecumenical partnerships, etc. Faith communities that engage in interreligious learning come from diverse theological perspectives, but they share a vibrant faith and commitment to work for the good of all people. Though grounded in their own faith traditions, these faith communities do not limit their attentions solely to their own membership, but provide leadership in their local communities and beyond. These faith communities develop skills in community advocacy and in building alliances and partnerships. They know how to listen to the needs of their partners; they know the difference between "acting for" and 'working with" other individuals and groups; and they know how to shape a shared agenda. These faith communities seek connections and resources on an ongoing basis, remaining open to new partnerships and ways of growing deeper interreligiously.

8. *Plan Monitor, and Evaluate.* Most of the faith communities and organizations in this study, regardless of size or resources, have implemented some kind of formal plan to support interreligious learning. The most successful interreligious learning plans are those with clarity of purpose and with enough flexibility to allow for needed changes and the surprises that occur in the course of all human relationships. Without ongoing evaluation that includes discernment, reflection, adjustments, and modifications, any plan will eventually lose its energy or purpose. As discussed throughout this book, planning processes that begin with bringing all parties together for joint projects is optimal for supporting interreligious learning, as is openness to new opportunities as they emerge. Team-building skills, including clear communications and a spirit of mutual respect, are critical for cooperative interreligious encounters. All those interviewed for this book cited the importance of people from different religious traditions planning collaboratively as integral to interreligious learning.

9. *Practice Reconciliation.* God calls all humanity to a life of rich diversity. Our capacity, the capacity of faith communities to build relationships with God, each other, our neighbors and the larger world, is consistent with the vision of many of the religions of the world. Throughout the New Testament, Jesus is frequently found reaching out to and in communication with people from religions and cultures different from his own. Faith Communities practice reconciliation when they seek to heal the divisions and enmity between peoples within the community and beyond. Interreligious conversations are a vehicle for groups to relate positively to each other and to heal negative prejudices and historic divisions. The process of living out interreligious relationships impacts our hearts, our minds, and our lives and brings about new understandings. To practice reconciliation means, in part, to perceive that our differences and our interdependence are a divine gift. It means that peace will not be built on separatism or political arguments, but on the transformation of hearts. Compassionate listening skills, mediation skills, and conflict transformation skills are all integral to the practice of reconciliation.

NEW HORIZONS IN INTERRELIGIOUS LEARNING

The lessons of the faith communities and religious organizations studied here point to a need for the creation of intentional interreligious learning communities where people can be affirmed in their own religious, social, and cultural identities and at the same time be creatively transformed through authentic engagement with others. We need each other. More research on interreligious learning for all ages needs to be done within and across religious traditions, particularly those approaches which develop religious literacy along with cultural competency. To be sure the contours and the articulation of interreligious learning vary across traditions. At the same time, traditions share in interreligious learning that is based in personal narratives, religious literacy, interreligious encounters, sharing sacred spaces, compassionate action, and initiating intentional interreligious learning communities. The growth in many regions in the creation of interreligious sacred spaces is related to the need for more reflection on the ways we can pray together in our particularity and in a spirit of hospitality, and at the same time avoid the misappropriation of the practices of other faith traditions. The intersection of interreligious learning and online learning pushes the borders of our delivery systems for all religious education. How to build bridges in faith communities with interreligious families and as well those who claim multiple religious identities are two practical needs related to growing religious pluralism. We now know that faith communities that support interreligious learning create spaces for deep conversations and for encounters to take place and for relationships to be transformed. They are places where we can relate to the wider world, and where we can claim our own voices, as well as hear and speak to others. Faith communities which actually encourage a plurality of voices also tend to be places where power-sharing is critical to the way decisions are made and common life organized. They are sacred spaces which respond with compassion to the needs and concerns of their neighbors. They are places where we can begin to find God beyond the borders of our limited understandings about the Divine and share in the stories of our companions along the way as we form partnerships for the good of the world.

REFLECTION QUESTIONS

1. As you complete this book, which stories interested you the most and why?

2. This last chapter offers some reflections on the images of "bridges" and "borders" as they relate to building interreligious community. What are some additional images that relate to your own sense of interreligious learning?

3. Reflect on the "Ten Things Faith Communities and Religious Organizations Can Do to Support Interreligious Learning." Where can you begin? Are there other suggestions that you might add to the list?

References

BOOKS

Abu-Nimer, M., and D. Augsburger. 2009. *Peace-Building By, Between and Beyond Muslims and Evangelical Christians*. Plymouth, UK: Lexington.

Armstrong, Karen. 2010. *Twelve Steps to a Compassionate Life*. New York: Knopf.

Angelou, M. 1993. *On the Pulse of the Morning*. New York: Random House.

———. 2009. *Letter to My Daughter*. New York: Random House.

Baker, D. G. 2010. *Greenhouses of Hope: Congregations Growing Young Leaders Who Will Change the World*. Herndon, VA: Alban Institute.

Barnes, M. 2012. *Interreligious Learning: Dialogue, Spirituality and the Christian Imagination*. Cambridge: Cambridge University Press.

Berling, J. A. 2004. *Understanding Other Religious Worlds. A Guide for Interreligious Education*. Maryknoll. NY: Orbis.

Blundell, P. A. 2010. *Inter-Religious Dialogue: Toward an Educational Framework*. Saarbrücken, Germany: VDM.

Boys, M. C. 2000. *Has God Only One Blessing? Judaism as a Source of Christian Self-Understanding*. New York: Paulist.

———. 2005. *Seeing Judaism Anew: Christianity's Sacred Obligation*. Lanham, MD: Sheed & Ward.

Boys, M. C., and S. Lee. 2006. *Christians and Jews in Dialogue: Learning in the Presence of the Other*. Woodstock, VT: Skylight Paths.

Broadbent, L., and J. Logan. 1988. *A Birthday to Celebrate: A Story of Guru Nanak*. Times to Remember. Norwich, UK: Religious and Moral Education.

———. 2009. *At Home and the Synagogue*. Places in Worship. Norwich, UK: Religious and Moral Education.

Brockman, D. R., and R. L. F. Habito. 2010. *The Gospel Among Religions: Christian Ministry, Theology, and Spirituality in a Multifaith World*. Maryknoll, NY: Orbis.

Browning, D. S., and M. J. Bunge. 2009. *Children and Childhood in World Religions*. New Brunswick, NJ: Rutgers University Press.

Browning, D. S., and B. J. Miller-McLemore. 2009. *Children and Childhood in American Religions*. New Brunswick, NJ: Rutgers University Press.

Buber, M. 1973. *Werke III*. Munich: Kosel.

References

Buller, L. 2005. *A Faith Like Mine: The Celebration of the World's Religions Seen through the Eyes of Children*. London: DK.

Caldwell, E. F. 2011. *God's Big Table. Nurturing Children in a Diverse World*. Cleveland: Pilgrim.

Cobb, J. 2012. *Religions in the Making: Whitehead and the Wisdom Traditions of the World*. Eugene, OR: Cascade.

Cohn-Sherbok, D. 2001. *Interfaith Theology: A Reader*. Oxford: One World.

Conde-Frazier, E., S. S. Kang, and G. A. Parrett. 2004. *A Many Colored Kingdom: Multicultural Dynamics' for Spiritual Formation*. Grand Rapids: Baker.

Constant, A. 1998. *Man of Peace: The Story of Mahatma Gandhi*. Faith in Action Series. Norwich, UK: Religious and Moral Education.

Coppola, D. L. 2006. *What Do We Want the Other to Teach About Us? Jewish, Christian and Muslim Dialogues*. Fairfield, CT: Sacred Heart University Press.

Crosbie, M. 2000. *Architecture for the Gods*. New York: Watson-Guptill.

DeYoung, C. P. 1995. *Coming Together: The Bible's Message in an Age of Diversity*. Valley Forge, PA: Judson.

Dula, P., and A. E. Weaver. 2007. *Borders and Bridges: Mennonite Witness in a Religiously Diverse World*. Telford, PA: Cascadia.

Eck, D. L. 1993. *Encountering God: A Spiritual Journey from Bozeman to Banares*. Boston: Beacon.

———. 2001. *A New Religious America*. San Francisco: Harper.

Ellsberg, R. 1991. *Gandhi on Christianity*. Maryknoll, NY: Orbis.

Frew, D. H., editor. *Sacred Spaces: 2004 Interfaith Sacred Space Competition*. San Francisco: Interfaith Center at the Presidio, 2004.

Galloway, K. 2000. *Maker's Blessing*. Glasgow, UK: Wild Goose.

Gopin, M. 2012. *Bridges Across an Impossible Divide: The Inner Lives of Arab and Jewish Peacemakers*. New York: Oxford University Press.

Hall, D. J. 1991. *Thinking the Faith*. Minneapolis: Fortress.

Hauerwas, S. 1983. *The Peaceable Kingdom: A Primer in Christian Ethics*. Notre Dame, IN: University of Notre Dame.

Heckman, B., and R. P. Neiss. 2008. *Interactive Faith: The Essential Interreligious Community-Building Handbook*. Woodstock, VT: Skylight Paths.

Hedges, P. 2010. *Controversies in Interreligious Dialogue and the Theology of Religions*. London: SCM.

Hedges, P., and A. Race. 2009. *Christian Approaches to Other Faiths*. Norwich, UK: SCM.

Hefner, R. W., and M. Q. Zaman. 2007. *Schooling Islam: The Culture and Politics of Modern Muslim Education*. Princeton, NJ: Princeton University Press.

Heft, J. L. 2006. *Passing on the Faith: Transforming Traditions for the Next Generation of Jews, Christians and Muslims*. New York: Fordham University Press.

Heim, S. M. 1995. *Salvations: Truth and Difference in Religion*. Maryknoll, NY: Orbis.

———. 1998. *Grounds for Understanding: Ecumenical Resources for Responses to Religious Pluralism*. Grand Rapids: Eerdmans.

Hoffman, G., C. Monroe, L. Green, and D. Rivers. 2008. *Compassionate Listening: An Exploratory Sourcebook About Conflict Transformation*. Indianola, WA: The Compassionate Listening Project.

Hornung, M. 2007. *Encountering Other Faiths: An Introduction to the Art of Interreligious Engagement*. Philadelphia: Interfaith Center of Greater Philadelphia.

Hyde, M. O., and E. G. Hyde. 2009. *World Religions 101: An Overview for Teens*. Minneapolis: Twenty-First Century Books.

Idliby, R., S. Oliver, and P. Warner. 2006. *The Faith Club: A Muslim, A Christian, A Jew— Three Women Search for Understanding*. New York: Free Press.

Inge, J. 1993. *A Christian Theology of Place*. Sussex, UK: Ashgate.

Ingram, P. 2009. *The Process of Buddhist-Christian Dialogue*. Eugene, OR: Cascade.

Interfaith Youth Core. 2009. *Interfaith Leaders Toolkit*. Chicago: Interfaith Youth Core.

Jones, W. P. 2000. *Worlds Within A Congregation: Dealing with Theological Diversity*. Nashville: Abingdon.

Kaplan, J. 2004. *Interfaith Families: Personal Stories of Jewish-Christian Intermarriage*. Westport, CT: Praeger.

Keely, B. A. 1997. *Faith of Our Foremothers: Women Changing Religious Education*. Louisville: Westminster John Knox.

King, M. L. 1968. *Where Do We Go From Here: Chaos to Community*. Boston: Beacon.

Knitter, P. 1990. *No Other Name: Christian Attitudes Toward World Religions*. Maryknoll, NY: Orbis.

———. 2002. *Introducing Theologies of Religions*. Maryknoll, NY: Orbis.

Kujawa-Holbrook, Sheryl A. 2002. *A House of Prayer for All Peoples: Congregations Building Multiracial Community*. Bethesda, MD: Alban Institute.

Kwok, P. L.. 2012. *Globalization, Gender, and Peacebuilding: The Future of Interfaith Dialogue*. New York: Paulist.

LeBaron, M. 2002. *Bridging Troubled Waters: Conflict Resolution from the Heart*. San Francisco: Jossey-Bass.

Lee, J. Y. 1995. *Marginality: The Key to Multicultural Theology*. Minneapolis: Fortress.

MacKenzie, D., T. Falcon, and J. Rahman. 2009. *Getting to the Heart of Interfaith*. Woodstock, VT: Skylight Paths.

Mays, R. K. 2008. *Interfaith Dialogue at the Grass Roots*. Philadelphia: Ecumenical.

McCarthy, K. 2007. *Interfaith Encounters in America*. New Brunswick, NJ: Rutgers University Press.

McLaren, B. D. 2012. *Why Did Jesus, Moses, the Buddha, and Mohammed Cross the Road? Christian Identity in a Multi-Faith World*. New York: Jericho.

Moore, D. L. 2007. *Overcoming Religious Illiteracy: A Cultural Studies Approach to the Study of Religion in Secondary Education*. New York: Palgrave Macmillan.

Mosher, L. A. 2005. *Belonging*. Faith in the Neighborhood 1. New York: Seabury.

———. 2006. *Praying: The Rituals of Faith*. Faith in the Neighborhood 2. New York: Seabury.

———. 2007. *Loss*. Faith in the Neighborhood 3. New York: Seabury.

———. 2012. *Toward Our Mutual Flourishing: The Episcopal Church, Interreligious Relations, and Theologies of Religious Manyness*. New York: Peter Lang.

Nhat Hanh, Thich. 1999. *Call Me by My True Name*. New York: Parallax.

Numrich, P. D. 2009. *The Faith Next Door: American Christians and Their New Religious Neighbors*. New York: Oxford University Press.

Patel, E. 2012. *Sacred Ground. Pluralism, Prejudice, and the Promise of America*. Boston: Beacon.

Patel, E., and P. Brodeur. 2006. *Building the Interfaith Youth Movement: Beyond Dialogue to Action*. Lanham, MD: Rowman & Littlefield.

Peace, J. H., O. N. Rose, and G. Mobly. 2012. *My Neighbor's Faith: Stories of Interreligious Encounter, Growth, and Transformation*. Maryknoll, NY: Orbis.

References

Pew Forum On Religion and Public Life. 2008. "Statistics on Religion in America Report." In *Religious Landscape Survey*. http://religion.pewforum.org/reports.

Pollefeyt, D. 2007. *Interreligious Learning*. Leuven, Belgium: Leuven University Press.

Prothero, S. 2007. *Religious Literacy: What Every American Needs to Know—and Doesn't*. New York: HarperOne.

———. 2010. *God Is Not One: The Eight Rival Religions that Run the World*. New York: HarperOne.

Puthiyottil, C. 2001. *Our Neighbors: An Introduction to Cultural Diversity and World Religions*. Minneapolis: Augsburg Fortress.

Quinn, F. 2012. *Welcoming the Interfaith Future: Religious Pluralism in a Global Age*. New York: Peter Lang.

Race, A., and P. M. Hedges. 2009. *Christian Approaches to Other Faiths: A Reader*. London: SCM.

Rhodes, J. D. 2001. *World Religions*. Burst—Topics for Today's Teens. Nashville: Abingdon.

Ridgely, S. B. 2011. *The Study of Children in Religions*. New York: New York University Press.

Rogers, F., Jr. 2011. *Finding God in the Graffiti: Empowering Teenagers through Stories*. Cleveland: Pilgrim.

Roozen, D. A., and H. Hadsell. 2009. *Changing the Way Seminaries Teach: Pedagogies for Interfaith Dialogue*. Hartford: Hartford Seminary.

Rumi, J. 1997. *The Illustrated Rumi*. Translated by C. Barks. New York: Broadway.

Rüppell, G., and P. Schreiner. 2003. *Shared Learning in a Plural World: Ecumenical Approaches to Inter-Religious Education*. Münster: LIT.

Sachs, J. 2002. *The Dignity of Difference*. New York: Continuum.

Schneiders, S. 2003. *Written that You May Believe*. New York: Crossroad.

Sharp, M. A. M. 2013. *Misunderstanding Stories: Toward a Postcolonial Pastoral Theology*. Eugene, OR: Pickwick.

Smith, D. I. 2000. *Learning from the Stranger: Christian Faith and Cultural Diversity*. Grand Rapids: Eerdmans.

Smith, J. D. and G. S. Rosenthal. 2010. *Let us Reason Together: Christians and Jews in Conversation*. Louisville: Witherspoon.

Smith, J. I. 2007. *Muslims, Christians and the Challenge of Interfaith Dialogue*. New York: Oxford University Press.

Smock, D. 2002. *Interfaith Dialogue and Peacebuilding*. Washington, D.C.: United States Institute of Peace.

Speight, M. 1989. *Creating Interfaith Community*. New York: General Board of Global Ministries, the United Methodist Church.

Sterkens, C. 2001. *Interreligious Learning: The Problem of Interreligious Dialogue in Primary Education*. Leiden: Brill.

Suchocki, M. H. 2003. *Divinity and Diversity: A Christian Affirmation of Religious Pluralism*. Nashville: Abingdon.

Sutcliffe, S., and B. Sutcliffe. 1994. *Committed to Judaism: A Jewish Community*. Norwich, UK: Religious and Moral Education Press.

Tenzin Gyatso [The Dalai Lama]. 2001. *An Open Heart: Practicing Compassion in Everyday Life*. New York: Little, Brown & Co.

Thistlethwaite, S. B. 2012. *Interfaith Just Peacemaking. Jewish, Christian and Muslim Perspectives on the New Paradigm of Peace and War*. New York: Palgrave Macmillan.

Thompsett, F. H. 1989. *We Are Theologians*. Cambridge: Cowley.

Torry, M., S. Thorley. 2008. *Together and Different: Christians Engaging with People of Other Faiths*. Norwich, UK: Canterbury.

Volf, M. 1996. *Exclusion and Embrace: A Theological Exploration of Identity, Otherness and Reconciliation*. Nashville: Abingdon.

Volf, M., G. bin Muhammad, and M. Yarrington, 2010. *A Common Word: Muslim and Christians on Loving God and Neighbor*. Grand Rapids: Eerdmans.

Weil, S. 1952. *The Need for Roots*. New York: Putnam.

Wistrich, R. S. 1994. *Anti-Semitism: The Longest Hatred*. New York: Pantheon.

World Council of Churches. 1986. *My Neighbor's Faith and Mine: Theological Discoveries through Interfaith Dialogue*. Geneva: World Council of Churches.

Wuthnow, Robert. 2010. *Boundless Faith: The Global Outreach of American Churches*. Berkeley: University of California Press.

Yong, A. 2008. *Hospitality and The Other: Pentecost, Christian Practices, and the Neighbor*. Maryknoll, NY: Orbis.

Yust, K. M., A. N. Johnson, S. E. Sasso, and E. C. Roehlkepartain. 2006. *Nurturing Child and Adolescent Spirituality: Perspectives from the World's Religious Traditions*. Lanham, MD: Rowman & Littlefield.

ARTICLES AND CHAPTERS

Amin, S. M. 2001. "Kindness to a Non-Muslim Neighbor: Tips for Interaction." *Islam Online*.

Australian Consultation on Multi-Faith Worship. 1995. "Guidelines for Multi-Faith Worship."

Balmer, R. 2006. "Finding Common Ground." *Alban Weekly* (November 20).

Barksdale, S. 2007. "Minneapolis Interfaith Service for Bridge Victims Draws More than 1,400." *Episcopal News Service* (August 6).

Binyon, M. "The Tent Where Ideas Are Canvassed and Passions Lulled." *The Times* (July 31).

Boudreau, S. 2009. "Diversity in Education and the Marginalization of Religion." In *Diversity and Multiculturalism: A Reader*, edited by S. R. Steinberg, 297–306. New York: Peter Lang.

Broadway, B. 2002 "'Spiritual Siblings': Md. Jewish Congregation, Presbyterian Church Join in Building a Better Home." *Washington Post* (May 4).

Brussat, F., and M. A. Brussat. "The Spiritual Practice of Hospitality." http://www.spiritualityandpractice.com/practices/wartime.php?id=18218.

Butler Bass, D. "The 2013 Jean L. Wickett Lecture." Claremont School of Theology, March 5, 2013.

Byrne, C. 2011. "Freirean Crititical Pedagogy's Challenge to Interfaith Education: What Is Interfaith? What Is Education?" *British Journal of Religious Education* 33/1 (January) 47-60.

Caldwell, D. "The New Neighbors." *Beliefnet*. http://www.beliefnet.com/Faiths/2001/06/The-New-Neighbors.aspx.

Chittister, J. 2013. "Lectio with Joan Chittister." *Monastery of the Heart* website.

Council for a Parliament of the World's Religions. 1999. "A Call to Our Guiding Institutions: Presented on the Occasion of the 1999 Parliament of the World's Religions."

December 1-8, Cape Town, South Africa. http://www.parliamentofreligions.org/_includes/FCKcontent/File/CalltoGuidingInstitutions.pdf.

Diamant, J. 2010. "Prominent Muslims Make Pilgrimage to Auschwitz." *Christian Century* (September 3) 19.

Dias, E. 2010. "Training Pastors, Rabbis, and Imams Together." *Time* (August 22).

Duraisingh, Christopher. 2001. "The Multi-Colored Wisdom of God: A Pentecost Paradigm." *The Witness* (December) 13–14.

Eck, D. L. 1991. "Gandhian Guidelines for a World of Religious Difference." In *Gandhi and Christianity*, edited by R. Ellsberg, 77–90. Maryknoll, NY: Orbis.

Eck, D. L. 2006. "What is Pluralism." The Pluralism Project, Harvard University.

"Ecumenical and Interreligious Education." 1995. *Religious Education* 90/2, entire issue.

Evers, G. 2012. "Trends and Development in Interreligious Dialogue." *Studies in Interreligious Dialogue* 22/2: 228–43.

Galloway, K. 2007. "From the Holy City: Seeking the Heartlands." *Coracle* 4/29 (June-July 2007) 3-4.

Gandhi, M. K. "Satyagraha, Gandhi's Peace Prayer." http://www.slas.net/peace/satyagraha/index.html.

Greider, K. J. 2012. "Religious Pluralism and Christian-Centrism." In *The Wiley-Blackwell Companion to Practical Theology*, edited by B. J. Miller-McLemore, 452–61. Malden, MA: Wiley-Blackwell.

Grossman, C. L. 2006. "Moms Find Spiritual Friends in the Faith Club." *USA Today* (September 26).

Hartford Institute for Religion Research. 2000. "What Do You Know about Your Interfaith Neighbor?" http://hirr.hartsem.edu/research.

Hadsell, H. 2000."Introduction." *Meet Your Neighbors: Interfaith Facts*. Hartford: Hartford Seminary.

Hames, J. 2009. "Cathedral Artist Interweaves Many Images: Interfaith Art Project Highlights Philadelphia's Community's Diversity." http://library.episcopalchurch.org/article/cathedral-artist-interweaves-many-images.

Hirsch, D. D. 2003. "The Rabbi Came to Church." *Presbyterians Today* (September 21).

Interfaith Funders. n.d. "'Good for the Soul, Good for the Whole': Faith-Based Community Organizing and the Renewal of Congregations." Syosset, New York.

Jackson, B. W., and E. V. Holvino. 1988. "Developing Multicultural Organizations." *Journal of Religion and Applied Behavioral Science* (Fall) 14–19.

Jenkins, P. 2010. "Religion by the Numbers." *Christian Century* (July 23) 45.

Kaiser, J. E. G. 2010."'Do What Is Just': Today's Jewish Social Justice Movement is Renewing Its Strength with Faith and Grassroots Power." *Sojourners* (February) 30.

Kujawa-Holbrook, S. 2010. "A New Paradigm for Theological Education." *Huffington Post* (June 9).

Kwok, P. L. 2011 "Interfaith Encounter." In *The Blackwell Companion to Christian Spirituality*, edited by A. Holder, 532–49. Malden, MA: Wiley-Blackwell.

Landsberg, M. 2010."Seminary to Span the Divides of Faith." *Los Angeles Times* (August 17).

LeSueur, S. "Church, Synagogue Recreate Ancient Site for Summer Program." *Episcopal Teacher* (Summer) 1, 7.

Lipman, S. 2010. "In Los Angeles, Future Rabbis, Imams and Ministers Will Train Together." *The Jewish Week* (August 17).

MacIntosh, P. 1988. "White Privilege: Unpacking the Invisible Knapsack." Wellesley College Center for Research on Women, Wellesley, MA.

Messina, I. 2005. "Connecting the Paths." *Tucson Weekly* (September 5). http://www.tucsonweekly.com/tucson/connecting-the-paths/Content?oid=1070749.

Mizejewski, G. 2001. "Different Faiths, Same Goal." *The Washington Times* (February 12).

Nhat Hahn, Thich. 2010. "Returning Home." *Shambala Sun* (January 10) 67.

Parks, S. D. 1989. "Home and Pilgrimage: Companion Metaphors for Personal and Social Transformation." *Soundings* 72: 315.

Patel, E. 2009. "Acts of Faith: Interfaith Leadership in a Time of Religious Crisis." *Virginia Seminary Journal* (Fall) 32, 40.

Paulson, M. 2008. "Architectural Prize for Andover Newton." www.Boston.com, August 8.

Penn, J. 2009. "Interfaith Youth Program." Unpublished: 2.

"Pluralism Sunday." 2012. *Progressive Christianity.* http://progressivechristianity.org/tcpc-weekly-liturgy/pluralism-sunday-2013/.

Podger, P. 2006. "Sharing Sacred Space." www.Roanoke.com, November 26.

Pratt, D. 2012. "The Praxis of Dialogue: Can We Yet Go Further?" Unpublished paper delivered at the University of Bern.

Prothero, S. "Religious Literacy: What Every American Should Know." Pew Forum Faith Angle Conference, Key West, Florida, December 3, 2007.

Public Religion Research Council. "The End of a White Christian Strategy." http://pastoralia.org/church/the-end-of-a-white-christian-strategy.

Quinn, F. 2003. "Are All Religions Equal? Yes or No? or the Path Beyond Pluralism: New Steps in a Converging Religious Dialogue." Unpublished paper.

Radcliff, D. 1997. "Psychological Foundations of Multicultural Religious Education." In *Multicultural Religious Education*, edited by B. Wilkerson, 93–128. Birmingham, AL: Religious Education Press.

"Research: Multifaith Education in Seminaries." 2009. http://www.auburnseminary.org/seminarystudy/.

Rohr, R. 2007. "Gandhi's Place." www.carradicalgrace.org.

Rondeau, M. 2008. "Love Thy Neighbor: Clergy Seek Donations for Food and Fuel." *Bennington Banner* (September 6).

Rutz, M. 2010. "Upstate Becomes Buddhist Pilgrimage Site." The Buddhist Channel, July 2. http://www.buddhistchannel.tv/index.php?id=61,9323,0,0,1,0#.Us8IQ2RDvqE.

Satyagraha. "Gandhi's Peace Prayer." http://salsa.net/peace/satyagraha/index.html.

Schell-Lambert, A. 2009. "An Inter-Religious Eco-Justice Model for the Local Community." DMin. Thesis, Episcopal Divinity School, Cambridge, MA.

Schlosser, L. Z. "Christian Privilege: Breaking Sacred Taboo." *Journal of Multicultural Counseling and Development* 31/1 (January 2003) 44-51.

Schreiber, L. 2005. "News/Reports." *Moment Magazine* (December 13).

Sensoy, O. 2000. "Kill Santa: Religious Diversity and the Religious Holiday Problem." In *Diversity and Multiculturalism: A Reader*, edited by S. Steinberg, 321–29. New York: Peter Lang.

Stassen, G. 2009. "Ten Just-Peacemaking Practices that Work." In *Peace-Building By, Between and Beyond Muslims and Evangelical Christians*, edited by M. Abu-Nimer and D. Augsburger, 61–79. Lanham, MD: Lexington.

"Statement of Muslim American Imams and Community Leaders on Holocaust Denial." 2010. www.faithindialogue.com/imams-statement.

Stendahl, K. 1993. "Religious Pluralism." *The Journal of Religious Pluralism* 2.

Sudilosky, J. 2005 "Women Building Peace." *The Lutheran* (February) 45.

Tennyson, A. 1892. "Akbar's Dream." In *The Death of Oenone, Akhbar's Dream, and Other Poems*. London: Macmillan.

Tenzin Gyatso [The Dalai Lama]. 2010. "Many Faiths, One Truth." *New York Times*, May 24. http://www.nytimes.com/2010/05/25/opinion/25gyatso.html?_r=1&.

———. 2010. "Only Genuine Compassion Will Do." *Buddhadharma* (Summer) 26.

Tisdale, S. J. 2006. "Beloved Community." *Tricycle* (Fall) 57.

Tutu, D. 2010. Quoted in www.tutufoundationuk.org (accessed November 19, 2010).

Vecsey, L. 2009. "White House Seder Tradition 'Started' in Harrisburg." *PennLive* (April 8). http://www.pennlive.com/midstate/index.ssf/2009/04/white_house_seder_tradition_st.html.

Watts, R. 2002. "Following Jesus to the Mosque." *Presbyterians Today* (May) 13.

World Council of Churches. 2009. "Ecumenical Considerations for Dialogue and Relations with People of Other Religions: Taking Stock of 30 Years of Dialogue and Revisiting the 1979 Guidelines." http://www.wcc-coe.org/wcc/what/interreligious/cd40-04.html.

Wrey, L. 2004. "Zen Buddhist Group Welcomes Everyone." *Roanoke Times & World News*, (November 4).

"Youth Groups Embrace Interfaith Work." 2010. Unitarian Universalist Association of Congregations, October 1. http://www.uua.org/interconnections/interconnections/171862.shtml.

INTERVIEWS

Chesson, Kathleen Kline to SKH, September 14, 2009; December 21, 2010.

Foraker, G. with SKH, June 8, 2009; September 12, 2010.

Haberman, David to Anita Schell-Lambert, February 28, 2008.

Hermna, Joyce to SKH, June 14, 2008.

Kanzler, J. to SKH, June 25, 2008.

Kern, Alexander to SKH, June 14, 2009.

Kitagawa, John to SKH, July 12, 2010.

Levy, Robert to SKH, February 12, 2009.

Malmberg, Robert E. to SKH, June 20, 2008.

Medina, Ernest to SKH, March 1, 2010.

Peace, Jennifer to SKH, February 12, 2009.

Penn, Janet to SKH, June 14, 2008.

Purdy, James to SKH, October 10, 2009.

Rahman, Mawdudur to SKH, November 24, 2010.

Razvi, S. A. to SKH, June 16, 2008.

Rhodenhiser, James C. to SKH, February 12, 2009.

Schell-Lambert, Anita to SKH, January 10, 2008; September 10, 2009.

Streit, Jep to SKH, October 22, 2010.

Yarbough, Denise to SKH, September 18, 2007.

Appendix:

An Interreligious Transformation Continuum for Christian Congregations and Organizations

v	1. Exclusivist	2. Inclusivist/Religious Tolerance	3. Compliant	4. Pluralist	5. Redefining/Multiple Religious Belonging	6. Transformed/Interfaith Community
Characteristics & Practices	Supports a Christian status quo. Excludes people of other religions from policies, practices, and decision-making at all levels. "The Replacement Model"—Christianity intended to replace all other religions; fundamental question is soteriological—humans are *saved* by grace alone; by faith *alone*; by Christ *alone*; by scripture *alone*. One standard of truth (Bible).	Maintains the privilege of Christianity as the religion which has traditionally held power, with the exception of limited contact with other religions. Believes that God can be found outside the Christian church. "The Fulfillment Model"—maintains that Christianity is the fulfillment of other religions, or "default."	Supports religious pluralism on a "symbolic" level, yet essentially reflects an assimilation model. Sees itself as interfaith and religiously "diverse" but with little systemic change in culture, structures, policies, and decision-making.	Sees doctrinal differences as a barrier to the ethical obligation to engage with other religions. Develops intentional interfaith organization, and strives for deeper understanding and accountability. More common to organizations than to particular congregations or denominations.	Makes intentional choices to rebuild organizational and cultural life in the desire to become an interfaith (or multi-religious, inter-religious) organization. Includes and goes beyond "The Acceptance Model" in neither holding one model as superior nor seeking commonalities—makes room for co-existing truths. Sees the need for a commitment to change; to mechanisms in place to facilitate change; and, for collective action	Holds a future vision where religious differences no longer limit human potential. Institutional life fully reflects shared power with diverse religious, cultural, and economic groups.

Actions	Denies the realities of religious diversity, as well as the impact of Christian hegemony on other religious groups. Little for Christians to gain from other religions (even harmful). Lifestyle commitment desire to share good news to the world to convert.	Is aware of other religions, yet does not act due to fear, ignorance, or other factors. May operate multi-religiously in an unacknowledged way, and/or view beliefs, practices, rituals through a Christian lens.	Is relatively unaware of ongoing patterns of privilege, paternalism, and control, or fears change. Takes action to learn more about other religious, and may participate in multi-religious, interreligious or interfaith programs and/or practices, rituals.	"The Mutuality Model" -- recognizes the need for unlearning religious oppression is an ongoing and lifelong vocation. Desires to move beyond traditional "inclusion" to authentic dialogue, yet structures continue to maintain Christian privilege.	Audit and restructure all aspects of community life for full participation of different religions. Form intra-organizational groups and coalitions to speak out on issue. Authentic, stressful dialogue. Multiple religious belonging.	Full participation in decisions that shape institutional structures & vision.
Social Justice	Few social justice initiatives, but may give money to charity. Extensive outreach may be connected with efforts to evangelize.	Passively engage with other religions in the spirit of "noblesse oblige".	Focus on social justice projects and some advocacy. A fairly common response is to invite participation from persons from other religions.	Participation in an intentional change process to address and change the power imbalances between religious groups. Learns about neighbors through one's own religious experience.	A collaborative approach to social justice, as "people of faith," stand with oppressed as allies and learn how to be allies.	Porous boundary between the organization and wider faith communities.

chart continues on the next page

v	1. Exclusivist	2. Inclusivist/Religious Tolerance	3. Compliant	4. Pluralist	5. Redefining/Multiple Religious Belonging	6. Transformed/Interfaith Community
Change Strategies	Begin by learning to appreciate religious diversity and raise awareness of oppression issues. Raise consciousness about religious diversity in own community. Begin to "unpack" the idea of wider salvation.	Moving to the next stage, beyond tolerance, requires knowledge of religions, dialogue skills, an understanding of the dynamics of oppression and the need for collective action.	Conflict avoidant stage, as Christian privilege is not addressed. Desire to support the recruitment of people from other religious groups, but it remains largely symbolic. Misappropriation is a particular concern.	Generally, with specialized assistance, begins to audit and dismantle exclusive and/or oppressive practices, yet remains within the norms of a dominant Christian worldview.	Structural changes that are shaped by people from a variety of religions through sharing power and decision-making. Also involves redefining the community's, vision, practices, etc.	Works to form alliances and networks in support of efforts to eliminate social oppression and educate others to do the same.

Monocultural → Multicultural → Religious Pluralist → Full Interfaith Community

Religious and cultural diversity seen as negative → Religious and cultural differences are recognized and tolerated → Religious and cultural differences are assets

Educational Tasks — Encounter Difference — Respond From Own Location — Conversation/Dialogue — Develop Relationships — Internalize the Process

Adapted and Expanded by Sheryl Kujawa-Holbrook, 2003, 2008, 2009

Sources: Knitter, Berling and Avazian, Branding, Griffin, Hardiman, Harro, Holvino, Jackson, and James.

About the Author

SHERYL A. KUJAWA-HOLBROOK, IS a priest of the Episcopal Diocese of Los Angeles, an educator, historian of religion, and practical theologian. She is currently vice president of academic affairs and dean of the faculty, and professor of practical theology and religious education at Claremont School of Theology, and professor of Anglican Studies at Bloy House, the Episcopal Theological School at Claremont. In addition to her thirty years of experience as a teacher, trainer, workshop, conference and retreat leader, she is the author of thirteen books and numerous articles and reviews. Before her academic career, Kujawa-Holbrook worked worldwide for the Episcopal Church in education and ministries with young people. She is on the boards of the Journal of Interreligious Dialogue (JIRD), the Kaleidoscope Institute (KI), and Religious Freedom USA, and the book review editor of *Anglican and Episcopal History*. In 2010–2011 Kujawa-Holbrook was a fellow in the Christian Leadership Initiative sponsored by the American Jewish Committee (AJC) and the Shalom Hartman Institute, Jerusalem, Israel. Her interreligious works include, *Pilgrimage—The Sacred Art: Journey to the Center of the Heart*, SkyLight Paths 2013. She is the editor and co-author of, *For One Great Peace: An Interfaith Study Guide*, Abrahamic Faiths Peacemaking Initiative (2012); and editor and co-author, *Interfaith Peacemaking Curriculum*, Abrahamic Faiths Initiative (2012). *God Beyond Borders: Stories of Interreligious Learning from Faith Communities* is the first in the Horizons In Religious Education Series sponsored by the Religious Education Association (REA).